Frederic William Farrar

Essays on a liberal education

Frederic William Farrar

Essays on a liberal education

ISBN/EAN: 9783742860354

Manufactured in Europe, USA, Canada, Australia, Japa

Cover: Foto ©Suzi / pixelio.de

Manufactured and distributed by brebook publishing software (www.brebook.com)

Frederic William Farrar

Essays on a liberal education

ESSAYS

ON

A LIBERAL EDUCATION.

EDITED BY

REV. F. W. FARRAR, M.A. F.R.S.

ASSISTANT-MASTER AT HARROW, LATE FELLOW OF TRINITY COLLEGE, CAMBRIDGE, AND
HON. FELLOW OF KING'S COLLEGE, LONDON.

SECOND EDITION.

London:
MACMILLAN & CO.
1868.

PREFACE.

THE principles and methods of Liberal Education are at the present time undergoing considerable discussion, and it cannot be otherwise than useful to direct general attention to the changes already in progress, and to other reforms which have become either imperative or desirable. Liberal Education in England is not controlled by the Government, nor is it entirely in the hands of tutors and schoolmasters; it is an institution of national growth, and it will expand and improve only with the expansion and improvement of our national ideas of what education ought to be. We have endeavoured, so far as lies in our power, to hasten this expansion and improvement by showing in what light some of the most interesting questions of Educational Reform are viewed by men who have had opportunities for forming a judgment respecting them, and several of whom have been for some time engaged in the work of education at our Universities and Schools.

LIST OF SUBJECTS AND AUTHORS.

ESSAY I.

ON THE HISTORY OF CLASSICAL EDUCATION.

By Charles Stuart Parker, M.A. *Fellow of University College, Oxford.*

Page 1

ESSAY II.

THE THEORY OF CLASSICAL EDUCATION.

By Henry Sidgwick, M.A. *Fellow of Trinity College, Cambridge.*

Page 81

ESSAY III.

LIBERAL EDUCATION IN UNIVERSITIES.

By John Seeley, M.A. *Fellow of Christ's College, Cambridge, and Professor of Latin in University College, London.* Page 145

ESSAY IV.

ON TEACHING BY MEANS OF GRAMMAR.

By F. E. Bowen, M.A. *Late Fellow of Trinity College, Cambridge, and Assistant Master at Harrow.* Page 179

ESSAY V.

ON GREEK AND LATIN VERSE-COMPOSITION AS A GENERAL BRANCH OF EDUCATION.

By the Rev. F. W. Farrar, M.A. F.R.S. Page 205

ESSAY VI.
ON TEACHING NATURAL SCIENCE IN SCHOOLS.
BY J. M. WILSON, M.A. F.G.S. F.R.A.S. *Assistant Master in Rugby School, and Fellow of St. John's College, Cambridge.* Page 241

ESSAY VII.
THE TEACHING OF ENGLISH.
BY J. W. HALES, M.A. *Late Fellow and Assistant Tutor of Christ's College, Cambridge.* Page 293

ESSAY VIII.
ON THE EDUCATION OF THE REASONING FACULTIES.
BY W. JOHNSON, M.A. *Fellow of King's College, Cambridge, and Assistant Master at Eton.* Page 313

ESSAY IX.
ON THE PRESENT SOCIAL RESULTS OF CLASSICAL EDUCATION.
BY LORD HOUGHTON, M.A. *Trin. Coll. Cambridge, and Hon. D.C.L. Oxford.*
Page 365

ESSAYS

ON

A LIBERAL EDUCATION.

I.

ON THE HISTORY OF CLASSICAL EDUCATION.[1]

BY CHARLES STUART PARKER.

I. Greek as a Common Language.—II. The Early (Greek) Church and the Classics.—III. Latin as a Common Language.—IV. The Mediæval (Latin) Church and the Classics.—V. The Revival of Letters in Italy.—VI. The Revival of Letters in Germany.—VII. The Reformation and Classical Education.—VIII. Classical Education in England.—IX. English Theories of a larger Education.—X. Experience of Germany.—XI. Experience of France.—XII. Present State of Liberal Education in England.

ALTHOUGH there are many theories of classical education as it now exists, history can give but one account of its origin. It arose from the relations in which the Greek and Latin languages have stood, in the past, to the whole higher life, intellectual and moral, literary and scientific, civil and religious, of Western Europe. Greeks and Romans, as well as Jews, are our spiritual ancestors. They left treasures of recorded thought, word, and deed, by the timely and judicious use of

[1] For parts of this paper, materials have been taken from Von Raumer's and from Schmidt's "Geschichte der Pädagogik."

which their heirs have become the leaders of mankind. But they left them in custody of their native tongues.

I. After Alexander, the Greek tongue spread widely through the East, and became the means of blending Oriental with Western modes of thought. Commerce prepared the way for liberal intercourse. Ideas were exchanged freely with reciprocal advantage. But the Greek, offering new philosophy for old religion, obtained for Europe the more precious gift—

Χρύσεα χαλκείων, ἑκατόμβοι' ἐννεαβοίων.

No faith attracted more attention than that of the Jews. Their sacred books were carefully translated into the Greek language, and afterwards, by fanciful adaptation, and by real insight, expressed in terms of Greek thought. Greek philosophy meanwhile, embracing with reverence the long-sought wisdom of the East, went beyond the measure of Pythagoras, Socrates, or Plato, and often beyond the guidance of sober reason, in ascetic abstraction from the things of sense, and ardent longing after spiritual truth.

Christianity itself had Greek for its mother-tongue. St. Paul, a Roman citizen, writes in Greek to the Christians of Rome. The Epistle to the Hebrews is Greek, and so is that of St. James "to the twelve tribes scattered abroad." Indeed, it is now maintained that Greek had become the ordinary language of Palestine, and was spoken by our Lord himself.[1]

Nor did Western Christendom lay aside this tongue, provided by God to publish and preserve the Gospel, until the Greek mind had left its lasting impress on the doctrines of the Universal Church.

[1] Roberts' Discussions on the Gospels.

For great part of three centuries, the Churches of the West were mostly "Greek religious colonies."[1] Their language, their organization, their liturgy,[2] their Scriptures, were Greek. The Apostolic Fathers, the apologists and historians of the early Church, the great theologians, orthodox and heretic, wrote and spoke Greek. The proceedings of the first seven Councils were carried on, and the speculative form of the Christian faith defined, in that language. It was hardly possible to handle the profounder questions in any other. Augustine is at a loss for words to speak of them in Latin. Seven centuries later Anselm undertakes the task with diffidence; nor is it clear whether in his own judgment he succeeds or fails.[3]

Thus, when Christianity became the State religion, and the emperor, in such broken language as he could command, took a modest part in the discussions of Nicæa, it was a last and signal spiritual triumph of captive Greece over Rome.

II. The ancient Church encouraged the study of heathen literature, but with a paramount regard to morality and Christian truth. Plato, Cicero, and Quintilian had pointed out the danger of using the poets indiscriminately as school-books; and the Father who

---

[1] Milman's Latin Christianity, i. 27.

[2] It is significant that the word *liturgy* is Greek, as are *hymn*, *psalm*, *homily*, and *catechism*, *baptism* and *eucharist*, *priest*, *bishop* and *pope*.

[3] His chief difficulty is to translate ὑπόστασις—"tres nescio quid ... non possum proferre uno nomine ... congruo nomine dici non potest ... sicut non sunt tres substantiæ, ita non sunt tres personæ." Yet he uses *substantia*, apologising: "Græcos secutus sum, qui confitentur tres substantias in una essentia, eadem fide, qua nos tres personas, in una substantia." There are not, and there are "tres substantiæ:" there are not, and there are, "tres personæ." Such are the verbal contradictions which arose from the unfitness of the Latin tongue to render Greek thought.

slept with Aristophanes under his pillow would not have placed him in the hands of boys. But even Tertullian allowed Christian boys to attend the public schools under pagan masters.

Origen made the study of heathen poets and moralists preparatory to that of higher Christian truth. His master, Clement, taught that philosophy [1] was the testament or dispensation given to the Greeks, the schoolmaster to bring them, as the Mosaic law brought the Jews, to Christ. And his teaching was generally accepted. To this day "along the porticoes of Eastern churches, both in Greece and Russia, are to be seen portrayed on the walls the figures of Homer, Thucydides, Pythagoras, and Plato, as pioneers preparing the way for Christianity."[2] When Julian forbade the Christians to institute public schools of rhetoric and literature, in which pagan authors might be read, the bishops protested.

In short the liberality of these early Fathers, their eagerness to recognise a high moral and intellectual standard, wherever it could be found in heathen writers, as "the testimony of a soul by nature Christian," and their faith that such excellent gifts are from God, furnish an admirable example of the spirit in which the Church may deal with questions of education, whether they relate to Greek philosophy and the classics, or to modern inductive science and free thought.

During this first Christian age, Greek was the common

---

[1] A faith afraid of philosophy, in his view, is a weak faith. Faith is a summary mode of knowledge (σύντομος γνῶσις); knowledge is the scientific and reasoned form of faith (ἐπιστημονικὴ πίστις, ἀπόδειξις). Faith comes first, but let us add to our faith knowledge.

[2] Stanley's Eastern Church, p. 35.

language of literature, while Latin, after Tacitus and Pliny, rapidly declined. The "Meditations" of the Emperor Marcus Aurelius are composed in the vernacular of the freedman Epictetus. No Latin names can be placed beside those of Lucian and Plutarch, Arrian and Dion Cassius, Ptolemy and Galen. At Athens and Alexandria, the great conservative and liberal universities,[1] studies in grammar and criticism were conducted side by side with philosophy and science. In both alike the Greek tongue was employed. Of all the considerable intellectual production which went on throughout the Roman world, jurisprudence alone was Latin.

III. But if Greek was the chosen language which carried literature, science, and wisdom, Christian, as well as heathen, to the highest pitch in the ancient world, Latin also was an appointed means of transferring them to Western Europe.

The imperial art of Rome laid the solid foundations on which, when the flood of barbarism began to subside, much of the old fabric was laboriously reconstructed, before the thoughts of man took a wider range. In Spain and Gaul Latin became the mother tongue. But in uneducated mouths it resumed that process of decay and regeneration, the natural life of a language spoken and not written, which only literature can arrest. Hence in time, Italians, as well as Spaniards and French, had to learn book-Latin as a foreign language.[2] It was

[1] Merivale's Roman Empire, vol. vii.
[2] Dante (De vulgari Eloquentia) distinguishes the literary from the vulgar tongue as being acquired by long and patient attention to rule. "Grammatica locutio est secundaria. Ad habitum hujus pauci perveniunt, quia non nisi per spatium temporis et studii assiduitatem *regulamur et doctrinamur* in illa." His own Latin was uncouth.

to them what the writings of our forefathers would be to us, if "Englisc" literature excelled English as Roman did "Romance." But other than literary interests maintained the old Latin as a common language beside the provincial dialects of the new.

The laws of the Western Empire, the last and greatest product of the ancient Roman mind, were adopted by the Gothic, Lombard, and Carlovingian dynasties, and in the twelfth century the first great European school at Bologna was thronged by students of Roman law.[1] At one time there were twenty thousand, from different countries, dividing their attention between civil and canon law, the Pandects and the Decretals. Both were studied with a view to advancement in life, but especially to Church preferment.

Indeed it may be said, with as much truth as is required in metaphor, that the ark which carried through the darkest age, together with its own sacred treasures, the living use of ancient Latin, and some tradition of ancient learning, was the Christian Church.

What at first had been everywhere a Greek became in Western Europe a Latin religion. The discipline of Rome maintained the body of doctrine which the thought of Greece had defined. A new Latin version, superseding alike the venerable Greek translation of the Old Testament and the original words of Evangelists and Apostles, became the received text of Holy Scripture. The Latin Fathers acquired an authority scarcely less binding. The ritual, lessons, and hymns of the Church were Latin. Ecclesiastics transacted the business of

[1] Roger Bacon and Dante both complain that no one would study anything but jurisprudence. (Dr. Döllinger's Universities Past and Present.)

civil departments requiring education. Libraries were armouries of the Church: grammar was part of her drill. The humblest scholar was enlisted in her service: she recruited her ranks by founding Latin schools. "Education in the rudiments of Latin," says Hallam, "was imparted to a greater number of individuals than at present;" and, as they had more use for it than at present, it was longer retained. If a boy of humble birth had a taste for letters, or if a boy of high birth had a distaste for arms, the first step was to learn Latin. His foot was then on the ladder. He might rise by the good offices of his family to a bishopric, or to the papacy itself by merit and the grace of God. Latin enabled a Greek from Tarsus (Theodore) to become the founder of learning in the English Church; and a Yorkshireman (Alcuin) to organize the schools of Charlemagne. Without Latin, our English Winfrid (St. Boniface) could not have been apostle of Germany and reformer of the Frankish Church; or the German Albert master at Paris of Thomas Aquinas; or Nicholas Breakspeare Pope of Rome. With it, Western Christendom was one vast field of labour: calls for self-sacrifice, or offers of promotion, might come from north or south, from east or west.

Thus in the Middle Ages Latin was made the groundwork of education; not for the beauty of its classical literature, nor because the study of a dead language was the best mental gymnastic, or the only means of acquiring a masterly freedom in the use of living tongues, but because it was the language of educated men throughout Western Europe, employed for public business, literature, philosophy, and science, above all, in God's providence, essential to the unity, and therefore enforced by the authority, of the Western Church.

IV. But the Latin of the Middle Ages was not classical, and in the West Greek became an unknown tongue. Cicero did less to form style than Jerome; Plato was forgotten in favour of Augustine; Aristotle alone, translated out of Greek into Syriac, out of Syriac into Arabic, out of Arabic into Latin, and in Latin purged of everything offensive to the mediæval mind, had become in the folios of Thomas Aquinas a buttress, if not a pillar, of the Christian Church.

The neglect of heathen writers began in an age when the clergy were contending against Paganism as well as barbarism. In quieter times the best Latin classics reappear, and instead of hymns such as *Dies Iræ* or *Veni Creator Spiritus*, there are crops of tolerable verse in classical metres. Still, the aim of mediæval differs from the aim of classical education. It may be well therefore to know what, at the worst, the former was, before seeing it in conflict with the latter.

Among Churchmen, Gregory the Great has been selected as an example of "prepossession against secular learning carried to the most extravagant degree." His conception of its use and value may be gathered from his commentary on the First Book of Kings. The Israelites went down to the Philistines to sharpen every man his share, and his coulter, and his axe, and his mattock. So Christians must go down into the region of secular learning to sharpen their spiritual weapons. Moses was trained in the learning of the Egyptians: Isaiah had a better education than Amos: St. Paul was a pupil of the great Gamaliel. There are depths of meaning in Holy Scripture which no unlearned person can explore. The liberal arts, therefore, are to be studied so far, as by their aid revealed truth is profoundly understood.

Secular learning, not as complementary but as subordinate to Holy Scripture; such was the professed aim, in barbarous times, of "one who has been reckoned as inveterate an enemy of learning as ever lived." But the practical meaning of such an aim depends on the zeal and judgment with which it is pursued. And in practice, Gregory did not show much regard even for the first of liberal arts. Witness his account of his own habits as a writer:—"I am at no pains to avoid barbarous confusions. I do not condescend to observe the place or force of prepositions and inflections. My indignation is stirred at the notion of binding the words of the heavenly oracle under the rules of Donatus."[1] Such language from a Pope was not likely to promote the right understanding of Scripture.

Charlemagne reproves his bishops for bad grammar in their letters to him. He too desired to promote secular learning in subordination to Holy Scripture. It was for this that he founded his cathedral and conventual schools.[2]

Neither churchmen as such, nor statesmen, were the enemies of grammar. Nor were the lawyers greatly to

[1] From the first Christianity spoke the language of the people; many of the Fathers affect rudeness of speech. "I am a disciple of fishermen."—*Basil.* "Once for all, I know *cubitum* is neuter; but the people makes it masculine, and therefore so do I."—*Jerome.* "We are not afraid of the grammarian's rod."—*Augustine.*

[2] "Psalmos, notas, cantus, computum, grammaticam, per singula episcopia et monasteria discant."

blame. One of them, indeed, is accused of having said, "De verbibus non curat jurisconsultus." But this is doubtless a foolish sneer at men whose learning, while directly useful to society, was not less important for moral and political science, studies of high rank in liberal education.

The true and tough antagonist that must be vanquished before Cicero and Virgil could prevail, was neither the old Church Latin, with its ornate rhetoric, nor Law Latin, which neglected style. It was the more recent Latin of the schools that provoked, fought, and lost the battle against Latin of the Augustan age. The scholastic philosophy, like German metaphysics, had a style and dialect of its own. It had constructed an apparatus of abstract terms, which were supposed to correspond, like those of modern science, with the most essential distinctions of things. With this key it endeavoured to unlock even the mysteries of theology, and penetrating the secret of existence, to command the whole realm of knowledge. It thus combined moral and religious speculation with the promise of natural science. It was accepted by thousands of active minds as a comprehensive system of thought, exalted above the shafts of ignorant ridicule or literary censure. It was for this that eager students, in the thirteenth century, crowded the Universities of Paris and of Oxford. Engrossed with the sublime objects and powerful method of the new philosophy, they neglected rhetoric for logic.

"A party," says Hallam, "hostile to polite letters, as well as ignorant of them—that of the theologians and dialecticians—carried with it the popular voice in the

Church and universities. The time allotted by these to philological literature was curtailed, that the professors of logic and philosophy might detain their pupils longer." Their Latin did not aspire to be the Latin of Cicero, but a Latin for expressing truths to which Cicero had not attained. With the Latin of Cicero in the domain of higher education, School Latin could make no terms. If it did not conquer it must die.

This indifference to literary form was carried so far as to provoke reaction. The lesser Schoolmen and their pupils became ridiculous by their slovenliness and blunders in the Latin of every-day life. The earlier names stand above this reproach. Lanfranc and Anselm have the good word of Hallam: he praises the letters of Abelard, while preferring those of Heloisa. But the decadence was rapid: the tongue habitually spoken in the universities became to cultivated ears a jargon. The *Oxoniensis loquendi mos*[1] was proverbial, and only less intolerable than that of Paris. In a satirical poem of the thirteenth century, entitled "The Battle of the Seven Arts," Grammar is encamped in Orleans, Logic in Paris. Grammar, in whose ranks are the ancient poets, is beaten out of the field. In the great library of Paris, when the fourteenth century began, there was not a copy of Cicero, nor any poet but Ovid and Lucan. The study of civil law was also forbidden. School theology and school philosophy reigned supreme.

V. Driven out of France, the poets rallied in Italy. Three great Florentines embraced their cause—the first, himself an adept in the wisdom of the schools.

---

[1] A Visitor, in 1276, officially condemned the phrase *Currens est ego*. Oxford logic can still match it, in English, if not in Latin.

The homage of Dante to Virgil, in the great work in which (rejecting Latin) he laid the foundation-stone of the Italian language, did much to kindle in his fellow-countrymen that affectionate[1] veneration for their ancient poet which has never perhaps been so deeply felt elsewhere as in his native land. Well for Italy, if all the objects of her literary worship had been as noble, or the worshippers as pure in heart.

Boccaccio, half a century later, devoted himself at Virgil's tomb to literature and art, read Homer in Greek, and acquired reputation by his Latin eclogues. He also wrote, and repented having written, the tales which are regarded as the first-fruits of Italian prose.

But the chief leader of the revolution which overthrew the Schoolmen was Petrarch, whose whole soul was in the enterprise of reinstating the ancient masters of language. He, while Schoolmen despised him as an unlearned poet, set the first example of that enthusiastic collection and preservation of classical manuscripts, for which Italy has earned unceasing thanks. In childhood his fine ear had been taken captive by the music of a Ciceronian sentence. He lamented bitterly that through ignorance of Greek he was deaf to the melodies of Homer. Virgil he studied with such zeal, that he was suspected of learning the black art, and employing the

---

[1] The feeling finds touching expression in a hymn sung at Mantua on the Feast of St. Paul. The Apostle, on landing in Italy, is taken to see the poet's grave:—

"Ad Maronis mausoleum
Ductus, fudit super eum
Piæ rorem lacrymæ:
Quem te, inquit, reddidissem,
Si te vivum invenissem,
Poetarum maxime."

great magician's charms in the composition of his own verse. His Latin epic, "Africa," enchanted even the University of Paris. But, though invited to receive the poet's wreath at the hands of philosophers, he preferred honour in his own country; where he was conducted with extraordinary pomp and popular enthusiasm, attended by dancing satyrs, fauns, and nymphs, and escorted by all the gods of Olympus, to the Capitol, and crowned by the Senator of Rome. Thence proceeding to the ancient Christian Basilica, and kneeling before the altar, he offered his garland of ivy, laurel, and myrtle to St. Peter.

Later in life, he felt that the Latin epic was not a masterpiece, and that his Italian sonnets better deserved the crown. But his countrymen of that age did not think so. The artist could best judge of his own execution; Italy knew what had been her ideal. Her imagination was fixed on the revival of the past. Scipio, not Laura, had shared the poet's triumph. More than a century had yet to pass before the mother-tongue came into literary favour; more than two centuries before the Academy, passing by Dante, made Petrarch the standard for verse, Boccaccio for prose. For the present Italian scholars laboured heart and hand to establish the classical form of culture.

They received invaluable aid from the Greeks who settled in Italy during the half century before and immediately after the capture of Constantinople. Although the vulgar tongue of Greece was now Romaic, educated society had retained the ancient language. Its resuscitation in Western Europe created a new epoch. "For seven hundred years," says Aretino, speaking of Chrysoloras, the first Greek professor at Florence (1396), "no Italian has been acquainted with Greek literature, and yet we know that all learning comes from the Greeks." The poets more than doubled their ranks, and made common cause with the mighty philosophers of Greece. Cosmo founded a Platonic Academy: the Professor of Greek literature at Florence lectured on "the great master of the wise." The Latin Aristotelians asked with indignation how a philosopher could be expounded by one who was none. Politian replied, that a king's interpreter need not be a king.

With the general literature and philosophy of the Greeks, their natural history, physics, mathematics, medicine, and other sciences,[1] were revived. Everything contributed to restore the past. Greek was learnt as a living language. Latin was spoken in polite society. There was no modern history, philosophy, or science which could compete with the treasures daily discovered in the virgin soil of ancient manuscripts. Both form and substance had the charm of novelty for all men, so that the same thoughts were active in the minds of old and young. The revival of antiquity flattered the political instincts of the people. And it was highly for the honour of Italy to lead the other nations of Europe to the admiring study of her greatest writers.

On the other hand, a passion for attaining to the new standard of literary excellence led many scholars to neglect the more solid parts of a liberal education. Zeal for the ancient languages did more at first to repress and cramp than to foster and direct the growth of the

[1] The founder of modern astronomy, and the first President of the College of Physicians (Linacre), were eager students in Italy.

mother-tongue. And the good sense of the many was perverted in straining after an ideal attained at most only by the few. Their art does not conceal the want of nature: their works bear the fatal stamp of second hand.

In all endeavours to revive the past it is easy unawares to overstep the line which divides imitation from caricature. The revival of a pagan ideal in a Christian country caused constant embarrassment in the choice between the unclassical and the incongruous. When Dante wrote

"Oh sommo Giove,
Che fosti 'n terra per noi crocifisso,"

he did not violate good taste or Christian feeling more than Pope, when in his "Universal Prayer" he unites the names

"Jehovah, Jove, or Lord."

But Boccaccio's phrase for the Resurrection, "il glorioso partimento del figliuolo di Giove dagli spogliati regni di Plutone," is scarcely more irreverent than it is absurd. And Boccaccio is outdone by Bembo, who not only speaks of Leo X. as vicegerent of "the immortal gods," but even when writing in the Pope's name presumes to call the Holy Spirit "Zephyrus cælestis," and the Virgin Mary "dea Lauretana."

And, worse than bad taste, with the return to pagan models in literature and art, there was a return, not indeed to pagan belief, but to pagan unbelief and pagan vice. The sixth Cæsar, as Pontiff, did not wear a thinner veil of religion than the sixth Alexander. The most profligate heathen had written nothing so bad that an Italian scholar of the worst sort did not think it worthy of transcription, comment, and imitation. The state of morals deterred many in this country from sending their sons to Italy for classical instruction. The Italians themselves had a motto, " Inglese italianato è un diavolo incarnato."

Some of the dangers attending the revival of classical literature were plainly seen at the time. Petrarch writes —" Above all, let us be Christians. Let us so read philosophy, poetry, and history, that our hearts may be ever open to the Gospel of Christ. The Gospel is the one sure foundation on which human industry may securely build all true knowledge." Vittorino, the most renowned Italian of those times for his educational labours, made his pupils read Christian as well as heathen books. He also instructed them in logic and metaphysics (not of the scholastic type) mathematics, and the fine arts, and watched carefully over their moral character. But his zeal for the classics was such that he had little regard for the mother-tongue. Lorenzo endeavoured by precept and example to enforce cultivation of the mother-tongue, but found fashion too strong for him except among his personal friends. In Florence the first and most peremptory command of fathers to sons and masters to pupils was, on no account to read anything vulgar.[1]

Pico di Mirandola wrote a defence of the Schoolmen in excellent classical Latin, and disputed at Rome in the Latin of the schools. To perform such an exercise

[1] "Che eglino, nè per bene, nè per male, non leggessero cose volgari."— *Foscolo* (quoted by Ranmer). This proscription would include the "Legends of the Fourteenth Century," lately republished. Written for the people, they are admirable for vigour and directness of style, and would have been a good corrective of literary pedantry, as well as heathen vice.

in Ciceronian Latin would have been as impossible as to conduct the Nicene debates in the Latin of the later empire.

But Italian scholarship generally seemed rather to bathe itself with ever new delight in the refreshing waters of the past, than to evolve the intense spiritual fire which was needed to sever the gold from the dross, and unite the classical with the Christian ideal, old things with new.

Nor can it fail to be observed how slight and superficial was the part played by the Italian people at large in the movement. Classical education in Italy seems to be the education of princesses and of princes, of noble ladies and young men of rank and fortune. Such was the work of Guarino, who had distinguished Englishmen among his pupils; such in the main was the work of Vittorino, whose establishment, beautifully decorated by art, and surrounded by gardens and woods, was known as the Casa Giojosa. Vittorino, however, spent all his own means and interested his high-born pupils in assisting poor scholars, some forty of whom he contrived to feed, clothe, and instruct, as well as to visit hospitals and prisons. It may be that there was more such instruction of the people than appears. At least the general fact cannot be mistaken. Although in the revival of Letters Italian enthusiasm and Italian scholarship, aided by the Greeks, supplied at first all the working power, it was not until the pursuit of the new ideal had been carried beyond the Alps that it changed the whole course of school education.

VI. Looking from Italy to Germany, we see a complete contrast of race, of mother tongues, of history, of religious temper, and generally of national character. It was only natural that Italian scholars should doubt, and leave it for Germans themselves to try, whether the noble and graceful literature of the ancient world, which, when once revived, seemed hardly more exotic than indigenous in Rome or Florence, could flourish in the Northern soil. Yet in truth, Germany presented the conditions necessary for its successful cultivation, though with underlying spiritual diversity, which must profoundly modify the type.

Christian Rome had subdued the barbarians, and had laid upon them, for all higher purposes of life, the yoke of a foreign language. Long did the luckless Germans toil to frame their lips aright: marvellous were their failures,[1] and marvellous their success. By frequenting foreign universities,[2] and by that infinite capacity for taking pains, which is the national genius of the German,[3] their educated men had attained to a Latin, which passed muster among the dialects of the schools.

In the fifteenth century, the Brethren of the Common Life, or Hieronymites, had perhaps a hundred

[1] The chief difficulties were inflections and pronunciation. In planting the Church, St. Boniface found one of his Germans baptizing "In nomine Patria, et Filia, et Spiritui Sancta." Reuchlin was recommended for an Italian mission as having a tolerable accent, "sonum pronuntiationis minus horridum." Würtemberg regulations of the 16th century enact that children whose German mouths by nature cannot pronounce all the letters, are not to be dragged by the hair, or immoderately flogged. Necessity had not yet given birth to the invention of pronouncing Latin by the rules of the mother tongue.

[2] Their own universities did what they could. Ingolstadt, for example, enacted "Quod nullum suppositum in communitatibus bursarum aut in aliis locis bursae Theutonicum loqui audeat." But they got no better Latin than they gave.

[3] "Das Genie ist der Fleiss."—*Schiller*.

establishments in the Low Countries and parts of
Germany and France, where they gave instruction in
reading, writing, speaking, and singing Latin. At
their chief college, Deventer, a scholar was punished
for letting fall a single word of Dutch. Their best
Latin probably resembled that of the "Imitatio Christi,"
a book of which Europe has been content to read two
thousand editions in the original, while it has but once
been translated "from Latin into Latin." The same
book may give some notion of their educational ideal,
which was sublime, but on a narrow foundation.
Everything was subordinate, not so much to Scripture,
as to the spiritual life. But their conception of spiritual
life wanted breadth. Their founder, Gerard Groot, a
mighty preacher in the mother tongue, had experienced
a strong reaction from magic, necromancy, and scholastic philosophy, which he had studied at Paris.
"Spend no time," he charges them, "on geometry,
arithmetic, rhetoric, dialectic, grammar, poetry, horo-
scopes, or astrology. Such pursuits are renounced by
Seneca, much more by a Christian of spiritual mind.
They avail not for the spiritual life. Of heathen sciences,
the moral are least to be shunned. The wiser heathens,
such as Socrates and Plato, applied themselves to
these." This injunction against all the liberal arts but
music, left the brethren ample time for spiritual exercises, and for a work which they had much at heart,
the elementary instruction of the people.

Experience so far corrected their narrowness, that
from their schools chiefly went forth the men who
sowed the seeds in Germany of the classical revival,
as well as of the religious reformation. Thomas à

Kempis (it is said) exercised much influence at their school at Zwoll over Wessel, who, though but a moderate Greek and Hebrew scholar, was the greatest theologian of his time.[1] Wessel, in his turn, if not Thomas à Kempis himself, was in intimate relations with Hegius, Agricola, Lange, and Dringenberg, who were all educated by the brethren. Of these, Hegius presided over the College of Deventer for thirty years (1438-1468), and trained many good scholars both in Latin and in Greek. He speaks with enthusiasm of the importance of Greek. "If any one wishes to understand grammar, rhetoric, mathematics, history, or Holy Scripture, let him learn Greek. We owe everything to the Greeks." Writing to Wessel to borrow the Greek Gospels, he thus ends his letter—"You wish to be informed more precisely about my teaching. I have followed your advice. *All learning is hurtful, when acquired with spiritual loss.*"

This was still the noble Shibboleth of the school. But it was found compatible now with classical education. Of all the scholars sent out from Deventer one only of any mark,[2] Adrian VI., had the reputation of being unfriendly to classical culture, such as he found at Rome after Leo X.

Agricola proved that it was possible for a German to attain to the highest standard of pure Latin and of classical erudition. He valued his liberty too highly

---

[1] Such was Reuchlin's estimate. Luther's confidence in his own convictions was greatly increased by their agreeing with Wessel's, so closely, that if he had known Wessel's writings sooner, he might have been accused (he himself says) of plagiarism.

[2] Another, Ortuinus Gratius, has an unenviable notoriety as the master at Cologne to whom the "Epistolæ obscurorum Virorum" are addressed.

to become a schoolmaster, but was much consulted in all questions of classical education.

Lange rooted out the old schoolbooks, and set up a flourishing classical school at Münster. "I have great confidence," writes Agricola, "in the success of your labours. I believe our own Germany will attain to such learning and culture, that Latium itself shall not be more Latin." The new ideal stands before his mind. Lange lived to see its advent. Reading in his old age the theses of Luther, "Now is the time at hand," he exclaimed, "when darkness shall be driven from the land: sound doctrine shall return to our churches, and pure Latin be taught in our schools."

Dringenberg was rector (1450-1490) of a school at Schlestadt, which sent out many brilliant scholars. Of younger Daventrians, Busch made himself an itinerant apostle of classical education, lecturing in England and France, as well as in Germany. He accomplished the public abolition of the mediæval schoolbooks at Erfurt, but was expelled from Leipsic and thrice from Cologne, strongholds of the old grammars, where he attempted similar reforms.

The most distinguished of Daventrian scholars, Erasmus, praises the character, learning, and ability of his master, Hegius, but attacks the brethren as exercising an illiberal influence over education. His ideal differs from theirs. Indeed, the one factor in the educational movement of his time which Erasmus most imperfectly represents, is the deep spiritual earnestness of the men, to whom, in common with many forerunners of the Reformation, he owed his early training. His merciless satires did much to stimulate that contempt for monks which was preparing at once what he intended and what he did not intend, a revolution in education, and the violent disruption of the Church. Even his Colloquies, for boys from eight years of age, which came into general use as a schoolbook, are full of open or covert attacks on monks, relics, pilgrims, and generally on all forms of religion which he regarded as superstitious: so much so, that the book was condemned by the Sorbonne, forbidden in France, burnt in Spain, and placed on the Index at Rome. Melanchthon allowed selections only to be used in schools.

As an educational reformer, Erasmus was not likely to be misled into the extreme of Italian fashion. He had greater work on hand than the greatest of Latin epics, or the purest of Latin styles. His extensive acquaintance with ancient literature made him despise prostrate adoration of individual writers. His sense of the superior importance of scriptural and theological studies raised him above enthusiasm for mere literary culture.

So far as the true interests of classical education were concerned, his sarcastic pen was seldom better employed than in writing his "Ciceronianus," an onslaught on the superstition of using none but Cicero's Latin. Of all moderns, Erasmus was in the best position to understand the necessities of Latin as a living tongue. For, while he wrote and spoke with singular fluency and spirit on almost every topic of the day, he vaunted his ignorance of Italian, and was equally ignorant of French, English, and German. In his "Ratio Studiorum," he strongly recommends translation from Greek into Latin, as giving insight into the comparative powers and idioms of each language, and showing what *we* have in common with the Greek. This casual expression indicates how completely Latin was regarded as the language of all education. The corresponding exercise in the present day would be careful written translation from the classics into the mother tongue.

His Greek grammar contributed to facilitate the study of the language in Germany. But his great work was his Greek Testament, which, though printed later than the Complutensian, was the first edition actually published, in 1516.

Reuchlin shares with Erasmus and Agricola the credit of introducing the study of Greek from Italy into Germany. The foundation of Hebrew learning was laid by Reuchlin alone, in his "Rudiments of the Hebrew Tongue," published in 1506.

These two great works, Reuchlin's "Rudiments," and the New Testament of Erasmus, stimulated to the utmost in Germany the study of Hebrew and Greek, which now resumed their dignity as the sacred tongues, dethroning the language which had long been their vicegerent in the Western Church. The same two books enabled Luther to complete his German Bible. But long before it was published the great struggle had begun, and the further fortunes of classical culture became involved in the progress and results of the Reformation.

VII. How closely the interests of classical as well as popular education were bound up with those of religious reform appears nowhere more plainly than in Luther's "Letter to the Burgomasters and Town-councillors of all the Towns of Germany, moving them to found and maintain Christian Schools. Anno 1524."

Extracts can give but a feeble impression of its drift and power. It is the stirring appeal of a leader of men, rousing the dull and rallying the noble to a war against Ignorance in her strongholds. But it is also the prophetic warning of a great seer, the burden of Germany. The argument comes on like an advancing tide: the movement of history is in it. Behold, all things are ready! The voice is the voice of Luther, but the call is the call of God.

"Of a truth Almighty God hath graciously visited us Germans in our own land, and brought us a right golden year. See what learned young fellows we have now, and grown men, fine scholars in the languages and all the arts. Ay, and useful too, if you would use them to teach the young folk. Do not your own eyes see that a boy can be taught now in three years, so that at fifteen or eighteen he knows more than all high schools and cloisters ever knew till now.

"My good friends, buy while the market is at your door. Make hay while the sun shines. God's grace is like the passing shower, which does not return where it has been. Therefore lay hold, and hold fast, whoever can: slack hands gather scanty harvests.

"The people that we want will not grow of themselves. We cannot carve them out of wood, nor hew them out of stone. God will not work a wonder to help us, when He has given us wherewith to help ourselves.

"But if we must have schools, say you, what is the use of teaching Latin, and Greek, and Hebrew, and other liberal arts? Cannot we teach the Bible and God's Word in German? Is not that sufficient for salvation?

"Why, if there were no other use of the tongues,

it ought to gladden our hearts and kindle our souls, that they are such a noble, beautiful gift of God, which he is bestowing now so richly on us Germans, more almost than on any other land.

"But true though it be that the Gospel came and comes only by the Holy Spirit, yet it came by means of the tongues, and thereby grew, and thereby must be preserved. For when first God sent the Gospel by the Apostles throughout the world He gave the tongues also. Aye, and beforehand, by the Roman rule, He had spread the Greek and Latin tongues in all lands, that His Gospel might bear fruit far and wide. So hath He done now. No one knew to what end God was bringing forth the tongues again, till now it is seen that it was for the Gospel's sake. To that end He gave Greece to the Turks, that the Greeks, driven out and scattered abroad, might carry forth the Greek tongue, and so a beginning might be made of learning other tongues also.

"As we hold the Gospel dear then, so let us hold the languages fast. If we do not keep the tongues, we shall not keep the Gospel. As the sun to the shadow, so is the tongue itself to all the glosses of the Fathers. Ah, how glad the dear Fathers would have been if they could have so learned Holy Scripture."

In the foreground of all Luther's thoughts on education, stands the knowledge of Holy Scripture, rightly understood by diligent use of human learning,[1] under guidance of the Holy Spirit, an attainment demanding, as he knew by experience in translation, a

---

[1] "Nihil aliud est Theologia, nisi Grammatica in Spiritus Sancti verbis occupata."—*Luther*.

different discipline from that which satisfied Gregory, or Gerard Groot, or, in his own time, the Vaudois, whom he censures for neglect of Greek and Hebrew. But the languages are in no servile subordination. Glorious and beautiful in themselves, they become holy by ministering freely to the mind of God. Holy is the Hebrew tongue, for to it first were committed the oracles of God. Holy is the Greek tongue, for it was chosen to be the well-spring of the Gospel. But hallowed also is every other tongue into which the waters from that well-spring have flowed. Whereas without the sacred tongues, and without the Gospel, Germany has sunk so low, that her wretched people, like poor dumb cattle, can neither read nor write good German, nor good Latin, and have well-nigh lost the use of their natural reason. Not only the sacred tongues, therefore, but German and Latin, not only religious, but secular literature is to be studied. Next to the Bibles in all tongues and the commentators, in a library, are to stand books which help to acquire the languages, such as the works of poets and orators, be they heathen or Christian, Latin or Greek. Education has been religious only, so that it has been held a kind of scandal for a scholar to marry. It must be so now no longer. Even if there were no soul, no heaven, and no hell, there would still be need for schools to train boys and girls into sensible men and women. Jurists as well as theologians are wanted. If those two professions were to cease, ere long, between war and crime, your tradespeople would be glad to grub with their fingers ten ells deep for a learned man. Recruits for the gown must be obtained as recruits are obtained to bear arms. If rulers may compel able-bodied youths to carry spear and gun, so may they compel boys of able mind to go to school for their own and their country's good, and be trained for holy orders or the law.

Luther's scheme of national education embraces high and low, rich and poor; or rather, perhaps, he hardly supposes that the high-born will deign to devote themselves to the learned professions. But every poor boy of good capacity is to be enabled, nay compelled, to study the learned tongues, and to fit himself to serve God in Church and State. Latin, and Greek, and Hebrew are not to be articles of luxury for the rich, but to be taught freely to all who will learn, in every town.

In denouncing the old schools, Luther's language becomes unmeasured. Nowhere is there one good school. Nothing has been learned in cloister-schools and high schools, but to be asses, blockheads, and dolts. Twenty, forty years one might learn there, and in the end know neither Latin nor German, or, perhaps, enough bad Latin to be a priest, and say mass.

The Universities also want "a good strong reform." They have become mere places of resort for free living and vain-glory. Little is heard there of Holy Scripture and the Christian faith. The blind heathen Aristotle is their master rather than Christ. If Luther's advice were taken, Aristotle's Physics, his Metaphysics, his "De Anima," and his Ethics, should all be turned out together, since no one yet has understood their meaning; his Logic, Rhetoric, and Poetics should be kept for training youths to speak and to preach. With these should be studied the learned tongues, mathematics, and good histories, which are of more worth than all philosophy for the guidance of life.

For the schoolmaster's office, Luther had unbounded respect. "If I were not a preacher of the Gospel," he declares, more than once, "I know no station on earth that I would rather fill than that of a schoolmaster or teacher of boys."

His just sense of the importance of education, and his broad views of its relations to the whole framework of society, give his opinions an intrinsic value, which goes far to make good the want of practical experience.

But if Luther, with all his zeal for the tongues, never taught them, he had a colleague who never preached, but devoted his whole life to the work of education, "the Preceptor of Germany," Melanchthon.

At twelve years of age Melanchthon went to Heidelberg, and was Bachelor of Arts at fourteen, having been taught wordy Logic and a smattering of Physics. At seventeen he took his Master's degree at Tübingen, and lectured on Virgil and Terence. Four years later he became Professor of Greek at Wittenberg, where he spent the remainder of his days (1518—1560).

Wittenberg, though the youngest, was the leading University of Protestant Germany; and Melanchthon was both the leading spirit of Wittenberg, and chief adviser in the organisation of Protestant schools. His writings are a rich mine of facts concerning German classical education.

His report on churches and schools (1528) became the basis in Saxony of a reformed scholastic, as well as ecclesiastical establishment, independent of Rome. The example was followed in other German states.

The report recommends the following regulations for schools : [1]—

1. The children to be taught Latin only, not German, Greek, or Hebrew. Plurality of tongues does them more harm than good.

2. They are to be kept to a few books.

3. They are to be divided into three classes. The first to read Donatus and Cato, and learn a list of Latin words daily. The second class to read Æsop's Fables, and select colloquies of Erasmus, and learn Latin proverbs. Also, grammar is to be well worked into them, and learnt by heart. When they know the rules of construction, they are to "construe," as it is called, which is very useful, and yet little used. As they grow older, they are to learn by heart Terence, and after Terence, Plautus; the pure plays only, as the Aulularia and Trinummus. One day in the week to be set apart for Christian instruction: St. Matthew to be expounded grammatically. Older boys may read easy Epistles or the Proverbs, but not Isaiah, Paul to the Romans, St. John's Gospel, or the like. The third class, the picked intellects of the school, to read Cicero's Offices and Letters, and Virgil, and say Virgil by heart. When Virgil is done, they may read Ovid's Metamorphoses.

When they thoroughly know their etymology and syntax, they are to learn metre and compose verses. This exercise is a great help to understanding the writings of others, makes the boys rich in words, and gives dexterity in many things. Speaking Latin is also enforced. The master, as far as may be, to speak only Latin.

[1] What does not bear on classical education is omitted.

Melanchthon insists on the importance of grammatical knowledge, especially for the right interpretation of Scripture. How many controversies turn on the meaning of a word. Neglected Grammar has avenged herself on the monks,[1] by letting them take spurious things for genuine. He rejects the notion that scholarship may be attained by reading, without grammatical study. Such scholarship is never safe, nor thorough.

His Latin grammar, which went through fifty editions, was in general use in German schools of the sixteenth century. The rules were few, lest boys should be alarmed. His Greek Grammar was written at fourteen, and recast in maturer years. In the preface to a Hebrew Grammar, which had his sanction, he lays it down as certain, by consent of the learned, that no one can undertake anything considerable in sound scholarship without Hebrew.

His Manuals of Logic, Physic, and Ethics were for the most part[2] introductions to the Greek text of Aristotle, whose tenure of exclusive rights in liberal education was renewed in Germany for another century by Melanchthon's influence. His Rhetoric was a similar introduction to Cicero and Quintilian, following whom he regarded the orator's art as requiring profound learning, great gifts, long practice, and acute judgment. He felt the importance of Christian rhetoric in the age of the Reformation.

---

[1] One of their masters, expounding the text "Melchisedec Rex Salem panem et vinum obtulit," enlarged on the spiritual significance of salt.

[2] He added to the Physic what he knew of modern discoveries, introducing Physiology for instance to illustrate the "De Anima."

These schoolbooks, intended to lead the young student to the great classical masters of thought and language, were, in fact, much used to save the trouble of going to the fountain-heads. The use of Melanchthon's philosophical manuals became known as "the Philippic Method," and the imitation of his manner[1] as "the Philippic Style."

But, though the building never rose to its intended height, the ground plan shows that the great educator of Germany was far from adopting the dimensions of a merely literary training. He laid under contribution all departments of knowledge[2] and set forth the conception of a truly liberal and many-sided education, not without practical regard to the requirements of Church and State. It remained for experience to show how much of this was beyond the ambition or the reach of an ordinary student.

Melanchthon's own experience must have taught him much. In an inaugural lecture he contrasts the old course with the new. It is charged against the new studies by the adherents of the old, that "after much toil there is little fruit. Greek is taken up lightly for display; modern Hebrew is of small account; meanwhile, sound learning is falling into disuse, philosophy is forsaken."

On the contrary, the truth is that these philosophers have entirely missed the meaning of Aristotle, to understand whom in Greek is difficult, in the Latin translations of the Schoolmen is impossible. He himself (the

---

[1] "He far excelled Erasmus in purity of diction and correctness of classical taste."—*Hallam.*

[2] He prepared a Latin Manual of History, and enforced arithmetic and mathematics. Morhof calls him "verum πολυμαθείας parentem."

professor, aged twenty-one) for six years of his life almost ruined his mind in the school of these pseudo-Aristotelian Sophists, who are the very reverse of Socrates. For whereas the one thing which Socrates knew was that he knew nothing, the one thing which they do not know is that they know nothing.

Instead of their philosophy the University of Wittenberg teaches the genuine Aristotle in the Greek, mathematics, the classical poets, orators, and historians, and true philosophy.

Melanchthon himself lectured with success on Ethics, Logic, and Natural Science, using for each subject the Greek text of Aristotle, as the statutes required.[1] Luther speaks of the crowds that thronged his lecture-rooms from all countries, including England, Italy, and Greece. But, alas for Mathematics! Erasmus Reinhold, a distinguished friend of Copernicus, could not obtain a decent attendance at his lectures. Melanchthon's lectures on Ptolemy[2] met with the same fate. And, alas for the Greek classics! Homer begged for readers as in his lifetime he begged for bread. Wittenberg was deaf to Demosthenes, and would none of Sophocles. "I see," said Melanchthon at last, "that this generation has no ear for such authors. Scarce a few of my audience remain, to spare my feelings. I owe them thanks." At the Universities, as at the schools, much more attention was directed to Latin than to Greek. Terence, for whom there was a special professorship at Wittenberg, owes more even than Aristotle to Melanchthon, who

---

[1] "Enarrabit Ethicus Græca Aristotelis Ethica ad verbum ... Physicus enarrabit Aristotelis Physica."

[2] De Apotelesmatibus et Judiciis Astrorum.

used all his great authority to introduce the plays into schools.[1]

Of Melanchthon's pupils it must suffice briefly to mention those who did most to carry on the work of classical education. Camerarius, Rector at Nürnberg, is better known as a philologist, and as Melanchthon's biographer, than as a schoolmaster.

Trotzendorf, at Goldberg, laid a narrow classical foundation for professional studies. Latin verses and Latin letters were written every week. No phrase was to be used unless the author from whom it came could be pointed out. No language but Latin was spoken, even by the servants. Some of the scholars read St. Paul in Greek, and the Old Testament in Hebrew.

Michael Neander presided at Ilfeld over a school which Melanchthon considered to be the best in the country. His pupils (Neandrici) were noted at the Universities for taking the lead[2] from their first arrival. They began Latin at nine, Greek at thirteen, Hebrew at sixteen. He wrote many school-books, and took considerable pains with History, Geography, and Natural Science.

Hieronymus Wolf was Rector of a Gymnasium at

[1] "Hardly any book," he says, "is mo worthy to be in the hands of all mankind. In exact adjustment of the expression to the thought, he has surpassed them all. If St. Chrysostom delighted in Aristophanes (doubtless as a model of eloquence), how much more is Terence to be prized, whose pieces are free from the disgusting grossness of the Greek poet, and whose style is even more perfect. Therefore, I exhort schoolmasters to recommend this author in the most pressing way to young students. For he seems to me to form the judgment on affairs of the world better than most of the books of philosophers. And no other author will teach the boys to speak Latin with equal purity, or train them to a style which will stand them in better stead."

[2] He ascribed his success in teaching to simplicity: "Plerique fere abhorremus a simp implicitate quæ tamen discentibus est utilissima."

Augsburg, which undertook "to carry scholars so far in religion, the ancient languages, and philosophy, that they might be able to study at the University without the help of a tutor." He pronounced against making the younger boys[1] speak Latin, and against requiring verses *invita Minerva*.

Like Melanchthon, he remembered that the languages are but means to higher ends, solid learning, philosophy, and sound religion. "Happy were the Latins," he says, "who needed only to learn Greek, and that not by school-teaching, but by intercourse with living Greeks. Happier still were the Greeks, who, so soon as they could read and write their mother tongue, might pass at once to the liberal arts and the pursuit of wisdom. For us, who must spend many years in learning foreign languages, the entrance into the gates of Philosophy is made much more difficult. For, to understand Latin and Greek is not learning itself, but the entrance-hall and ante-chamber of learning."

But the school most characteristic of the century, was that of Strasburg, under Sturm, who was Rector forty-five years (1538-1583). He was brought up by the Hieronymites at Liége, and mentions having played there in the Phormio of Terence. Never did the brethren send forth one more zealous in imparting classical culture, or who more definitely conceived his work. His theory of education may serve as a standard for discrimination of later and more hybrid forms.

The end of all study, according to Sturm, is to combine piety with learning.[2] But piety being the

---

[1] "Nec minima pueri virtus est tacere, cum recte loqui nesciat."
[2] *Pietas literata* became a watchword of Protestant schools.

common duty of all men, the distinctive aim of the student is to attain wisdom and eloquence, the knowledge of things, and the power to set them forth in pure and graceful words. In the order of nature words come before wisdom.[1] A student should be trained six years at home, ten at school, and five at an academy. Of the ten years, eight are required for gaining purity and perspicuity, two for adding the graces of style. Readiness and skill in adapting words to things are the business of the five academical years.

Sturm conceives the means as clearly as the end. Of ten forms, each one has its special work. The youngest boys are taught the Latin name of everything they eat, drink, see, or handle in playground, school, or church.

As they rise in the school, the quantity of Latin text read is much increased. The practice of composition is incessant. The elder boys write exercises daily. Verses are begun in the fifth; the upper forms transpose odes of Horace and Pindar into other metres, and produce poems of their own. In prose, the fifth form re-translate from German into Latin, and compare with the original. The upper forms turn Greek orators into Latin, and Latin orators into Greek, with special attention to rhythm, accent, and effect, the master of the form always showing his own version. They write themes, descriptions, and letters, and declaim with or without verbal preparation. They also make careful written translations from Thucydides and Sallust. On Sundays, they turn German catechism into Latin. The elder boys

---

[1] "Ad loquendum homines quam ad cogitandum judicandumque promptiorem naturam habent."

read St. Paul in Greek,[1] and learn by heart his Epistle to the Romans. They learn no Hebrew, for the Rector is of deliberate opinion that a fair command of two languages is as much as can be expected from boys of sixteen.[2]

Materials, as well as models, for the composition are furnished by constantly reading and learning by heart the best authors, and by systematic excerption of phrases and "flowers." The rules of Logic are exemplified from Demosthenes and Cicero; those of Rhetoric also from Homer[3] and Virgil. Latin poetry is traced to its Greek sources; and parallel passages learnt by heart, in verse and in prose. Cicero and Terence[4] are the models for Latin prose. Imitation is reduced to rule. Like theft in Sparta, it is honourable if it is not found out.[5] The jackdaw's mistake was careless arrangement of his borrowed plumes. Stolen apparel should be disguised, by addition, diminution, or alteration.[6] But Sturm does not admit, that to take from Cicero is to steal. "Convey, the wise it call."

"Whose is the work of memory? Whose the skill in selection? Whose the craft in concealment? I come upon the words in Cicero's writings. I mark their value,

[1] The exposition was to be practical. "Non considerabis quid in suis faciant commentariis theologi, sed quid Romani fecerint cum ad illos Paulus scripsisset."

[2] "Multum illum profecisse arbitror, qui ante sextum decimum ætatis aunum facultatem duarum linguarum mediocrem assecutus est."

[3] "Credo ego, omnium oratorum ornamenta et instituta in Homero demonstrari posse, ita ut, si ars dicendi nulla extaret, ex hoc tamen fonte derivari et constitui possit."

[4] "Terentio post Ciceronem nihil utilius est. Purus est sermo et vere Latinus."

[5] "Primus conatus sit ut similitudo non appareat."

[6] "Occultandi vero modus in tribus consistit: additione, ablatione, mutatione."

note the place. I find an use to which they may be put: I go back to the place, transfer them, disguise them, appropriate them, 'borrow' them, if you will. Whose are they now? They have cost me more pains than they cost Cicero. Besides, Cicero does not grudge me them: did he not write for others, for all mankind?" Such, in spirit, is the German Cicero's defence of a practice which Erasmus condemned.

To gain colloquial readiness, all the boys speak Latin, even the obscure little Teutons in the dim regions[1] of the lowest forms. The masters are forbidden to address them in German. The boys are severely chastised[2] if they use their mother tongue. On the way to and from school, and in games, they are to speak only Latin, or Greek. A first fault may be pardoned, but contumacious use of the mother tongue is far too grave an offence.[3]

But the chief feature of the school is the theatre, in which the elder boys weekly tread the stage, and the younger boys[4] fill the benches. Had Melanchthon foreseen to what length a system of pressing Terence upon the attention of boys might be carried, his recommendation of the poet to schoolmasters would perhaps have been less urgent or more guarded. Though Sturm is careful with Horace and Catullus, his boys play all the pieces of Terence and of Plautus indiscriminately. By dividing the work, the whole repertory can be got

---

[1] "Qui in extremis latent classibus."
[2] "Hæc consuetudo custodienda severitate et castigatione" (ἓν διὰ δυοῖν).
[3] "Nullus veniæ locus, si quis hic peccet petulanter."
[4] This is not expressly stated; but as Sturm was jealous of the advantage which ancient Roman boys had in attending the theatre, it is not likely that he would allow his own boys to lose opportunities.

through in six months.[1] Day after day the actors are busy conning their parts, and week after week they throw themselves, with as much histrionic effect as by imagination or drill they can attain, into the stage characters and theatrical situations which pleased and edified pagan Rome. If Plato's Republic had been among the school-books of Strasburg, the boys would have understood his remarks on the drama. Sturm was aware of the objections made, and arranged also a law court, with quæstor, jury, and public complete, in which all the forensic orations of Cicero were to be delivered once a year, the best wits of Strasburg arguing on the other side. It must be added that the two highest forms learnt a little arithmetic and Euclid and use of the globes; and the whole school was trained in music and gymnastics.

Was this a satisfactory education in the sixteenth century? If not, wherein lay the mistake?

It will not do to answer the first question off-hand in the negative, and to set down Sturm as a pedant.[2] In the first place parents were not of that opinion; and (as a great modern journal argues) if parents are content to send their boys to a school as it is, why propose reforms? The school kept up its numbers: in Sturm's time there were several thousand pupils. It kept up its aristocratic connexion: there were two hundred

---

[1] The two upper forms also represented plays of Aristophanes, Euripides, and Sophocles.

[2] Bacon speaks slightingly of him: "Tunc Sturmius in Cicerone oratore et Hermogene rhetore infinitam et anxiam operam consumpsit." In Hallam's opinion, "Scarce any one more contributed to the cause of letters in Germany ... We could, as I conceive, trace no such education in France, certainly not in England."—I. 336.

boys of noble birth, twenty-four counts and barons, and
three princes. It did not neglect the children of the
poor; they were maintained at the public expense, or
by private charity.¹ It had an European reputation:
there were Poles and Portuguese, Spaniards, Danes,
Italians, French, and English. But besides this, it was
the model and mother school of a numerous progeny.
Sturm himself organised schools for several towns which
applied to him. His disciples became organizers, rectors,
and professors. In short, if Melanchthon was the in-
structor, Sturm was the schoolmaster of Germany.² Together with his method, his school-books were spread
broad-cast over the land. Both were adopted by
Ascham³ in England, and by Buchanan in Scotland.
Sturm himself was a great man at the imperial court.
No diplomatist passed through Strasburg without stopping to converse with him. He drew a pension from
the King of Denmark, another from the King of France,
a third from the Queen of England, collected political
information for Cardinal Granvella, and was ennobled
by Charles V. He helped to negotiate peace between
France and England, and was appointed to confer with
a commission of cardinals on reunion of the Church.
In short, Sturm knew what he was about as well as
most men of his time.⁴ Yet few will be disposed to

¹ "De quorum indole constat, certus numerus constituatur quibus respublica victum suppeditet: cæteri privatim a civibus conquirant necessaria."
² "Suo tempore communis fere scholarum per Germaniam moderator. Ejus
consilia non Germaniæ tantum urbes sed peregrinæ secutæ sunt. A cujus
methodo utinam non abiissent scholæ Germanicæ".—*Morhof,* vi. 1, 13; ii. 2, 19.
³ See his "Schoolmaster," lately reprinted; in Johnson's opinion "the best
advice ever given for learning languages."
⁴ His Life has been written in French by C. Schmidt.

accept his theory of education, even for the sixteenth century, as the best.

Wherein then lay the mistake? In what he asserts, or in what he assumes?

Sturm asserts that the proper end of school education is eloquence, or in modern phrase, a masterly command of language, and that the knowledge of things mainly belongs to a later stage. Although the "fair command of two languages" is to be turned to other account elsewhere, it is clear that at school Greek is made secondary to Latin, and Latin to the formation of style.[1] To become acquainted with the thoughts and things which are to be found in such rich variety in classical authors, is not the final end in view. Homer, Demosthenes, Thucydides, Aristophanes, Euripides, are read chiefly for their rhetoric, and as material for translation into Latin.[2] Latin is not learnt to read Cicero and Terence, but Cicero and Terence are read to learn Latin.

Sturm assumes that Latin is the language in which eloquence is to be acquired. Yet he plainly declares that eloquence is not tied down to the ancient tongue. "What can be more pure and graceful than the Italian prose of Boccaccio, or what more musical than Petrarch's verse? The French have their Comines, and the Germans their Luther; a man who, if there had been no Reformation, if he had never preached, never written anything but the pure and rich German of his Bible

---

[1] "Multa Herodotus, plura Thucydides, Xenophon nihil non habet quod sequaris."

[2] There was nothing then in German to translate, unless it were the Catechism, or Luther's Bible, or Tauler's sermons, which open German as Boccaccio's novels open Italian prose literature.

translation, for this alone would have been immortal."
Why then were German boys to neglect their mother
tongue, and spend ten years in laying the foundations of
eloquence in Latin?

It is easy to divine the answer. The attainment of
eloquence in one language was arduous, in more than
one (at least for the majority, to whose interests a
schoolmaster ought to look) impossible. A choice must
be made between Latin and German. Sturm chose the
common language[1] of educated Europe, and sacrificed the
mother tongue.

While classical schools were thus organized throughout
Protestant Germany, Catholics on their part were not
idle. Perceiving what strength Reformers derived from
alliance with the ancients, and discerning the true
value of classical studies, if kept subordinate to the faith
and interests of the Church, the Jesuits resolved to fight
against heresy with the nobler weapons of education
and learning, leaving to the Dominicans fire and sword.
They forthwith drew up a scheme, obtained the Pope's
consent, and used their utmost endeavours to secure that
throughout Europe as many as possible of the rising
generation might for the future be committed to their
charge.

The Jesuits had special motives for making Latin the
language of their schools, and judged it expedient to push
the practice so far as forcibly to suppress the mother-
tongues. They knew but one end, the interests of the
Church; one sacred text, the Vulgate; one Breviary,

---

[1] "Quod in tribus divini spiritus muneribus Deus voluit ubique esse, et esse perpetuum. . . . Hæc jam in medio proposita est industriæ hominum, ut quæ velit earn suis civibus respublica recuperare possit."

the Roman; one will, their General's. So, in their schools, they would have but one spoken language, Latin; one style, that of Cicero; one theology, that of Aquinas; one philosophy, that of Aristotle, interpreted, when possible,[1] in accordance with Aquinas. All this was matter of obedience. "Read, write, speak Latin," was one rule. "Imitate Cicero," was another. An independent style might foster independent thought, which might ripen into independent action.

Every class spoke Latin, and every class read Cicero. Cicero supplied the form and often the matter of exercises in prose. Virgil stood in the same relation to verse. Christiads were written in the style of the Æneid. The classics were read in expurgated editions. Instead of setting Christian youth to act heathen plays, the Jesuits wrote dramas, in which naughty boys, ghosts, drunkards, and devils supplied the excitement necessary to please. The boys were forbidden to attend any public spectacle, unless it were to see heretics burnt.[2]

Three classes learnt grammar, the fourth humanity, and the fifth rhetoric. The study of the classics was thus directed to the formation of an eloquent style, to be used in the service of the Church. Some attention was also given to the subject-matter and to miscellaneous knowledge, under the name of "polymathy," or "erudition." Much less Greek than Latin, and no Hebrew was read in the schoolwork (*studia inferiora*). In the higher studies, Aristotle's Logic, Physic, Metaphysic, and Ethics, with Euclid and the use of the globes,

---

[1] The Dominicans were furious at this qualification.

[2] "Neque ad publica spectacula, nec ad supplicia reorum, nisi forte hæreticorum, eant."—*Ratio et Institutio Studiorum*, 170.

formed the staple of liberal education. In the theological course, the exegetical lectures were on the Vulgate, with occasional reference to the Greek and Hebrew. The Hebrew lecturer chose some one of the easier books.

This well-devised system was worked by able writers of school-books and by skilful teachers. The education was gratuitous. Different measures of it were given according to the capacity of the pupils. The rapid progress made by Catholic scholars presented a striking contrast to the backward state in which they had often been kept by the mediævalism of the other religious orders. Protestants sent their sons to profit, without charge, by the zeal of the Jesuit teachers. Their reputation and their numbers grew apace. The first school was opened in 1546, six years after the foundation of the order. Before the century closed, there were two hundred. They overran Germany at once, making their headquarters at Vienna, Cologne, Prague, Ingolstadt, and Munich. In France they encountered more opposition. Yet they were soon known as the best classical scholars in the country. The Port Royalists, a century later, were in this respect their only rivals.

Sturm regards the method of the Jesuits as bearing a close resemblance to his own. He commends them for having undertaken what neither Hegius, nor Agricola, nor Reuchlin, nor Erasmus could persuade the old religious orders even to allow, the cultivation of true eloquence and sound learning. He rejoices in their zeal, both as provoking Protestants to vigilant rivalry, and as directly carrying on the good work.

But the chief testimony in their favour is that of

Bacon, who declares that he could sum up his thoughts on education by naming the Jesuit schools as the best.[1] He praises them especially for accustoming boys to act a part, which, though disreputable as a profession, is useful in life, and lauds their energy and skill in the formation of moral character, no less than in the cultivation of learning. This estimate stands in marked contrast with that of Leibnitz, who rates the Jesuits of his own time (a century later) as below mediocrity, and treats Bacon's admiration as a mistake.

VIII. In England, Greek literature had neither died out so soon, nor was so slow to revive, as in other countries.[2] The question between Latin and the mother-tongue was complicated for a time by the rival claims of Norman and Saxon, Latin being construed in grammar-schools into French till about 1350.[3] The Norman conquest also tended to mark strongly the contrast between the gentleman and the scholar. Hallam supposes that in 1400, or a generation later, an English gentleman of the first class would usually have "a slight tincture of Latin." But about the earlier date Piers Plowman bitterly complains that every cobbler's son and beggar's brat gets book-learning, and such wretches become bishops, and lords' sons and knights crouch to them. He thinks that lords should make bishops of their own brothers' children.[4] Probably nowhere did the Christian

---

[1] "Consule scholas Jesuitarum : nihil enim quod in usum venit his melius."

[2] See Sir George Young's Essay on the "History of Greek Literature in England."

[3] The change had its bad as well as good side. "The boys learn their grammar in less time than they were wont to do, but know no more French than knows their left heel, and that is harm to them if they shall travel in strange lands." So writes John of Trevisa, in 1387.

[4] See "Education in Early England," by F. J. Furnivall.

religion do more than in England to exalt them of low degree; and nowhere were gentlemen less disposed to humble themselves to be scholars, that they might be exalted to be bishops. The universities were much frequented by the sons of yeomen; and in the monastery and cathedral schools, and large parish-schools, any peasant boy of good capacity might learn Latin free of expense.

In the reign of Richard II. indeed, a petition was presented to Parliament by certain lords, praying that children of serfs and the lower sort might not be sent to school, and particularly to the schools of monasteries, wherein many were trained as ecclesiastics, and thence rose to dignities in the state.[1] But the clergy were strong enough to defend the cause of the poor. One of the most disgraceful acts for making agricultural labour compulsory, ends with the proviso that "every man and woman of what estate or condition that he be, shall be free to set their son or daughter to take learning at any manner school that pleaseth them within the realm."[2]

Gentlemen took care that their sons should learn "courtesy," to ride, sing, play upon the lute and virginals, perform feats of arms, dance, carve, and wait at table,[3] where they might hear the conversation (sometimes French or Latin), and study the manners of great men. In some of the great houses there were masters of grammar to teach Latin to the "young gentlemen of the

[1] Christian Schools and Scholars, ii. 234.
[2] 7 Hen. IV. c. 17, quoted in "Education in Early England."
[3] Cardinal Morton used to say of Sir Thomas More, "This child here waiting at table, whosoever shall live to see it, will prove a marvellous man."

household." Also many gentlemen studied at the inns of court, and some at foreign universities.

A letter from Pace to Colet, about the year 1500, shows the tone of another class of gentlemen. One is represented as breaking out at table into abuse of letters. "I swear," he says, "rather than my son should be bred a scholar, he should hang. To blow a neat blast on the horn, to understand hunting, to carry a hawk handsomely, and train it, that is what becomes the son of a gentleman: but as for book-learning, he should leave that to louts."

It is stated by a recent historian, that, as late as the reign of Edward VI. there were peers of Parliament unable to read. Well might Roger Ascham exclaim, "The fault is in yourselves, ye noblemen's sons, and therefore ye deserve the greater blame, that commonly the meaner men's children come to be the wisest councillors, and greatest doers, in the weighty affairs of this realm."

The history of the classical revival at the English universities is well known, and has lately been brought before the public.[1] It may suffice to remark that almost all the Oxford leaders, Selling, Linacre, Grocyn (a Wykehamist), Colet, and Lilly, had visited Italy, and were in close relations with Italian scholars; while, of the Cambridge leaders, Croke (an Etonian) had taught Greek at Leipsic and at Louvain, and Smith and Cheke were men of the world, and of some European reputation.[2] The lustre of these names, and the enthusiastic flatteries of

---

[1] In Seebohm's Oxford Reformers, and in Sir G. Young's Essay.

[2] Linacre was tutor to Prince Arthur at Oxford (1501), Cheke to King Edward VI. (1544). Smith was Secretary of State to Queen Elizabeth.

Erasmus, who found himself at home with a distinguished circle in each university, tend to conceal the fact that, for a long time, the number of classical scholars was but small. Indeed, it could not well be otherwise until some change should take place in the schools.

The two great schools founded before the revival, Winchester (1386), and Eton (1440), were on one model, being intended to lay a grammatical foundation for the studies of New College, and of King's. No record of the course of training in those days has been preserved.[1] In Wolsey's Statutes (drafted before 1477) for the Ipswich Grammar School, which was to prepare students for his college at Oxford, there is no mention of verses or of Greek.

An account of Eton in 1560 (?) shows what the school had become quarter of a century after the appointment of Udall as head-master. The sixth form alone learn Greek grammar. The younger boys read Terence, Cicero (Sturm's selection), Vives, and Lucian in Latin. Among the books of the upper forms, besides the Ovid, Virgil, Horace, Catullus, and Martial of modern days, are Cæsar, Lucan, and the epigrams of More.

Verses are written on subjects such as might still be set in the lower forms. There is some attempt to go to nature for poetic inspiration. Before writing on "the flowery pleasantness of spring," the boys are sent out at break of day to gather branches of maythorn, taking care not to wet their feet. In "fruitbearing autumn" the plentiful crops must be imagined and described before nutting is allowed. The verse was Latin, with an exception in favour of the gaiety of spring, which was

[1] In the Paston Letters, there are two Eton Latin verses of 1468.

allowed to vent itself in simple English; as still, when his heart is most full, an Eton boy may bid his school farewell in the unpractised accents of his mother-tongue. The other exercises were declamations, themes, versions, and variations. Excerption of flowers and phrases was also taught in school.

Epigrammatic contests were encouraged, and the writer describes with glee how at Montem new fellows were salted with salt, with Latin gibes, and with their own tears. On the long winter nights the boys acted Latin or English plays written by Udall, "the father of English comedy." In July a competitive examination was held, that the fittest in all Britain might be elected to the college.

From this account it is plain that classical education did not leap at once into full growth. If "English boys disporting themselves in Greek epigrams" existed anywhere save in the imagination of Erasmus, it can hardly have been at Eton. But before the end of the century a contemporary writer[1] states that at Eton, Winchester, and Westminster a great number of poor scholars were "well entered in the knowledge of the Latin and Greek tongues and rules of versifying." As regards other schools, the information extant relates to what was intended rather than to what was achieved.

What was intended in cathedral schools has been set forth in Mr. Whiston's book on cathedral trusts. If the preambles of Acts were history, it would appear that at all the cathedrals founded or reformed by Henry VIII. good stipends were provided for "readers of Greek, Hebrew, and Latin." When an endeavour was made at

[1] Harrison. See "Education in Early England," p. 58.

Canterbury to exclude the children of the poor from profiting by these endowments, Cranmer made a spirited protest, concluding as follows: "The poor man will for the most part be learned when the gentleman's son will not take the pains to get it. . . . Wherefore, if the gentleman's son be apt to learning, let him be admitted; if not apt, let the poor man's child that is apt enter in his room." But before long cathedral trust-moneys for the most part took another direction.

During the last thirty years before the Reformation there were more grammar schools erected and endowed in England than had been established in three hundred years preceding. These were results of the recovery from the Wars of the Roses, and of the classical revival, which had nowhere more influence than at court. The king himself was learned in the tongues, and took care that his family should be so. Erasmus praises the learning of Queen Catharine and the Latin letters of Mary. Ascham read Aristotle's Ethics in Greek with Edward, and made him translate from Cicero into Greek. Of Elizabeth's Greek he writes to Sturm in the highest terms. Lady Jane Grey, Lady Cecil, Lady Russell, and More's daughter Margaret are examples of the classical scholarship attained, so far as hawking and hunting permitted, in families connected with the court.

The Reformation greatly diminished the amount of education by the destruction of religious schools. It became necessary "to take diverse orders for the maintenance and continuance of scholars, priests, and curates," which led to the foundation of more grammar schools. But the rapacity of Edward's council left scanty funds to endow them. The reign of Mary was disastrous to education. The general want of schools, decay of the Universities, and decay of learning were represented to Elizabeth[1] in the strongest terms. But, except by private liberality, little was done to meet the want.

The statutes of the grammar schools or free schools founded by the Crown and by private benefactors are nearly all on one model, combining classical with religious instruction. The archetype may be found in Dean Colet's Statutes (1509) for St. Paul's. Scholastic Latin was to be strictly excluded, but not so Christian writers in good Latin. The head master was to be "learned in good and clean Latin literature, and also in Greek, if such may be gotten." Such was gotten, in the person of Lilly, the author of *Propria quæ maribus* and *As in præsenti*. Erasmus, who had been much consulted in the whole matter, and helped to draw up the grammar, considered this school to be the best in England.

The statutes of the school founded at Manchester (1525) by Bishop Oldham may serve further to set forth the conception of a grammar school. He had observed that "the children in the same country having pregnant wits had been most part brought up rudely and idly," and determined to give them an opportunity of learning grammar, as being "the ground and fountain of all the other arts and sciences . . . the gate by the which all other been learned and known in diversity of tongues and speeches." There is no special mention of Greek.

The Shrewsbury Grammar School, founded by Ed-

---

[1] Strype's Annals, i. 437. "At the beginning of her reign but few of the clergy had the least tincture of Greek learning, and the majority did not understand Latin."—*Hallam*.

ward VI. (1551), is described by Camden as "the best filled in all England, being indebted for its flourishing state to provision made by the excellent and worthy Thomas Ashton." Ten years later, Laurence Sheriff made similar provision for Rugby. Harrow was founded (1571) as "the Free Grammar School of John Lyon." He names for use many of the best Latin and Greek books, but only one Greek poet, Hesiod. The boys are "to be initiated in the elements of Latin versification very early." And "no girls shall be received to be taught in the same school." The head master "may take of the foreigners such stipends and wages as he can get, so that he take pains with all indifferently, as well of poor as of rich."

The statutes of the later free schools generally prescribe verses, and Greek. Archbishop Grindal, for example, requires for St. Bees (1583) "a meet and learned person that can make Greek and Latin verses, and interpret the Greek Grammar and other Greek authors." The only other Greek author named is "the little Greek Catechism set forth by public authority." Archbishop Sandys expects from the Hawkshead School, in Lancashire (1588), that "the chiefest scholars shall make orations, epistles, and verses in Latin and Greek for their exercises," and all the scholars "shall continually use the Latin tongue or the Greek tongue as they shall be able." Archbishop Harsnet wishes for Chigwell (1629) "a man skilful in the Greek and Latin tongues, a good poet. For phrase and style he is to infuse no other save Tully and Terence; and to read the ancient and Latin poets, no novelties or conceited modern writers."

Latin plays are not much mentioned in the statutes, but were frequently acted; at Shrewsbury weekly. In a few cases Hebrew is required of the head-master, as at Bristol, Southwark (1614) and Lewisham (1652). But in by far the larger number of schools Greek and Latin alone are specified, and in some it is expressly said that "Greek and Latin only," or "the classics only," are to be taught.

Charterhouse (founded 1611) is an exception. For, although the statutes (dated 1627) prescribe "none but approved authors Greek and Latin, such as are read in the best esteemed free schools," and Latin and Greek verses every Sunday upon some part of the Second Lesson, it is added that the scholars shall be taught "to cypher and cast an account, especially those that are less capable of learning and fittest to be sent to trades."

When grammar schools have received new statutes by Act of Parliament, there has seldom been an essential change. At Leeds, an attempt was made to introduce a more modern education. But it was decided in Chancery (1805) that "the Free School in Leeds is a free grammar school for teaching, grammatically, the learned languages, according to Dr. Johnson's definition." In general, little has been done to meet the requirements of a later age. Endowments have been wasted by the cessation of demand for free classical instruction.

It is remarked by Locke, that writing a good hand and casting accounts are seldom or never taught at grammar schools, and yet gentlemen send their younger sons there who are intended for trades, and tradesmen and farmers send their children, though they have neither intention nor ability to make them scholars. To ask why, he says, is thought as strange as to ask why they go to church : " Custom serves for reason."

In this way, schools which have almost ceased to supply the universities, have still kept together a certain number of scholars. But in some places even custom has at last died out : the schoolmaster draws his salary, and the school stands almost empty.

To give any other than a liberal education in these free schools, would be a departure from the purpose of the founders. They did not design to save the pockets of gentlemen by educating their younger sons for trade, or to enable the sons of farmers to become masters of the arts of writing and casting accounts. Their intention was to recruit the ranks of the universities and of the learned professions from among rich or poor. And to a great extent this was accomplished.

It should not be forgotten what the classical free schools scattered through England have done in times past to furnish her great men. Take only the names which meet the eye in turning over the pages of Carlisle,[1] omitting all the best-known public schools, that is, the most successful free schools, formed on the same type. From Abingdon and Norwich came Chief-Justices Holt and Coke; from Huntingdon, Cromwell; from Grantham, Newton; from Kingston, Gibbon; from Giggleswick, Paley; from Newcastle, Ridley, Akenside, Eldon and Stowell. From other schools, now not more distinguished than these, came Wallis, and Harvey, and Jenner, and Davy; Jewel and Laud; Stillingfleet, Waterland, Barrow, and Clarke; Kennicott, Lightfoot,

[1] " Endowed Grammar Schools." Published, 1818.

and Prideaux; Huskisson, Clarkson, and Wilberforce; Heber, and Martyn. It would be easy to lengthen the list from other and more recent sources. One name cannot be omitted. It was at a free school that Shakspeare received a liberal education.

IX. Thus Grammar and the Classics were established, and for three centuries have been accepted in practice as constituting, with religion, the whole course of liberal school education in England. But in theory the system has not passed unquestioned.

It deserves remark that Bacon did not urge reform in school education. He contents himself with praising the Jesuits, and gleaning a few neglected truths. The friends of rhetoric, as against science at schools, are so far entitled to count him on their side. Yet his advice to bring the mind into closer contact with facts, and to work from the concrete to the abstract, led other schoolreformers to insist upon the knowledge of things as well as words, and to protest against teaching abstract rules before a child knows the concrete facts of language. The truth is that intellectual revolutions begin among grown men, and are afterwards imported into schools. Classical studies were pursued for some time before they were organized for school education. So it has been with inductive science for a much longer time: because the classics were (corruptions excepted) at the first as perfect as they are now, whereas the inductive sciences came slowly into existence. Bacon anticipated, but could not create them. Had he attempted it, boys might have been taught to disbelieve Copernicus, and to despise Gilbert. Bacon might, indeed, have recommended mathematics, the very name of which tells what the

Greeks thought of their importance in education. But
his own training was unfortunately defective on that
side. Moreover, Bacon (though before his age in this
as in other respects) was not without a certain contempt for boys.

A generation later, Milton raised his eloquent voice to
proclaim the reforming of education as "one of the
greatest and noblest designs that can be thought on, and
for the want whereof this nation perishes." An idea had
long since in silence presented itself to him of a better
and larger education. As regards learning, his first
principle is that "language is but the instrument con-
veying to us things useful to be known." He therefore
condemns as the chief mistake at schools "a preposterous exaction, forcing the empty wits of children to
compose themes, verses, and orations, which are the acts
of ripest judgment." In his opinion the most rational
way of learning a language is first to commit to memory
the most necessary parts of grammar; next, to apply
the grammar in reading the most delightful book that
can be found, such as Plutarch's Lives; then to proceed
forthwith to the solid things which the language con-
tains, beginning with the easiest arts, that is, with those
which are most obvious to the sense. His list of authors
will seem absurd if the principle (of reading a language for its solid contents) be rejected, and out of date
at the present day if it be accepted. Agriculture, physiology, architecture, astronomy, and tactics are among
the subjects to be studied in Greek and Latin. Among
poets he first names Hesiod and Aratus, Lucretius, "the
rural part of Virgil," choice comedies, Greek, Latin, or
Italian, and "tragedies that treat of household matters."

Use of the globes, "any compendious method[1] of natural philosophy," mathematics, fortification, engineering, or navigation, anatomy, and the like are to be learnt from modern authors; geometry, "even playing, as the old manner was." Next follow ethics, economics, politics, the highest matters of theology, Church history, ancient and modern, and the Hebrew Scriptures. Then "choice histories, heroic poems, and Attic tragedies of stateliest and most regal argument, with all the famous political orations." Lastly, a course of logic, rhetoric, and poetics introduces the right season of forming the pupils to be able writers, "when they shall be thus fraught with an universal insight into things."

Although the scheme is impracticable, or, in Milton's words, "not a bow for every man to shoot in that counts himself a teacher," it shows that a great poet may be less disposed than a great philosopher to think that true command of language can be attained apart from knowledge of things.

A reformer more on a level with the public mind was Locke. In his view schools were teaching "things a great part whereof belongs not to a gentleman's calling, which is to have the knowledge of a man of business, a carriage suitable to his rank, and to be eminent and useful in his country according to his station."

He dissuades from sending a boy to school, which is "to hazard your son's innocence and virtue for a little Greek and Latin;" and advises that a tutor be procured who thinks learning and language the least part of education.

---

[1] One of Bacon's few remarks on Education is a warning against compendious methods.

Latin, however, of a certain sort being absolutely necessary for a gentleman, he is to "have it talked into him," by conversations with the tutor on geography, astronomy, chronology, anatomy, parts of history, and the like. If such a tutor cannot be found, the boy must learn by literal translations. Or his mother, without any previous knowledge,[1] may read with him a Latin gospel. Indeed, such Latin as Locke desires "might be learned almost in playing." Those who wish to be critically exact must study grammar. But ladies speak correctly without it. The only grammar which a gentleman needs is that of his own tongue, which alone he means to write. "And let him read those things that are well writ in English, to perfect his style in the purity of our language."

If the boy is sent to school, the master will want to teach him grammar. Locke advises the parent to explain "that you have no design to make him either a Latin orator or a poet, but barely would have him understand perfectly a Latin author."

As for verses, a boy has not, or he has, a natural turn for them. If he has not, you cannot give it him; if he has, the sooner it is suppressed the better. Such a taste will lead him into bad company and bad habits.

No man can pass for a scholar who is ignorant of Greek. But the question in hand is the education of a gentleman; to whom Latin and French, as the world goes, are by every one acknowledged to be necessary. When he comes to be a man, he can easily get Greek for himself.

---

[1] The *méthode maternelle* is in common use in French commercial schools. But a mother is supposed to know the language which she teaches.

As soon as a boy can talk, French should be "talked into him." Mathematics may also be useful. Locke himself knew a young gentleman who could demonstrate several propositions in Euclid before he was thirteen. "Natural philosophy as a speculative science" (says Locke) "I imagine we have none. . . . Yet the incomparable Mr. Newton has shown how far mathematics applied to nature may carry us in some particular branches of this incomprehensible universe. If others could give us so good and clear an account of other parts of nature, as he has of this our planetary world," the subject might become a proper part of a gentleman's education.

Locke's views resemble those of Montaigne, who wrote in the previous century. Montaigne's father had actually brought him up as a child to speak Latin only. But in Locke's time it was no easy matter for English gentlemen to do the like, Latin being then, in his own words, "a language foreign in their country, and long since dead everywhere." Montaigne had also learnt Greek (not much) from his father "almost in playing." He thought children's wits were none the sharper for dry rules of logic or grammar. "Magis magnos clericos non sunt magis magnos sapientes."

X. Theories, however, are of little weight as compared with experience. And for experience of any but the one-sided classical course of liberal education it is necessary to look beyond England.

In Germany, the first reformer of classical education was Ratich, who professed to have a system by which Hebrew, Greek, Latin, and other languages, might be learnt in a very short time. Dissatisfaction with existing education led several towns to employ him to organize their schools. The chief points of his method were to begin with the mother-tongue, to teach a language first and the grammar afterwards, to let nothing be learned by heart, but impress a lesson by frequent repetition, and the like. He saw the weak points of existing schools, but was not competent to reform them. He ended by being thrown into prison, and was only let out on signing a paper to the effect that he had promised more than he could perform.

A more successful reformer was Comenius (1592-1669), whose *Janua Linguarum* and *Orbis Pictus* obtained great celebrity and circulation. The latter was intended to combine a large and not exclusively classical Latin vocabulary with knowledge of things. He was led by reading Bacon to insist upon the latter. He held that all ranks should receive the same education, and that only two languages, the mother-tongue and Latin, should be carried to all possible perfection. He expected to see Latin become an universal language, not only for Europe, but for the world.

In the seventeenth century the Germans were learned rather than elegant scholars. But the Thirty Years' War brought down the standard so low that, after a short struggle to restore it, early in the eighteenth century Latin began to be laid aside as a spoken language at German universities and schools. Germans of rank would often desire that their sons should give up Greek to devote more time to French, which seemed about to become the common tongue of Europe. And little as the German language had then done in literature, there were rectors who held that it had its classical authors, and ought to be studied as carefully as the other tongues.

The cry of "Things, not words," gathered strength, and useful was opposed to liberal education. It was thought that boys intended for trade were out of place in the classical schools (Verbalschulen). The first Realschule was opened by Semler, at Halle, in 1739. At Berlin (1747) a Realschule, with a classical department, was founded, in which a liberal education might be combined with the study of any special subject, such as "breeding silkworms," or "ninety kinds of leather."

Rousseau's "Emile" (1762) stimulated the reaction in Germany against classical education, and led to the foundation of schools, of which a chief feature was Latin without the rod;[1] such as Basedow's "Philanthropin," at Dessau (1774), and later, the schools of Pestalozzi. Kant recommended and collected money for the former, and Fichte supported the latter. In Kant's opinion, "not slow reform, but swift revolution" was needed in schools. At the Philanthropin Greek was not taught at all, and Latin badly. Kant afterwards acknowledged it to be a failure, but thought the experience worth what it had cost. The Prussian minister, Zedlitz, at first believed in Basedow.

But Frederick II., being disposed to favour the classics,[2] Zedlitz appointed F. A. Wolf to be Professor of Philosophy and Education at Halle, in place of a disciple of

---

[1] Generally, Latin and rod were nail and hammer. For this reason Latin could only be taught to boys.

[2] "Lateinisch müssen die jungen Leute absolut lernen; davon gehe ich nicht ab."

Basedow, for whom the Chair had been founded. Wolf held the post twenty-three years (1783-1806), and educated some of the most distinguished German scholars, among others, Böckh, Bekker, and Heindorf; Halle having till then been under the reproach of producing no philologian. He accomplished this by founding a seminary for training professed scholars, many of whom became teachers at the classical schools. Insisting on thoroughness in everything, he opposed the introduction of miscellaneous knowledge. An ideal floated before him of making Greek, not Latin, the first language taught to boys. He believed that this was the right means to promote the highest culture of the German mind. But the whole current of the time was against him, and he gave it up as a beautiful dream. Practically, he advised that Greek and Hebrew should be taught only to those who showed special aptitude for language.

The experience of Austria[1] in liberal education is instructive. For more than two centuries (1550-1773) the Jesuits, Benedictines, and Piarists had almost a monopoly, the last-named order inclining to "things, not words." The Jesuits also taught natural science and mathematics, but failed to give efficient instruction. General dissatisfaction arose, and complaints were made that they loaded the memory without training the mind, taught poor Latin and no German, adhered to a course of study long since out of date, and objected to State control. Maria Theresa (1760) took vigorously in hand the general re-organization of schools. Cardinal Migazzi declared that the once glorious educational

[1] "Fortschritte des Unterrichtswesens," by Beer and Hochegger, 1867.

exertions and successes of the Order of Jesus had had their time, and like all things human, their schools had fallen into decay. Clement XIV. simplified things by abolishing the Order. A brilliant period followed, in which Austria took the lead in German popular education. Funds and buildings of classical schools were appropriated for normal and primary schools for both sexes; Maria Theresa's son, the future Emperor Joseph II., being of opinion that when all her subjects could read, write, and cypher, then would be the time to attend to learned education. The Empress, the aristocracy, and the great ecclesiastics assisted liberally from their private means. No more Latin was to be learned in these schools than was necessary for apothecaries, surgeons, and scribes, and to prepare for classical schools. But liberal education was not neglected. A scheme was drawn up by Professor Hess (1774), rejecting mediæval books, encouraging Greek and classical Latin, but requiring also the systematic study of German and the other mother-tongues, and insisting on mathematics and natural science. In favour of this reform, he appealed to the satisfactory experience of Saxony, Hanover, and Würtemberg.

The first difficulty was to find efficient teachers. The Piarists had their own ways of teaching "things, not words." And rather than employ Protestants, Austria fell back on the ex-Jesuits. Between the two, physical science had no fair trial. The new liberal education began to look like a failure; which distressed Joseph more than it distressed the Jesuits.

The death of Joseph (1790), the terror spread by the French Revolution, and the accession of Francis II.

brought about reaction. The professed principles of reform were not ill-sounding. Superficial studies were to be banished, physical science relegated to the philosophical course, and it was laid down that in liberal school education the proper study of mankind is man. Instruction in the German language and literature was to be retained. The clergy were to see that all this was done.

The year of another French Revolution (1848) brought another crisis. Plans of reform had long been under discussion : but in that year Austria first reached the stage of having a Minister of Public Instruction. Professor Bonitz, who was employed to reorganize the Gymnasia, defined it as the aim of liberal school education to impart a higher general culture, making such substantial use of classical literature, as to lay the foundation for University studies.

This conception of a "higher general culture," developed by the course of history, and recognised by all the educated nations of Europe, must determine the relation between the discipline of language and history, and the discipline of mathematics and natural science. Neither of these, considered as an independent force, can give the right movement to liberal education, the direction of which should not be determined by the classical languages alone, nor by these combined with the mother-tongue, but should result from the reciprocal and common action of all the higher studies. Bonitz regarded the application of this culture in its completeness by a single set of class teachers as "a didactic impossibility." On the other hand, he saw the danger of breaking up education into too many departments

His practical solution was to group kindred subjects. He insisted on previous examination of the teacher as essential to success; and a training college was founded at Vienna.

But this promising system of education was loudly denounced by the bureaucracy and aristocracy, the Catholic and some Protestant clergy, and the extreme national party. It was revolutionary, irreligious, outlandish, Prussian. It gave to Greek, the favourite tongue of Reformers, and German, a language in which Protestants were strong, an advantage over Latin, the language of the Catholic Church. The natural sciences would introduce the leaven of materialism; the severe examinations would fill the pulpits and tribunals with hard-working children of the poor. No person of rank or fortune would subject his son to such danger and such annoyance. With these complaints were mingled outcries from the non-German populations against an attempt to Germanise their children through the schools. The system had not elasticity enough for the diversity of language and civilization in a polyglot empire.

For five years, however (1850-1855), it flourished, and proved itself to be no mere ideal. Then a Concordat threw education back into the hands of the clergy. The aid of Jesuit teachers was accepted again on their own terms, without the indispensable check of examination. The other religious orders claimed the same exemption. Except for laymen, tests of efficient teaching were at an end. In this state the liberal education of Austria remains, a comprehensive scheme administered under narrow clerical influence.

In Germany generally, no one who has not studied

at an university can enter the higher civil service.¹ There are 58 universities, with 18,971 students. No one can matriculate without a certificate of fitness from his school. The number of Gymnasia, including those of German Austria, is 520, with 114,545 pupils;² besides preparatory schools (Progymnasia) in the smaller towns. The classical masters teach also the German language and literature, and sometimes French and English. For mathematics and natural science there are special masters. In some schools an hour a week is given to speaking Latin. Oral translations into Latin and Greek are practised, as well as written themes and versions, and Latin and Greek verse. Hebrew is optional, except for theological students, for whom the course includes composition in Hebrew prose.

The final examination (Maturitäts-prüfung) in Prussia occupies a week. The papers are a German essay, a Latin essay, and Mathematics (five hours for each), a Latin version, a simple Greek version, and translation from French. An oral examination follows, in Greek and Latin poetry previously but not lately read, and in unseen prose, with Latin questions and answers; also in Religion, in Mathematics, and in History. The essays are on subjects suited for boys, and means are taken to discourage "cram."

XI. The University of Paris did not lose its mediæval character till the Revolution. Francis I. "the father of French literature," had founded (1531) a Royal

---

¹ See Dr. Minssen's Report (1866) to the French Minister of Instruction; and (for Prussia), Mr. Bernard's Appendix to the Report on Public Schools; also Wiese, "Das höhere Schulwesen in Preussen."

² The number of boys in the Prussian Gymnasia was doubled in twenty years (1840-1860).

College, with professors of "the three principal tongues." And among the restorers of ancient, especially of Greek learning, the great names of Budæus, Turnebus, Stephanus, Scaliger, and Casaubon belong to France. But in Paris, the new studies were opposed by the old religious orders. The Jesuits, to the best of their power, maintained the cause of classical education and learning, and were long supported by the Bourbon court. Yet the scholastic theologians and the Gallican party finally prevailed. After some vicissitudes, in 1762 the order was abolished, and their colleges handed over to the University.

But throughout the provinces, from first to last, education flourished in their hands. They established themselves even in towns of less than 5,000 souls: and the tradespeople, great and small, finding good free schools at their doors, sent their children to learn whatever was taught there. The knowledge of Latin thus became for three centuries in France the mark of social standing as a townsman.[1] Together with Latin, the Jesuits took care to inculcate Church principles and Catholic doctrine. Yet it was in their schools that large numbers of the people acquired intelligence to take part in the religious reforms of the sixteenth and seventeenth, and the philosophical and social movement of the eighteenth century. One of their most brilliant disciples was Voltaire.

In the Revolution, education, like all other things, was wildly tossed upon the waves of change. Each successive government, every party, clerical or secular,

---

[1] "Le cachet de la bourgeoisie."—*Cournot.*

reactionary or progressive, saw and acted on the principle that in education lies the making of the future.[1] Notwithstanding undue predominance of political aims, much may be learned from the experience of France, for nowhere have more distinguished men taken in hand the organization of schools.

The Constituent Assembly entrusted the task to Talleyrand, who declared against exclusive classical education, as failing to train the whole mind. He considered that the best example of logical thought, and the best exercise for the reasoning powers, were to be found in mathematics, especially when studied in combination with the first principles of natural science. He proposed to strengthen the memory by history, and to stimulate the imagination by oratory, poetry, music, and drawing. Morality was to be placed on grounds of reason, virtue being taught as a science, and recommended as an advantageous calculation. His measures never took effect.

The Legislative Assembly employed Condorcet, who advised that mathematics and natural science should altogether supersede the classics; of which a superficial study was worthless, and a long and profound study pernicious rather than useful. His plan also came to nothing. The Convention accomplished little; and the Directory less.

Napoleon, as first Consul, laid the foundations of the present system. The Lycées, corresponding to the German Gymnasia, were organized on the principle that liberal education has two factors, literary culture

[1] See "Fortschritte des Unterrichtswesens;" and About, "Le Progrès."

and the discipline of exact science. The one was represented by Latin, the other by mathematics;[1] further subjects of instruction, such as Greek and history, and logic and natural science, being regarded as supplementary to these. Inspectors were appointed, and the preparation of school-books entrusted to able hands. To secure an efficient staff of teachers, Napoleon reorganized the Normal School of the Convention, in two departments, of Literature and of Science, and instituted competitive examinations for the appointments. He also (1806) established the University as an independent corporation charged with the supervision of education throughout the country, meaning thus to create a bulwark against destructive theories and incessant change.

The Restoration abolished the Normal School, and was laying the axe to the root of University independence, when Napoleon returned from Elba. Some years later the state obtained control by making the Minister of Public Instruction Grand Master of the University.

The government of Louis Philippe, under Guizot, on Cousin's recommendation, reformed primary education after the Prussian model, introducing the elements of natural science. But when it came to re-organizing secondary education, warm debates arose in the Chamber of Deputies (1835-6) on the comparative claims of literature and of science, of dead and of living tongues. It was argued against the classics, not only that they are practically useless for purposes of agriculture, trade, and the like, but also that some of the

[1] "On enseignera essentiellement dans les lycées le Latin et les mathématiques." (Decree of 10 Dec. 1802.)

most distinguished literary men of France had known little Latin, and less Greek.[1] The interests of the classics were eloquently defended by Guizot and Saint-Marc Girardin. But perhaps the most remarkable speech was the reply called forth from Arago by the shallow assertion that there is no humanizing principle in exact science.

The practical question was complicated by the fact that the Chamber was dealing at once with the interests of liberal and of commercial education, there being no proper organization for the latter.

Secondary education in France was mainly directed to the attainment of the *baccalauréat ès lettres*,[2] which confers the privileges of a first degree in that faculty, whereas the German certificate only entitles to matriculation. By new regulations in 1840, the test was made more severe, the candidate being shut up for two hours, with a dictionary, to translate from Latin, and then examined orally for three quarters of an hour in explanation of Latin, Greek, and French authors, and in philosophy, literature, history, mathematics, and physics. The questions were drawn from bags containing fifty on each subject, and, to render the work of preparation more definite, were published beforehand by the examiners, and (with answers) by private enterprise.

A longer and more searching examination was instituted for the title of licentiate in letters or in the sciences, at the Normal School, which was also re-organized by the government of Louis Philippe. With this part of their

---

[1] Racine and Boileau were Greek scholars; Corneille, Voltaire, Montesquieu, and Buffon, were not.
[2] The *baccalauréat ès sciences* was not established till 1852.

work they were so well satisfied, that Cousin recommended it as a model to the Prussians, who, however preferred their own system.

In lay schools for liberal education licentiates only could be teachers. Whether this should be enforced on religious schools also, at least if they were to educate laymen, was one of the most difficult questions with which Guizot had to deal. The clergy were indignant at the notion that the soundness and efficiency of their teaching, and especially of their scientific teaching, should be submitted to the judgment of laymen. Laymen, on the other hand, insisted on the rights of the University and of the State, and on the interests of solid learning and scientific truth. In the midst of the debate came the Revolution, which has left the clergy free.

In the later educational experience of France, perhaps nothing is more likely to be instructive to England than the episode of Bifurcation (1854–1864).

The system was a compromise between two conflicting tendencies. On the one hand, there was a great and growing demand for useful, and especially for mathematical and scientific education, not only among the industrial and mercantile classes, but among candidates for admission to the civil and military technical schools. On the other hand, Latin at least having always been deemed essential in middle-class education, there was great unwillingness that a considerable section of society should be withdrawn from the humanizing influence of classical literature.

Under the pressure of these opposite forces, Fortoul, then Minister of Public Instruction, departed from the fundamental principle of liberal education laid down by Napoleon, the intimate union of literature and science. The students were divided into Humanists and Realists. During the first five years they were to be educated together; during the last four they were to be in separate sections; working together, however, in French classics and composition, Latin translation, rhetoric, history, modern languages, and part of their philosophy. The Humanists were to be excused from higher mathematics and higher physics; the Realists in part from philosophy and Latin, and entirely from Greek. Latin and Greek were also to begin no longer in the first and second, but in the second and third years, and French grammar to be learnt before Latin.

After three years' experience, it was thought better to begin Latin and Greek grammar as early as before, and to put Latin composition later in the course. After another two years, it was found necessary to separate as far as possible all the literary work of the two sections, the Realists being a drag upon the Humanists. In the ninth year, a new minister (Duruy) condemned severely the loose mathematics of the Humanists, and decreed that the two sections should work together in both mathematics and literature for six instead of five years; and separately in both during their last three years, though learning under the same roof. Four months later he abolished bifurcation.

How then does he meet the practical demands which drove his predecessor to the adoption of this system? The answer, as regards liberal education, may be found in his instructions and circular dated in March, 1865. The general course has been arranged with more regard to science than hitherto, so that while the mind is enlarged by literary studies, the judgment may be strengthened by severer method. And mathematical courses have been added, in which a student, after completing the general course, may be prepared in one year for the ordinary Military School of St. Cyr, or in two years for the Polytechnic School, which qualifies for staff appointments. Non-liberal secondary education, (*enseignement secondaire professionnel*) has been separately organized.

M. Cournot, formerly inspector general of studies, writing in 1864, thought a greater sacrifice necessary to save classical education. He states that Professors of Greek literature in their French lectures dare not quote Greek, and recommends throwing overboard not only Greek composition (which would not lighten the vessel much), but Greek altogether, except the "dose" prescribed by the ancient University of Paris, which was such that a few Greek words should not arrest a French reader. He proposes to substitute German (which has grammar as well as literature) rather than English. He abandons also Latin verse, and even unwillingly parts with Latin essays, except for the grand prize at the "Concours général des lycées," at Paris, and perhaps as a "spécialité humaniste" in great provincial schools. It remains to be seen whether Government can maintain classical education at a higher level in France.

XII. While in Germany and in France three centuries have wrought these reforms, in England there has been but little change. The method indeed of classical education has been improved, and the standard raised.

Better dictionaries and editions have smoothed the learner's path. Nine head-masters have agreed upon the simplest form in which the abstract rules of the Latin tongue can be taught to children. The study of great poets, and orators, and historians, is not made so much an exercise of rhetoric or of grammar. Less regard is paid to figures, flowers, and phrases; and more to feelings, thoughts, and things. But Milton would still find verses and themes "wrung from poor striplings,[1] like blood out of the nose, or the plucking of untimely fruit." And it is still necessary to ask ourselves these questions:—Are the classics read to learn Greek and Latin, or are Greek and Latin learnt to read the classics? Is the end in view to write Greek and Latin, or to read them, and write the mother-tongue? Are learning Greek and Latin grammar and no English grammar, reading Greek and Latin authors and no English authors, and writing Greek and Latin exercises and no English exercises, the best means to form an English style? Are the French and Germans wrong in teaching French and German otherwise, or are their mother-tongues less nearly related to Greek and Latin? Or are our language and literature less worthy to receive attention than theirs?

Although the great English schools do not yet teach English, something has been added to the old purely classical course. Mathematics, and in some schools modern languages,[2] have recently become part of the school-work.

---

[1] Not always the striplings who show them up as their own.

[2] The study of modern languages was much encouraged at Eton by the judicious liberality of the late Prince Consort, and the support of the head-master. At Rugby, Dr. Arnold made the change.

Besides this, the Report of the Public Schools Commission, while decidedly supporting classical education, recommended that two hours in the week of schoolwork should be given to natural science, and the same to music or drawing. And several schools [1] have been found willing to try the science.

But the schools generally say that in these matters they are not independent, and that they must look very much to the Universities. Two-thirds of their boys, it is true, will not go to college. And modern subjects are recognised in the civil, military, and naval examinations, by success in which honour and advancement may be obtained. For manufacture, also, science is in request; as modern languages are for commerce. But "it ought to be the aim of the public schools to give an education of the best kind, not of the second best." And the best kind of education must be defined by the Universities, which train the masters and dispense the chief endowments. Do the Universities, then, insufficiently reward natural science, and modern history and languages, especially English?

To begin with the last. At Oxford,[2] the Chancellor's, the Arnold, the Stanhope, and the two Theological Essay prizes are high distinctions, bestowed upon able treatment of subjects in English prose. There are also prizes for English verse. And in examinations for scholarships, fellowships, or university honours (except in mathematics and perhaps in natural science), a good English style conduces greatly to success. So far, Oxford must reject the blame for discouraging the study of English at

---

[1] Some account of the experience of one is given in this volume.

[2] Cambridge studies are discussed in another essay.

schools. It is otherwise with matriculations and pass-examinations. No English composition is required, and if bad spelling, bad grammar, and bad style in English translations were taken into strict account, the number of failures would be much increased.

Modern languages are encouraged by free lectures, and by university scholarships. Several names are usually published for honour, together with those of the successful candidates. The examiners for Modern History honours also give weight to knowledge of foreign historians in their own tongue. But the University has hitherto declined to make modern languages a substantial part of the examination. And the colleges do nothing to teach, require, or reward this kind of knowledge.

Modern History is fully recognised, and obtains distinction and endowments. It is also in high favour with passmen as a means of getting their degree. No study has done more to bring out latent ability where classical tutors expected nothing of the kind.

The Natural Sciences have a good staff of professors, a museum and library, and an honour-list of their own, with such crumbs of endowment as may fall from the richly furnished tables of the classics. But narrow classical scholars have been disposed to regard the new studies with indifference, if not with jealousy. Nay, in some quarters there is the same mistrust of natural science as there used to be of Greek, lest it should disturb foregone conclusions.

An indictment also lies against Oxford for the discouragement of elementary mathematics in general education.[1]

[1] See a Letter to the Vice-Chancellor, by T. D. Acland, Esq. M.P.

Lastly, what kind of classical knowledge is encouraged at Oxford, and what amount is absolutely required? As regards candidates for honours, the answer is satisfactory. A large and thorough knowledge of the masterpieces of ancient poetry, and eloquence, and history, and thought,—the language being held in due subordination to the subject-matter,—earns the highest distinctions and the richest endowments. And a comparison of the class-lists with any list of leading statesmen in or out of Parliament, will show that this training, especially when combined with mathematics, is not unserviceable in public life. But even in classics very little is required from the many, and one of the chief problems which has lately exercised the mind of Oxford has been to convert passmen into classmen.

This has been partially solved by releasing them after two years from general education, if they will obtain honours in any special subject. But the last general examination in the second year, instead of being carefully arranged, is, for the present, huddled into the hands of persons appointed for another purpose, who require nothing more than correct translation. A state of things so contrary to the sound tradition of Oxford cannot long remain unchanged.

But the time has arrived for taking a broader view of the whole question. The country possesses already the Reports of Commissions on University Education, on the Public Schools, and on Primary Education in England and in Scotland. The series is now about to be closed by the publication of the Report on Middle-class Schools. The data will then be complete for the great problem of organizing English National Education.

If the Universities are equal to their duties, it is upon them that the noblest part of the task must devolve.

The free schools, which will occupy a prominent place in the forthcoming Report, were founded expressly to give a liberal, then conceived as a classical, education. It will be a duty of the Universities to see that, if possible, the endowments be not diverted from this purpose. With other schools in which modern languages and natural science are as fully recognised as the classics, the Universities have now for ten years spontaneously maintained a friendly connexion, by the Local Examinations. The title "Associate in Arts" implies that Oxford accepts education given in these schools as liberal. Balliol College, in the present year, has set the example of offering assistance and special facilities for the University education of the most successful candidates.

It may be thought that with primary schools at least the Universities can have no relations. But at Edinburgh, in the session 1865-66, of the students in the humanity classes, twenty-nine per cent came direct from primary schools. And at Aberdeen, in the bursary competition of 1865, forty-three per cent of the candidates mentioned in the Order of Merit had been first educated in parochial schools. A difficult question arises between liberal education in parish schools, and the requirements of the Revised Code. The Scottish Universities will take care that it be not solved by extinction of the liberal education in Scotland. But let the English Universities consider whether, with improved primary education, a similar question may not arise in England; whether there ought not to be, as of old, a ladder, by which a boy of rare intellectual powers may climb from his parish school to an University education.

A change in the school and university course also touches the question of liberal education for women. The sacred precincts of the classics have been tabooed against such intruders as Lady Jane Grey. But they are admitted to modern studies. Sometimes in natural science, and often in modern languages, history, and literature, girls now know more than their brothers. For them, then, as well as for their brothers, instruction must be made more thorough. The most narrow mind cannot deny that what they learn at all they should learn well.

Again, the cry is raised that material interests of England are in danger, from national neglect of science in education. At present wealthy manufacturers and merchants are much disposed to send their sons to the best liberal schools, though not to the Universities, if they are intended for trade. But if liberal schools will not teach modern subjects, and if the Universities will not fully recognise their importance, there is a risk in such quarters as these of losing liberal education altogether. Nor is England so short of material wealth and so over-stocked with liberal education that she can afford to run this risk.

Thus in many ways the question of the "course" of liberal education has a most important bearing on a larger question, which, if the Universities do not boldly face it, may be settled for them by a Reformed Parliament. If the Universities and the Church mean to remain national, they must do as the Legislature has done. They must open their eyes to see the true dimensions of a nation.

There is no reason to consider the matter otherwise than deliberately and calmly, but there is reason to consider it promptly, for the Report on Middle-Class Schools will require immediate legislation.

There is reason also to consider it profoundly. For the present relations between religion and critical scholarship, and between religion and science, are not such as can be safely left to a few learned and still fewer scientific men.

The time has come again (if it ever passed away) when the knowledge of tongues is of importance for the maintenance of sound religion. Much of our embarrassment in Biblical criticism is due to our ignorance of Hebrew and German. For Latin as a common language has died out, and German has now for a long time been the tongue in which all questions relating to antiquity are discussed with most research and learning. Nor does this only touch the clergy. Laymen ought to look into these questions for themselves.

The time also has come to deal with the misunderstandings between education and science, and between religion and science. The professors must look through the telescope of Galileo. This also concerns laymen as well as clergy. At present what Erasmus said of the scholars of his time is in effect what scientific men[1] say of our classical scholars: *Incredibile quam nihil intelligat litteratorum vulgus.*

[1] See especially a paper "On the Education of the Judgment," by Mr. Faraday.

The time has come, and it need not be doubted that our ancient Universities will prove themselves equal to this modern duty. If only their attention is fully directed to the question, if they view it in its broader aspect, if they look perhaps a little to what has been done in other countries, and then resolve what they will do themselves, there is reason to expect that their decision will be wise, and will be wise in time. But they have before them no less a problem than to organize National Liberal Education.

II.

THE THEORY OF CLASSICAL EDUCATION.

BY HENRY SIDGWICK.

IT is my wish to examine, as closely and completely as I am able to do within the limits of an essay, the theory of classical education: meaning thereby the body of reasons which, taken together, may be supposed to persuade the intelligence of the country, that the present course of instruction in the Greek and Latin languages and literature is the best thing that can be applied in the minds of English boys, in the year 1867, A.D.,—or at least better than anything that it has been proposed to substitute for it. Such a theory is somewhat difficult to extricate and expound in the case of this as of other institutions established long ago, in obedience to an impulse that has ceased to operate, under intellectual and social conditions which have since been profoundly modified. It is always, I think, a shallow view of history which represents such institutions as existing by *vis inertiæ* alone; *vis inertiæ* is a blind and irrational force, which we have to calculate and allow for in explaining to ourselves why institutions exist; but it is powerless (especially in an age like our own), unless combined with a respectable array of more rational forces. These forces are found in the convictions of intelligent and open-minded men who work the system, that it is supplying actual needs of the present age, is doing good work which the existing society wants done. But since it has never been incumbent upon any set of men, as a distinct and inevitable duty, to set forth what these needs and this work are; since it is evident to the most superficial inquirer that the system was originally established—or grew up—to meet very different needs, and to do very different work, its real *raison d'être* as an existing institution has to be elicited in the irregular, and, to a speculative mind, unsatisfactory way of volunteer conservative advocacy. The reasoning of advocates is generally apt to be vague, sweeping, rhetorical: but the arguments constructed to support what exists are perhaps the worst, as they are constructed under less pressure, with less felt need of intellectual exertion, and are inevitably addressed to the more docile and less critical portion of the public. A good reason, no doubt, is none the worse for being made to order; still it is natural to regard such reasons with suspicion, and the suspicion is often justified by closer examination. For, whatever be the cause, the arguments for classical education are often stated, even by able men, in a manner hardly worthy of their ability. They seem often so trivial and shallow, so partial and fragmentary, so vague and sweeping; they seem to suggest such narrow views of culture, such imperfect acquaintance with the intellectual development of mankind, so slight an effort to comprehend all the conditions of the infinitely important problem with which they deal. At the same time, the advantage that experience gives can hardly be too highly estimated. The result of handing over education to the most comprehensive theorist, with whatever gifts of lucid expression, would be, I doubt not, disastrous. The history of education is the battle-ground and burial-ground of impracticable theories: and one who studies it is soon taught to abate his constructive self-confidence, and to endeavour humbly to learn the lessons and harmonize the results of experience. But a teacher's experience must be measured not by the length of time that he has been engaged in his work, but by the amount of analytical faculty and intellectual labour that he has applied to the materials with which it has furnished him; by the way in which he has availed himself of the opportunities of observation and experiment which he, beyond all other men, has possessed. It not unfrequently happens—and perhaps it is not surprising—that even successful schoolmasters, immersed in the business of their profession, are found to have learnt the theory of what they are doing casually and long ago from other men, and to have let it remain in their minds in undigested fragments, not really brought to the test of, and therefore not modified by, experience. When such men become advocates, we soon detect their incapacity to give us any real instruction. Of course, many of a very different stamp have written in defence of classical education, and probably in the works and pamphlets that now exist on the subject, amounting to a considerable literature, all possible arguments have been brought forward. Still the wish that forms itself in the mind on the perusal of these works is, that the period of advocacy should if possible now close, and that not one or two, but a number of intelligent educators should take the arguments provided for them, turn them, and revolve them carefully, and by close, sober, accurate observation, obtain their exact value; and then express this in carefully guarded and limited statements. The very mistakes and contradictions of such observers would elicit truth, and we should soon feel a legitimate confidence, which we can hardly feel now, that our systematic treatment of youthful intellect, if not absolutely the best conceivable, was at least approximately the best attainable.

In beginning to treat of classical education, it is perhaps desirable to make a protest against the notion which seems to prevail in some quarters, that the course of instruction which now bears that name is an organic whole, from which it is impossible to cut off any part, without converting the rest into something of very inferior value. A boy is considered to have been made a complete classical scholar when he has been taught to translate elegantly and correctly from Latin and Greek into English prose; to compose correct and elegant Latin and Greek prose, and Latin and Greek verse. Classical study, the result of which does not include all these accomplishments, is supposed to be deficient in thoroughness.

Now there seems no adequate reason why Latin and Greek should be regarded as a sort of linguistic Siamese twins, which nature has joined together, and which would wither if separated. No doubt, the study of one is a good preparation for the study of the other; but it has no special need of it for its own completeness. The qualities of the two languages, and the reasons for which it is desirable to study them, are in many respects very different : and it is only by a palpable looseness of thought that they can be joined together in discussion as frequently as they are. When, for instance, Dr. Woolley[1] says that these two languages are the "master-keys that unlock the noblest tongues of modern Europe," he forgets how little Greek has to do with any of these tongues, except in forming their scientific terminology. When again the "severe regularity" of both languages is eulogized, it is forgotten how strong the tendency is in Greek to deviate from the normal type of the sentence, and to frame constructions which are not difficult to understand, but which can be brought under no grammatical rules. Moreover, the assumption is often made that, because there are strong arguments to prove that the thorough learning of *one* dead language is a valuable element of education, and that this language ought to be *either* Greek or Latin, therefore there is justification for teaching both Greek and Latin—I will not say thoroughly, but so as to engross the lion's share of time and trouble.

Again, it seems undeniable, that a person may learn to read even a dead and difficult language with correctness and ease combined, without ever attempting to compose elegantly or even idiomatically in it ; without, in fact, writing more than a sufficient number of exercises to fix thoroughly in his mind the more important part of the grammar. Many students of Sanskrit, Hebrew, and other languages, do not do as much as this, and yet obtain a sufficiently firm grasp, for their purposes, of the languages they study. The fact seems to be, that if the sole end in learning a language be to

[1] Late Principal of the University of Sydney.

read it easily, with correct apprehension of its meaning, the only means absolutely necessary is to read a great deal, and take care that the meaning is correctly apprehended. But perhaps the most singular assumption is, that it is an essential part of the study of Greek and Latin to cultivate the faculty of writing what ought to be poetry in these tongues. No one of the large and increasing body of students, who concentrate their energies upon other ancient languages: no one of the professors, who elucidate with the most subtle and delicate apprehension the most obscure and difficult poems in these languages: ever dreams of trying to develop such a faculty, except as the merest pastime. The composition of verses, and of elegant prose, may, or may not, be a desirable element of education; but these exercises must be defended independently on their own merits, not as forming an essential part of instruction in Greek and Latin.

In the discussions on classical education, we find debated, and decided generally, though not always, in the same way, a preliminary question of great importance—namely, whether education ought to be natural or artificial. I use these as the most convenient words, but they require some explanation. By a "natural" education is meant, that which teaches a boy things in which, for any reason whatever, he will be likely to take an interest in after life. It may be, that for commercial or professional reasons only, he will be forced to take an interest in certain subjects; in that case his education must at some time, and to some extent, begin to be commercial or professional, and not liberal. One can hardly be content that any human being should be trained entirely for his *métier*, and have no share of what may be called liberal education,—for every human being will have at least so much leisure, as to make it important for himself and for others, that he should be taught to use it rightly. But taking the term in its ordinary sense, and applying it to those who are able to defer the period of professional study till at least the close of boyhood, a liberal education has for its object to impart the highest culture, to lead youths to the most full, vigorous, and harmonious exercise, according to the best ideal attainable, of their active, cognitive, and æsthetic faculties. What this ideal, this culture may be, is not easy to determine; but when we have determined it, and analysed it into its component parts, a natural education is evidently that which gives the rudiments of these parts in whatever order is found the best; which familiarises a boy with the same facts that it will be afterwards important for him to know; makes him imbibe the same ideas that are afterwards to form the furniture of his mind; imparts to him the same accomplishments and dexterities that he will afterwards desire to possess. An artificial education is one which, in order that man may ultimately know one thing, teaches him another, which gives the rudiments of some learning or accomplishment, that the man in the maturity of his culture will be content to forget. This is the extreme case, but in proportion as a system of education approximates to this, in proportion as the subjects in which the boy is instructed occupy a small share of the thoughts of the cultivated man; so far that system may be called artificial, rather than natural. Now I think it must be allowed that, however much, historically and actually, the *onus probandi* may rest on those who oppose an artificial system of education, and wish to substitute a more natural one, yet, logically, the position of the combatants is reversed, and the *onus probandi* rests on those who maintain the artificial system. If a boy is to be taught things which, it is distinctly understood, are to be forgotten, the good that they do him during the time that they remain in his mind ought to be very clearly demonstrated. In order to escape the severity of this demonstration, the advocates of classical education are sometimes inclined to make an obviously unfair assumption. They assume that "training the mind" is a process essentially incompatible with "imparting useful knowledge." And no doubt the attack on classical education has frequently been of so vulgar and ignorant a character, that this assumption might be, if not fairly, at least safely, made. The clamour has been, "useful knowledge at any rate, and let the training of the mind take care of itself." Against assailants of this sort the defence of classics was, and deserved to be, victorious. But the question is now posed in a suitable form. It is now urged that the process of teaching useful knowledge affords as valuable a training in method as any other kind of teaching. However difficult it may be to appraise exactly two different kinds of training, this task distinctly devolves on those who would teach knowledge that they admit to be useless.

But in the case of classics the uselessness is by no means admitted. Though I think it may be fairly said that classical education is supported chiefly as an artificial system, it is supported partly as a natural system. Though many of its advocates would urge that it ought to be maintained for the training alone, even though the knowledge imparted were all to be forgotten, the majority urge also that this knowledge is in various ways of permanent value. In estimating the utility of the results of classical study, we naturally range these results under two heads: the knowledge of language gained, and the acquaintance with literature. The latter is the more splendid result, that which affords more scope to the eloquence of advocates, and is more impressive to the outside world; but the former is the more certain and universal acquisition, and the one upon which most stress is laid by educators. Whatever else is denied, the bitterest reformer cannot deny that boys do acquire some knowledge of two dead languages. We may therefore fitly commence our examination by inquiring what this knowledge is worth.

In the first place, although the classicists are, on the whole, the stanchest supporters of a liberal as opposed to a professional education, they also point out that a knowledge of Greek and Latin is useful professionally. This line of argument has been taken by able and accomplished men;[1] but I am not sure that it has, on the whole, been of service to the cause. The professional advantages are found to be unequally distributed among the different professions; and in some cases there is an almost comical discrepancy between the labour expended and the utility acquired. A clergyman has to interpret the Greek Testament, and therefore it is important that he should be able to read it in the original. It might perhaps, from a professional point of view, be better that he should be familiarised a little

---

[1] I may mention Sir W. Hamilton (Edinburgh Review), and the Rev. W. G. Clark (Cambridge Essays, 1855).

less with the Attic, and a little more with the Hellenistic dialect; but still Greek is, after all, Greek.[1] When, however, this point is strongly pressed, we cannot avoid contrasting the great anxiety shown that a clergyman should know Greek, with the complacent indifference with which his total ignorance of Hebrew is usually contemplated.

We may admit, again, that a lawyer — even an English lawyer—ought to be able to read Roman law in the original. It is not clear that he is likely to advance himself in his profession by the study, but it is for the benefit of society that he should engage in it. He ought, therefore, to be acquainted with Latin grammar, and a certain portion of the Latin vocabulary. As to doctors, can we gravely urge that they ought to understand the language in which their prescriptions are written, and that they find it instructive to read Galen and Hippocrates in Greek?[2] To men of science, it is pointed out that their ever increasing technical terminology is systematically formed from Greek and Latin words. This is true; and it is also true that a man of science might obtain a perfect grasp of this terminology by means of a list of words that he would learn in a day, and the use of a dictionary that he might acquire in a week. It may be further remarked,

---

[1] Some writers seem to extend the necessity of learning Greek, for the purposes of religion, much more indefinitely. "No religious nation," says Mr. Thring, "can give up Greek." I do not suppose that Mr. Thring means more than that it is desirable that there should be, besides the clergy, a body of learned persons studying Greek (and Hebrew), so as to keep the study safe from any professional narrowness. In this I should heartily agree. But it is a very aristocratic view of religion that makes it depend in any degree on a knowledge of Greek.

[2] See Cambridge Essays, 1855.

that though a clergyman might conceivably dispense with Latin, a learned clergyman, one from whom original research in the field of ecclesiastical tradition is expected, cannot dispense with it; and generally every antiquarian student, every one who inquires into the early history of any European nation, or of any department of modern science, will require to read Latin with ease. Science has at length broken its connexion with what was so long the learned language of Europe; but it is still the key to what, in contradistinction to science, is usually called erudition. To sum up: Greek is of use (we may say indispensable) to clergymen: Latin to lawyers and learned men. The other infinitesimal fragments of utility may be disregarded for our present purpose; and, finally, in all these cases, it is only the power of reading that is of use, and not that of writing the language.

Much more importance is claimed for the knowledge of the classical languages as an element of a truly liberal culture : as the best introduction to the study of Philology, as including the best instruction in the universal principles of Grammar, and as indispensable to a real knowledge of English and of other modern languages. It seems rather important to attach as clear and precise ideas as we can to the words "Philology" and "Grammar": as the looseness with which they are sometimes used creates an inevitable confusion of thought. Grammar is sometimes regarded as either an introduction to, or an extension of, Logic. It is called "the logic of common speech."[1] Now it would appear that Grammar, in this sense, includes only a

[1] Report of the Public Schools Commission.

small portion of what is taught as the grammar of any particular languages. It teaches some of the facts and laws of thought and expression which Logic also teaches (both studies being united by a common root) and also certain other facts and laws, which the theory of syllogistic reasoning is not obliged to notice, but which are equally universal, and — if I may use the term without provoking a controversy — equally necessary. Such are the distinctions of substantives and adjectives, of transitive and intransitive verbs, the existence and classification of the relations expressed by the other parts of speech, the distinctions of tenses and voices, of principal and subordinate, declarative and conditional sentences, &c. It is clearly impracticable to separate this part of any particular grammar from the rest: because it is difficult to say what is, and what is not, universal: since each man is biassed in favour of the distinctions which his mother tongue brings into prominence; and since there are many distinctions, which, when they are once pointed out we not only see to be true, but cannot conceive how we could ever have overlooked. The most philosophical branch of Philology is that which busies itself with such real but not indispensable (what we may call potentially universal) distinctions of thought: collecting them when they lie scattered in the grammar of particular languages, and clearly defining, arranging, and comparing them. This seems a study both extremely interesting in itself, and intimately connected with — we may even say a branch of—mental philosophy. And, no doubt, in learning Latin or Greek many such distinctions are taught to an English boy, of which the closest observation of his mother tongue would leave him ignorant. But it cannot be denied that nine-tenths of his time is occupied in storing up facts which in no sense belong to universal grammar : in learning, not new shades and distinctions of thought, but simply special ways of expressing old shades and distinctions, facts which are so patent in his own language, that Latin instruction is an extremely tedious and circuitous process of teaching him to observe them. In learning the usage of a new language we always find some things which seem to us convenient and rational, and which we should like if possible to incorporate into our own : but the greater part of what we learn appears accidental and arbitrary, while a good deal we regard as provokingly useless and troublesome. There is probably always a scientific explanation of this last, as the result of ages of growth, but there is often no philosophical explanation of it as belonging to a present instrument of thought. When, therefore, we are told that "the principles of universal grammar which are necessary as the foundation of all philosophical acquaintance with every language, carry the young scholar forward till his mind is deeply imbued with the literature, &c."[1] we see what large deductions must be made from this statement. A boy does no doubt learn principles of universal grammar which he will always desire to retain : but he learns them along with a large assortment of formulæ which, when he has once ceased to study Latin, he will be willing as soon as possible to forget.

By Philology is generally understood the study of language historically, of its changes, its laws of growth

[1] Dr. Moberly.

and development. It deals chiefly with the vocabulary and accidence of languages, as distinguished from the philosophical study of Grammar, of which I have spoken, that deals chiefly with the syntax. It is a study to which the thorough learning of either Latin or Greek forms an excellent introduction; but Latin from its relation to English possesses peculiar advantages in this respect; and these advantages would be much increased if French were learnt along with Latin, and every opportunity taken of pointing out the mutual relations of the three languages, Latin, French and English. No cultivated man can fail to feel the interest and charm of Philology, or would wish to say a word in its disparagement. Its materials are abundant, its processes productive, the aid it affords to History and Anthropology most valuable. Still it must be classed among the sciences that are studied from "pure curiosity"[1] alone; and, however noble an impulse we feel this to be, however true it is that any great increase of its force marks a step in human progress, yet such studies must be ranked, in importance to society, below sciences like Physics, Chemistry, Astronomy, animal and vegetable Physiology, which (besides the gratification they afford to curiosity) have had, and promise still to have, the greatest influence on the material welfare of the human race. And if we cannot (as we certainly cannot) include all the sciences in the curriculum of general education, it seems (from this point of view) that those studied from pure curiosity are precisely those that ought to be left to students of special bias and faculty, every care

---

[1] I use the word in the more elevated signification which the corresponding term in French bears.

being taken to yield to this bias and foster this faculty. If then it appear desirable on other grounds that boys should learn Latin (or Greek), the fact that they will be thereby initiated into the study of Philology is a real additional advantage; but taken by itself it does not constitute a very strong reason for learning either language.

We are told, however, in the strongest and most unqualified terms, that we cannot understand our own language without a knowledge of Latin and Greek: and this in two ways—both in respect of its grammar, and in respect of its vocabulary. This claims to be so cogent a proof of the direct utility of these ancient languages, that it deserves our most serious consideration. We shall find, I think, that it has been urged by the advocates of classics with more than usual exaggeration. The limit of extravagance seems to be reached in the following utterance of Professor Pillans (which is quoted with approbation in the Report of the Public Schools Commission): "It (English) is, besides, so uncompounded in its structure, so patchwork-like in its composition, so broken down into particles, so scanty in its inflections, and so simple in its fundamental rules of construction, that it is *next to impossible to have a true grammatical notion of it, or to form any correct ideas of grammar and philology at all*, without being able to compare and contrast it with another language, and that other of a character essentially different." Why the rules of a language should be hard to teach because they are simple, because the character of the language is analytical and not synthetical, because in it the relations of words and sentences are expressed almost entirely by particles, without the aid of inflection: why in such a language it should be "impossible" to convey "correct ideas," not only of the facts and principles of universal grammar (which are *ex vi termini*[1] common to all languages), but also of the formulæ in which its special usage is summed up, is not attempted to be shown. That a person who had learnt English grammar only would have a very limited idea of grammar is undeniable, but it is obvious that his idea might be correct as far as it went. The learning of the rules of Latin usage would, no doubt, sharpen our perception of the rules of English usage; and this indirect utility (which belongs rather to the second part of our subject) I do not wish to undervalue. And it may be advantageous to excite a boy's interest in the laws of language first, by making him feel that, without the observation of these laws, he cannot obtain the results that are demanded from him. But to assert that Grammar could not be taught analytically, instead of synthetically, seems contrary to common sense and experience alike.[2]

When we take the vocabulary, as well as the grammar,

---

[1] As the word universal is generally used, I have indicated another application of it, in the signification, as I have expressed it, of "potentially universal."

[2] Some persons have a vague idea that it is not worth while trying to teach English and some other modern languages systematically, because they are "hybrid;" as if a language could be "hybrid" in its grammar, however mixed in its vocabulary, and as if Latin was not hybrid, in the same sense, though not to the same extent, as English. Others cannot divest themselves of the notion that familiar phenomena must be simple, and seem almost irritated when shown how varied and complex are the rules of using their vernacular. For instance, a French writer complains "l'on raffine la grammaire française: on questionne un enfant. . . . sur des distinctions subtiles auxquelles Pascal et Bossuet n'ont jamais songé:" as if Virgil ever thought of a tertiary predicate, or Thucydides of the peculiar usage of ὅπως μή.

of English into our view, we find still more startling statements as to the difficulty of mastering our mother tongue. Mr. Thring tells us that "it is scarcely possible to speak the English language with accuracy or precision, without a knowledge of Latin and Greek." "It is not possible to have a masterly freedom in the use of words, or a critical judgment capable of supporting its decisions by proof without such knowledge." These are the words of a vigorous writer, and their substance I find stated, though less extravagantly, by several others. They seem to me well to illustrate the ignorance of the real nature of language, and the laws of its apprehension, in which our long tutelage to Latin and Greek has left us.

The fact is, that the study of Latin (for Greek, except in respect of scientific terminology, has much less to do with the question, and would hardly have been placed on a par with Latin here, but for the hasty and random way in which the stock arguments on this subject are continually repeated,) cannot tell us what the English language is, it can only help us to understand how it has come to be what it is. In order to learn to speak English with accuracy and precision, we have but one rule to follow,—to pay strict attention to usage. The authority of usage, the usage of cultivated persons, is in all disputed points paramount. The history of language is the history of continual change, and just as in learning Latin and Greek (or any other language), the tyro finds a knowledge of derivation frequently puzzling and misleading, the usage of words having often strayed from their original signification by long routes that can be only conjecturally traced: so in the case of words that we have derived from the Latin, the meaning of the Latin term has often been so modified, that it would be the merest pedantry to pay attention to it. No doubt we are all liable to make mistakes in our own language, especially in the case of terms which we meet with so rarely, that the natural process by which we learn the rest of our mother tongue cannot completely operate. And as these words are often derived from the Latin, a Latin scholar has a certain additional protection against such mistakes: he will naturally fall into them rather less than another man, who pays no particular attention to the subject. But he is liable to fall into a different set of errors, if he ever attempts, as pedants have attempted, to make his knowledge of Latin override English usage. Mr. Thring regrets the loss of the original meaning in the case of words like "edify" and "tribulation;" and no doubt the historic interest in the derivation of these words is very great, and the non-classical reader has every reason to be grateful to books like those of Archbishop Trench, that open this new field of interest to him. But for a man in search of accuracy and precision, seriously to try and shackle himself by attention to these lost significations—to refuse, for instance, to use the word "tribulation," except when the idea of "threshing" seemed suitable, would be pedantic frivolity. To the masters of English style, natural instinct and unconscious tact as to the living force of language, is the chief and primary guide; while English dictionaries and English classics are the only corrective and court of appeal in case this tact breaks down. In short, the application of Latin to the historical interpretation of English, is a branch of

Philology—a most entertaining and instructive branch—which I should be glad to place within the reach of every one, but which must be regarded, like the rest of Philology, as an intellectual luxury. When we are threatened, that, without a knowledge of Latin and Greek, our language would be to us "a strange collection of inexpressive symbols,"[1] we are at first alarmed; but on reflection, we perceive that our verbal signs would become "inexpressive," in the sense that they would only express the things signified; and the menace does not seem so terrible. We reflect also, that the historical study of language is of very modern growth, and that Greek and Latin must have been "strange collections of inexpressive symbols" to the writers of the master-pieces and models which we are invited to cherish.[2]

Some exception to what I have said ought to be made in the case of scientific nomenclature; because, as this is the one part of our language of which the growth is deliberate, and determined by the learned—not natural, and determined by the mass of the nation—

[1] Edinburgh Review, cxx.
[2] Mr. Joseph Payne, in a pamphlet remarkable for sobriety of statement, breadth of view, and close observation of the educational process, brings forward a somewhat different argument to show the advantage a Latin scholar has in reading English. He quotes several uses of English words derived from the Latin, in our older authors, (such as "civil," "resentment," "prevent,") which a classical scholar understands at a glance, but which puzzle or mislead a man uneducated in classics. But these uses ought to be found in dictionaries, and noticed by commentators. Every man reading older authors in his vernacular, ought to know that a part of their vocabulary is archaic, and ought to be on the watch for the archaic terms. I cannot think that the trouble is very considerable of acquiring as complete an acquaintance with these archaisms, as is necessary for literary purposes. A knowledge of Latin would only save a part of this trouble; much more would be done by the direct teaching of English literature which I advocate in this essay.

it has a living and progressive connexion with Latin and Greek which no other part of the language has. But even here it is necessary to make distinctions. It seems too sweeping to say that "no man can expound any subject matter with scientific precision, unless he is acquainted with the *etymologies* of the terms he employs."[1] The newer terms of scientific phraseology have been formed generally in a systematic way, upon fixed principles, and we may assume that, for the future, all additional technical terms will be so formed. Therefore, though it is not absolutely indispensable to the scientific student to possess the key to this phraseology (as he can learn the meaning of each word from its usage and place in the system to which it belongs), it will save him a great deal of useless trouble if he does possess it. But in the case of many of the older terms of science, formed irregularly or on false principles, a knowledge of the derivation will be useless or misleading. They have often great interest for the historical student: to the scientific man, the sooner they become mere counters the better. I have already indicated with what ease men of science might learn all the Greek and Latin words necessary to give them the required key. Instruction in such words ought to form a distinct part of the direct teaching of English, to which all these arguments for learning Latin and Greek seem to point, as an educational desideratum.

I have said that Latin was important chiefly with a view to the historical study of our own language, and not in order to obtain a complete grasp of it, as a living instrument of thought. It ought to be added,

[1] Cambridge Essays, 1855.

that though Latin forms one element in this historical study, it forms *only* one element, and that the other elements—and, indeed, we may say the study itself—have been surprisingly neglected in our educational system. Hardly in our Universities does any one dream of learning Early English, and though we teach some French and German in our schools, we teach them merely colloquially and practically, without any reference to their historical development or their linguistic relations. This neglect (which some efforts have been made to repair during late years) will be commented upon more in detail elsewhere in this volume. I have referred to the point here chiefly because it affords an example how the arguments for learning classics, being "made to order," are found, as far as they are worth anything, to prove more than they were intended to prove, and to support, not the existing course of instruction, but something of which that would form only one part.

In the eyes of many persons, however, the most important of the direct utilities supposed to be conveyed by a classical education is still that for which a classical education was originally instituted, acquaintance with the Greek and Latin literatures. In the first place, just as the ancient languages were called a master-key to unlock all modern European tongues, so the ancient writings are said to be indispensable to the understanding of all the best modern books. "If," says Dr. Donaldson, "the old classical literature were swept away, the moderns would in many cases become unintelligible, and in all lose most of their characteristic charms." A moment's reflection will show this to be a most strange and palpable exaggeration. For instance, Milton is the most learned of our poets: nay, as a poet, he is generally said to be obtrusively learned, learned to a fault. Yet how grotesque an absurdity it seems to assert that "Paradise Lost" would "lose most of its characteristic charm" to a reader who did not understand the classical allusions and similes. The real state of the case seems analogous to that which we have just discussed. A knowledge of classics is indispensable, not to the general reader, but to the historical student of modern authors: without it he can enter into their ideas and feelings, but not the antecedents which determined those ideas and feelings. He cannot reproduce the intellectual *milieu* in which they lived; he can understand what they said, but not how they came to say it. But for the general reader, who has no wish to go so deep, classical knowledge does not do much more than save some trouble of referring to dictionaries and histories, and some ignorance of quotations which is rather conventionally than really inconvenient. Many allusions to the classics explain themselves; many others are explained by the context; and the number of those that remain incomprehensible to a person who has read histories of Greece and Rome, and knows as much about the classics as he must inevitably pick up from a good course of English literature, is not very considerable. We may grant that "literature can only be studied *thoroughly* by going to its source."[1] But the conception conveyed in this word *thoroughly* assumes an exalted standard of reading, which, if carried out consistently, would involve an overwhelming encyclopedic study of literature. For the modern authors

[1] Dr. Temple.

whom the stream of fame has floated down to us, and whom we do read, contain numerous allusions to preceding and contemporary authors whom we do not think of reading, and require, in order to be *thoroughly* understood, numerous illustrations from preceding and contemporary history which we have no leisure to procure. We content ourselves with the fragmentary lights of a casual commentator. I do not see that it would be so dreadful if classical allusions were apprehended by the general reader in the same twilight manner. It may be very desirable that we should read everything more accurately and thoroughly; but let us have one weight and one balance. The historical study of literature, for the completeness of which I allow classics to be indispensable, is a most interesting and improving pursuit, and one which I hope will gain votaries yearly. But, after all, the branch of this study which seems to have the greatest utility, if the space we can allot to it is limited, is surely that which explains to us (as far as is possible) the intellectual life of our own age; which teaches us the antecedents of the ideas and feelings among which, and in which, we shall live and move. Such a course, at this moment of history, would naturally contain a much larger modern than ancient element: it would be felt in framing it more imperatively necessary to represent French, German, and English thought of recent centuries, than to introduce us to any of the older influences that combined to determine our immediate intellectual antecedents.

But the intrinsic value of Latin and Greek literatures seems to many to outweigh all other considerations. It is true that these literatures are no longer supposed to contain all knowledge; even their claim to give the best teaching in mental, ethical, and political philosophy, the last relic of their old prestige, is rapidly passing away: still they undeniably convey, with great vividness, a knowledge of what the Greeks and Romans were, how they felt, thought, spoke, and acted; and some persons of great eminence consider it of the highest importance that Greek and Roman life in all its phases should be kept continually before the mind of the modern world.[1] Persons of very opposite views agree in inculcating this. Clerical advocates tell us that to feel the real force of Christianity, we must acquaint ourselves with the vices of the ancient world, and learn how impotent, ethically speaking, the unassisted human intellect is; while enthusiasts of a different stamp point to the narrow rigidity, the withering pettiness, the complacent humdrum of our modern life, and urge that ancient literature teaches just that passionate love of country, love of freedom, love of knowledge, love of beauty, for which they pant. I do not wish to undervalue either kind of instruction, but I cannot say that I see the absolute want of either: I cannot but think that if we were debarred from Latin and Greek, a careful teaching of modern history, and a careful selection of modern literature would supply our youth with all the stimulus, example, and warning, that they require. Further, even if it be granted that we cannot dispense with the lessons of the ancient world, it is easy to exaggerate the disadvantages of learning them through

[1] This has been urged by Mr. Mill with his usual impressiveness, and is illustrated in a beautiful essay of Villemain's, called "Demosthènes et le Général Foy."

the medium of modern languages. We must remember
how many excellent translations we have of ancient
authors, some of which take rank as English classics;
and how much of our very highest historical ability has
been devoted to this period of history. Of course, every
student who takes up the period as a speciality, will
desire to know the languages thoroughly well, in order
to have an opinion of value upon disputed points; and
even the general reader always feels the additional
vividness, and, therefore, the additional pleasure and
stimulus and improvement, that a knowledge of the
original gives. But it would be absurd to say that an
Englishman (particularly if he can read French and
German) has any difficulty in accurately and thoroughly
informing himself what sort of people the Greeks and
Romans were. And it might, I think, be truly asserted,
however paradoxically, that even under our classical
system, the greater part of the vivid impressions that
most boys receive of the ancient world are derived from
English works; from Pope's Homer, Macaulay's Lays,
the English Plutarch (if they have the good fortune to
get hold of that delightful book), and afterwards from
Arnold, Grote, and Merivale.

But the æsthetic importance of ancient literature is
even more insisted on than the value of its moral
teaching. If we do not teach a boy Latin and Greek,
it is said, we cut him off from the highest literary enjoyment, and we prevent him from developing his taste
by studying the best models. It would avail little to
call in question (had I space and inclination to do so)
the surpassing excellence of ancient literature. For my
present purpose, I must regard this point as decided by

an overwhelming majority of persons of culture. But it will not be denied that in the English, French, and German languages,[1] there is a sufficiency of good literature to fill the leisure of a person engaged in any active calling, a sufficiency of works calculated to give a high kind of enjoyment, and to cultivate, very adequately, the literary taste. And if such a person was ever visited by a painful hankering after the time-honoured volumes that were sealed to him, he might console himself by taking note how often his contemporaries who had enjoyed a complete classical education, were in the habit of taking down these master-pieces from their shelves. For I cannot help thinking that classical literature, in spite of its enormous prestige, has very little attraction for the mass even of cultivated persons at the present day. I wish statistics could be obtained of the amount of Latin and Greek read in any year (except for professional purposes), even by those who have gone through a complete classical curriculum. From the information that I have been able privately to obtain, I incline to think that such statistics, when compared with the fervent admiration with which we all still speak of the classics, upon every opportunity, would be found rather startling. I am willing to admit that those who have a genuine preference for the classics, are persons of the purest, severest, and most elevated literary taste; and I cannot conceive that these relics will ever cease to be reverently studied by those who aspire to be artists in language. But this by no means proves that they ought to occupy the place they do

---

[1] I only omit Italian because it is rarely taught at schools, and I am not prepared to recommend that it should be more generally taught.

in the training of our youth. "It is admitted," says a Quarterly reviewer (summing up very fairly the Report of the Public Schools Commission), "that education must be literary, and that of literary education, classical learning must be the backbone." Whether I should agree with this or not, depends upon the sense in which "backbone" is interpreted: at present classical learning forms, so to say, the whole skeleton; and the result is, that, to a very large number of boys, what is supposed to be a purely literary education, what is attacked as being exclusively a literary education, is, paradoxical as it may sound, hardly a training in literature at all. For surely it is essential to the idea of such training that it should have some stimulating power; that it should inspire a fondness for reading, educe the capacity for enjoying eloquence and poetry, communicate an interest in ideas; and not merely guide and chasten such taste and interest if they already exist. The instruments of literary training ought to be not only absolutely admirable, but relatively attractive. If we wish to educate persons to enjoy any kind of art, I do not say that we are not to put before them things hard to appreciate, but we must certainly put before them also things that they will find easy to appreciate. I feel sure that if the schoolmaster is ever to be, as I think he ought to be, a missionary of culture; if he is to develop, to any extent, the æsthetic faculties of other boys than those who have been brought up in literary homes, and have acquired, before they come into his hands, a taste for English classics, he must make the study of modern literature a substantive and important part of his training. It may be said that some part of ancient literature, especially Greek, is ever young and fresh; and no doubt, in most good schools, some boys are made to feel this, and their path becomes flowery in consequence. But the majority want, to stimulate their literary interest, something that can be read with more ease, in larger portions: something, moreover, that has a visible connexion with the life of their age, which exercises so powerful a control over their imaginations. I do not know that, if difficulties of language were put aside, some ancient historians, such as Herodotus, might not be more attractive to boys from their freshness and *naïveté*, than any modern ones. But just when the difficulties of language are beginning to be got over, boys cease to relish this *naïveté*. They want something that speaks to their opening minds and hearts, and gives them ideas. And this they are seldom able to find to a great extent, in the ancient works they read. This is true, I know, of some at least among the minority who study classics at school and college with all the stimulus of uniform success; much more is it true of the majority who fail or are but indifferently successful. If such boys get imbued with literary culture at all, it is not owing to the classical system; it is due to home influence, to fortunate school friendships, to the extra-professional care of some zealous schoolmaster. In this way they are taught to enjoy reading that instructs and refines, and escape the fate of the mass, who temper small compulsory sips of Virgil, Sophocles, Tacitus, and Thucydides, with large voluntary draughts of James, Ainsworth, Lever, and the translated Dumas.[1]

[1] I must be pardoned for using the names familiar to my generation. I have no doubt there are other favourites now.

I wish this occasional and irregular training to be made as general and systematic as possible; and I feel sure that whatever classical teaching was retained, would become more efficacious by the introduction of the new element; and this not merely because every new mental stimulus that can be applied to a boy is immediately felt over the whole range of his work, but because the boy would gain a special motive for learning Latin and Greek, which he had hitherto been without, and the want of which had made his studies (to use the words of a Quarterly reviewer) "a prolonged nightmare." He might not at once begin to enjoy the classics: his progress might be still so slow, and his attention so much concentrated on the form of his authors, as to allow him but a feeble interest in their substance. But he would be cheered by the hope of this interest becoming daily stronger: he might distinctly look forward to the time when Sophocles would be as dear to him as Shakespeare, when Cicero and Tacitus would stir him like Burke and Macaulay. Again, some modern literature has a direct power of revealing to us the charm of ancient literature, of enabling us to see and feel in the older masterpieces what the *élite* of each generation could see and feel for themselves when the language was once understood, but what for the mass requires an interpreter. Some, for instance, would perhaps be ashamed to confess how shallow an appreciation they had of Greek art till they read Goethe and Schiller, Lessing and Schlegel. No doubt there are boys who find out the beauties for themselves, just as there are some to whom it would be a feast to be turned into a room full of fragments of antique sculpture. But our system is framed for the mass, and I feel convinced that the mass require to appreciate both the one and the other a careful preparation, the most important part of which would be supplied by a proper introduction into education of the element I am advocating.[1]

Further, I am disposed to think that the literary education of even the best boys is liable to suffer from the narrowness of the existing system. In the first place, there is a great danger in the predominance that classics are made to gain over their minds, by the indiscriminate eulogy and unreserved exaltation of the ancient authors *en masse*,[2] which they frequently hear. They are told, dogmatically, that these authors "are perfect standards of criticism in everything that belongs to mere perfect form," that "the laws that regulate external beauty can only be thoroughly known through them," that "they utterly condemn all false ornament, all tinsel, all ungraceful and unshapely work;" and the more docile of them are apt to believe these dogmas to a degree that warps and oppresses the natural development of their critical faculties. The truth is, that the best classical models only exemplify certain kinds of

---

[1] The *Quarterly Review*, a journal that does not often clamour for rash and premature reforms, says (vol. cxvii. p. 418):—

"Much more is it a thing to wonder at and be ashamed of, that, with such a literature as ours, the English lesson is still a desideratum in nearly all our great places of education, and that the future gentry of the country are left to pick up their mother tongue from the periodical works of fiction which are the bane of our youth, and the dread of every conscientious schoolmaster."

We may add that the question, whether native literature is to be systematically taught, has long been decided in the affirmative both in France and in Germany.

[2] I allow that there are some exceptions to this statement; for instance, one of the most exquisite artists in language, Euripides, has been perhaps unduly depreciated. Still I think I have fairly described the general tendency.

perfection of form, that several writers that boys read exemplify no particular perfection at all, and that some illustrate excellently well the precise imperfections that the enthusiast I have quoted enumerates.[1] How can it be said, for instance, that there is no "false ornament" in Æschylus, no "tinsel" in Ovid, no "ungracefulness" in Thucydides, no "unshapely work" in Lucretius? In what sense can we speak of finding "perfect form" and "perfect standards of criticism" in such inartificial writers as Herodotus (charming as he is) or Xenophon! There is perhaps no modern thinker, with equal sensitiveness to beauty of expression, who (in those works of his which have been preserved to us) has so neglected and despised form as Aristotle. Any artist in words may learn much from Cicero, and much from Tacitus; but the profuse verbosity of the one, and the perpetual mannerism of the other, have left the marks of their misdirection on English literature. I am simply repeating what are now the commonplaces of cultivated criticism, which can no longer be charged, on the whole, with being servile towards antiquity; but education is less emancipated, and as long as these sweeping statements of the perfectness of ancient literature are reiterated, a demand for careful limitation seems necessary.

But secondly, it can hardly be said that the artistic training which might be given by means of ancient literature (which I should be sorry to seem to undervalue) is given under our present educational system. A few attain to it self-taught: and even these are liable to all the errors and extravagances of such self-education.

[1] Mr. Thring.

But what effort is made to teach literary criticism to the great majority in our schools (or even in our universities)? Are they encouraged to judge as wholes the works that they so minutely analyse? to attain to any synthetical apprehension of their excellence? The point on which the wisest admirers of ancient art lay most stress is the completely organic structure of its products and the instinct for complex and finely articulated harmony that is felt to have guided the production. But in so far as schoolboys (with a few exceptions) are taught to feel the beauty of these products at all, it is the beauty of parts, and even of minute parts that they are taught to feel. And, from the mode in which these beauties are studied for purposes of composition it is not only a partial, but generally a perverted appreciation that is attained. In the effort to prepare his mind for composition, a boy is led to contemplate his authors under conditions as unfavourable to the development of pure taste and sound criticism as can possibly be conceived. He is led to break the diction of great masters into fragments for the purpose of mechanical ornamentation, generally clumsy and often grotesque. His memory (as an advocate exultingly phrases it) is " stored with precious things:" that is, it is stored with long words, sounding epithets, imposing circumlocutions, salient extravagances and mannerisms: so that his admiration is directed to a great extent to what is *bizarre*, fantastic, involved, over-decorated in the admirable models he studies: and even of what is really good he is apt to spoil his delicacy of apprehension, by the habit of imitating and introducing it unseasonably. I am aware how much careful training may do to correct these vicious tendencies: but they are likely to exist in overwhelming force as long as the imitative instinct is so prematurely developed as it is now, and applied to a material over which so imperfect a command has been gained.

This forms a convenient transition to another part of my subject: the examination in detail of the existing instruction in Latin and Greek, regarded primarily as a species of mental gymnastics, a method of developing the intellectual faculties: without reference to the permanent utility of the knowledge conveyed. When, however, the methods of classical instruction are spoken of as a "fine training," the word "training" may be used in two senses, which it is necessary carefully to distinguish. Sometimes, merely a rhetorical training is intended; the boy, it is said, is taught not only a special dexterity in the use of particular languages (his own included), but a complete grasp of language in general: he learns to dominate the instrument of thought instead of being dominated by it: "his mind is enabled to conceive form as an object of thought distinct from the subject-matter, and *vice versâ*, and hence generally to judge of the application of the one to the other in literature, with a degree of accuracy which is never attained except by those thus trained."[1] Sometimes, again, it is claimed that classics supply a complete general training to the mind: that, in the words of M. Cournot:[2] "Rien ne se prête mieux que l'étude grammaticale et littéraire d'une langue au développement graduel et méthodique de toutes les facultés intellectuelles de l'enfance et de l'adolescence. Cette étude exerce la

[1] Rev. W. G. Clark.   [2] De l'Instruction publique.

mémoire, la sagacité, le goût, le jugement sous toutes les formes, logiques ou non logiques, c'est-à-dire, soumises ou non à des classifications, à des déductions et à des règles précises. Elle forme l'homme tout entier." It will be convenient to take the narrower of these pretensions first: and examine whether composition in the ancient languages, and translation from them into our own, appear to form a complete course of instruction in the art of speech.

I think that few who have considered the subject can deny, that translation from a Latin or Greek author into English prose, under the guidance of a competent teacher, is a very vigorous and efficacious training in the use of our language, and gives very considerable insight into the nature of speech, and its relation to thought and fact. Our only doubt will be, whether the training and insight is not, by itself, one-sided; whether we do not require something else as a supplement, to give us a complete view and a complete grasp of language. "The art," says Dr. Moberly, "of throwing English with facility into sentence-moulds made in another language . . . what is this but to learn to have the choicest, most varied, words and sentence-frames of our own language constantly at command, so that, whatever varieties of thought and meaning present themselves to a man's mind, he will never be at a loss for expressions to convey them with an accuracy at once forcible and subtle to the mind of his hearers." This is no over-statement: but it leaves out of sight the dilemma in which even the matured scholar, and therefore infinitely more the tiro, is perpetually placed between exact English and elegant English, between the set of words that represents the precise meaning of the original (and is endurable in the vernacular), and the nearest English phrase that can be called tasteful. A schoolmaster must inevitably sacrifice accuracy or style, and he, as a rule, wisely determines to sacrifice style for the time. But if style is sacrificed here, it becomes desirable to cultivate it carefully in another part of the education. The result of laboriously forcing our language into "moulds" unnatural to it, will not be to give us an easy flow of it in natural moulds. Even when the process is carried further, as in the case of the more advanced students, and style is gradually more and more regarded, still the translator's dexterity remains a special dexterity, and does not amount to the whole art of composition. Translation is continually straining and stretching our faculty of language in many ways, and necessarily imparts to it a high degree of a certain kind of vigour; but the precise power that will be of most use to us for the purposes of life it does not, by itself, give, and it even causes us to form habits adverse to the ultimate acquirement of that power. Teaching the art of Rhetoric by means of translation only, is like teaching a man to climb trees in order that he may be an elegant dancer.[1]

[1] The conclusions of a thorough-going advocate of classical education in Germany, are as follows: "Das Uebersetzen der antiken Meisterwerke ist eine Schule für die Gewandtheit und Gediegenheit des Ausdrucks wie es keine zweite gibt. Die Verirrung aber, zu der diese Uebungen verkehrt betrieben führen könnten, die steife Nachbildung des griechischen und römischen Sprachgeistes, mit Verletzung des Deutschen, diese Verirrung wird verhütet durch das Lesen unserer deutschen Klassiker.... um den Schuler zur richtigen Ordnung der Gedanken anzuleiten, werden zu den Uebersetzungen aus den alten Versuche in eignen deutschen Ausarbeitungen hinzutreten müssen."— Raümer, "Geschichte der Pädagogik." And this seems to me a well-balanced view of the question.

I have allowed the efficacy of translation in teaching English expression; it must also be said that it develops very sufficiently the sense of one kind of excellence of form in all the more intelligent and appreciative minds: I mean of minute excellence, the beauty of single words and phrases. It does this simply because it enforces a close and reverent examination of masterpieces. We are apt to neglect many excellences in writings that we read with ease, simply because we read them with ease; and as we are forced in these times to read much hastily, we find some trouble in forming a habit of reading worthy things as they deserve. The best training for such a habit is to read fine compositions in some foreign language. But it must be remarked, that it is only at a certain stage in a youth's progress that Latin and Greek begins to give this training. In many cases the boy (and even the undergraduate) never becomes able to extract and feed on the beauties of his authors. A mind exhausted with linguistic struggles is not in a state to receive delicate literary impressions: instead of being penetrated with the subtle and simple graces of form, it is filled to the brim with thoughts of gender, quantity, tertiary predicates, uses of the subjunctive mood.

The training in æsthetic perception is thus by no means general, and it is, as I have before pointed out, very incomplete. But such as it is, it seems to me to be conveyed much more satisfactorily in the process of translation, than in that which is generally supposed to teach it, composition in Greek and Latin. We are told that a boy "cannot have appreciated the delicacy, taste, or the feeling of his models in literature, if he have not in some degree learned, from his own clumsy efforts and occasional better successes, at how almost immeasurable distance they stand from the rude rough things which otherwise he might be led to compare with them." I have spoken of the false and distorted view of literary excellence that this gives. A thoughtful boy feels the hardship of being made to imitate persons who have so unfair an advantage over him as the writers in a language now dead. An ambitious boy often loses all delicacy and truth of taste in the effort to assimilate all "useful" words and phrases which, however bad in taste they may be, will at least decorate and set off his own "rude rough things." The assertion that masterpieces cannot be appreciated without an effort to imitate them, seems to me contrary to common sense, to our experience in our own language, to our universal practice in studying foreign literatures, and to the analogy of other arts.[1] And the imitation that is encouraged at schools in the process of verse-writing is the very worst sort of imitation; it is something which, if it were proposed in respect of any other models than these, we should at once reject as intolerably absurd.

There is much more to be said for the exercise of writing elegant Latin prose, though I am not sure that it is not prematurely attempted in our present system of education. I do not think, as I have before said, that even this accomplishment is at all essential to the most accurate and complete knowledge of the Latin language. It cannot be too much insisted, that the faculty of

[1] There is some reason for urging that, a connoisseur in painting should have handled the pencil and the brush. But this is surely not in order to improve his taste, but to teach him closeness and correctness of observation, without which, in so directly imitative an art, a sense of beautiful effect may be misleading.

reading a language and that of composing in it are almost entirely distinct, and have to be acquired separately. A development of the latter faculty tends, no doubt, to improve the former to a certain degree; but it is a very roundabout way of improving it; if our object is to learn to read and translate, the time would be much better spent in reading and translating. I quite admit that by simply reading, without much sustained effort to translate, a language so remote from our own in its idiom as the Latin, a habit of loose apprehension is formed, and not only the refinements of expression are lost, but many mistakes are made in the substantial signification of sentences. But I should urge that written translation carefully looked over is, as a remedy for lax habits of reading, very far superior to any amount of composition.[1] Perhaps also too much has been made of the rhetorical utility of writing Latin prose: and too little of the logical training given to maturer students by the process of translation from English into Latin. The close and prolonged meditation over familiar words and expressions, which the effort to reproduce their full substance in an alien and difficult tongue entails, imparts a very delicate discrimination of the exact import of these current phrases. Moreover the effort to write so extremely synthetical a language as the Latin is very beneficial to an Englishman, as teaching him much about the real connexions of thought, the

---

[1] I have previously noticed the only function for which composition seems to me preferable to any other exercise —that of fixing firmly in the mind the grammar and the commoner rules of usage, which we require to have firmly fixed before we can read with ease and security. It does not seem to me indispensable even for this function; but it is probably a distinct abridgment of labour.

logical interdependence of sentences, which the analytical tendencies of his own language prevent his noticing. With reference to the rhetorical utility of this exercise, I will quote some remarks of Dr. Moberly, with which I partly agree, but which seem to me much too unqualified. "It is a very great part of the benefit to be derived from writing Latin prose, that a boy learns thence to write prose in any language.... He is taught what constitutes a sentence; how much meaning he may put into a sentence; how many clauses a sentence will bear.... One of the most common faults in composing English is that of stringing clauses upon clauses, without heeding the necessary rules of periodic structure.... I do not wish to recommend the building up of elaborate sentences after the manner of the writers of the seventeenth century, but I wish to observe that the slipshod style of modern English, with its loose clauses and involved parentheses, would be greatly corrected by a careful course of original composition in Latin.... Loose ungoverned clauses, dissimilar nominatives, and verbs hung together by unmeaning ands, no less than mixed metaphors and impossible figures, will not go into Latin. 'Try it in Latin,' might often suggest to a young writer the absurdity of what may seem to be rather fine in English.... The boy (who can write Latin) has obtained a master-secret which he can apply to many a difficult lock besides." There runs through all this the erroneous idea, which is pointed in the last sentence, that Latin style forms a kind of skeleton-key, or universal touchstone, for all other styles. No doubt by teaching any style thoroughly, we also teach, to a certain extent, how to penetrate the mysteries of any new style. But each language requires its own art of rhetoric; the "rules of periodic structure" are special for each: the questions "What constitutes a sentence?" &c. are answered as differently as possible in different languages. In some important points (mentioned by Dr. Moberly) practice in Latin forms a specially useful corrective to faults in English—it is like showing blemishes by a magnifying-glass: some things that are bad in English are clearly seen to be inadmissible in Latin. But precisely the same is true of French. Either language, properly used, may be made to improve our style in our own; any language (and not least these two), if carelessly used, may spoil it. It is indispensable that practice in writing the vernacular should proceed *pari passu* with the practice in an alien tongue, and receive as careful attention.

Again, Latin is a language in which the rhythmical effects are broad, palpable, easy to apprehend. This is also true of English, and (however hopeless it is in our broken utterance to emulate the continuous music of the more synthetical language), we might educate the ear very thoroughly by a careful study of our own masters of eloquence. Still, writing Latin, at a stage when elegance can be made a prominent object, seems well adapted to assist this education; and of course we attain a larger view of melody in general, by the study of literary models so widely different from our own.

Hardly any of the reasons that I have enumerated can be urged in favour of writing Greek prose. Useful as the Greek language is to teach subtlety and delicacy of thought, it is so much more lax in its laws of expression and structure than the Latin, that it has very little of the corrective effect of this latter upon English composition. Besides, one or two most charming and impressive Greek writers are exceedingly bad models. It will sound a paradox to mention Plato. Still, a style which is an intentional imitation (often an exaggeration) of the flexible and irregular movement of conversational utterances, can hardly be a good pattern for ordinary prose. Thucydides, again, with all the wonderful weight and pregnancy of his words, is the product of what few will deny to have been a thoroughly vicious school of rhetoric; and I think the unqualified admiration with which docile boys are, by many educators, led to regard his writing, frequently tends to injure or perplex the natural development of their taste. Besides, we are naturally very little sensible to the rhythm of Greek prose (which may perhaps be accounted for by our manner of reading it). It is hard for a boy even to pretend to himself that he appreciates the melody of even Demosthenes.

But, if it were granted that Greek composition supplied as valuable a training as Latin, there would be very little to be said for adding the one accomplishment to the other. We thereby burden the memory with much additional material, while we give the logical and rhetorical faculties but little additional training. It is becoming more and more evidently important in classical education to save time, without lowering the standard of excellence in the work required. One easy method of doing this, is to reduce the number of the kinds of composition cultivated.

On the whole, we are led to the conclusion that all these processes form a one-sided and incomplete training in the use of English, and require to be supplemented by some careful and independent teaching of English composition. It seems equally true, that in order to insure that complete view of the relation of language to thought, which, if we spend so much time in linguistic studies, we may fairly expect to insure, we can hardly dispense with some direct teaching of English. The immediate task set before a boy in all the processes of classical education, is to ascertain exactly the equivalence of two languages, not the relation of either to thought and fact. It is impossible that he should not indirectly gain much insight into this relation; but it is not impossible that in the case of many scattered words and phrases, he may learn to fit one language to another, without expressing a really clear idea in either. Moreover he reads at a time such small portions of the ancient authors, that there is very little opportunity for teaching him to grasp a long and elaborate argument as a whole; for training him quickly to apprehend the bearing not only of sentence on sentence, but of paragraph on paragraph. Again, just as it was urged that the appreciation of English literature, though it might perhaps be left to nature in the case of boys brought up by intellectual parents in a literary atmosphere, requires to be directly taught to boys without these advantages: so it may be said that the same boys are in danger of never learning a considerable portion of the English vocabulary. I do not exactly mean technical terms, but the half-technical, the philosophical, language which thoughtful men habitually use in dealing with abstract subjects. Of some of these terms such a boy may pick up a loose and vague comprehension from ordinary conversation, novels and newspapers; but he will generally retain sufficient ignorance of them to make the perusal of all difficult and profound works more weary and distasteful than their subject-matter alone would make them. If English authors were read in schools so carefully, that a boy was kept continually ready to explain words, paraphrase sentences, and summarize arguments; if the prose authors chosen gradually became, as the boy's mind opened, more difficult and more philosophical in their diction; if, at the same time, in the teaching of natural science, a great part of the technical phraseology (from which the main stream of the language is being continually enriched), was thoroughly explained to him; then we might feel that, by direct and indirect teaching together, we had imparted a complete grasp of what is probably the completest instrument of thought in the world.[1] I have admitted that, in the first stage in the analysis of language (assuming that we are right to begin it as early as we do now) the intervention of a foreign language may be valuable, in order that each step in knowledge may be felt as an increase of power. But I think that the last and crowning stage of this analysis, where the learner's view of the relation of language to thought is to be made as complete and profound as possible, being abstract and difficult, and involving a considerable strain on the reflective faculty, is generally best taught in the most familiar language, and therefore in the vernacular.

[1] Mr. Johnson, of Eton, in his interesting evidence before the Public Schools Commission (see Report, vol. iii. p. 159), expresses the opinion that, in the process of more careful cultivation of French, the English language might be (as he phrases it) "used up," and all its terms explained; whereas it is impossible to use it up in translation from Greek and Latin. This suggestion seems to me valuable and important, but I should still rely more on the direct teaching I speak of, though there is no reason why the two should not be combined.

I hope that I have shown my anxiety not to underrate the power over language developed by learning a foreign tongue, and especially one very alien in its laws and structure to our own. But I do not think it has been ever shown that this mode of development of our faculty of speech is absolutely necessary, or even, with reference to the place which language occupies in our life, obviously desirable. The normal function of language is not to represent another language, but to express and communicate facts. Scientific men are justly told by the classicists that all their discoveries would be useless without language; and the answer that the most inarticulate discoverers have generally found means to communicate their message to mankind, though a natural rejoinder, is not complete for our present purpose, for this inarticulateness is precisely the sort of evil which education ought to remedy. To describe a fact or series of facts methodically, accurately, perspicuously, comes by nature to some people, just as eloquence does; but it requires to be taught carefully to others. Only it is hard to see why the study of language, in this sense, should be separated at all from the study of subjects; why, as "things" cannot be taught without "words," the use of words should not be learnt *pari passu* with the knowledge of things. Indeed, it must be so learnt to some extent. The only question is, whether care and attention shall be bestowed on the process; whether the scientific teacher shall be content that his pupil should make it evident to him that his mind has grasped ideas, or whether he shall insist on those ideas being adequately expressed. If he does this latter, he will give gradually a training in language sufficient, not only for the ordinary uses in life, but even for the purposes of most professional students. The delicate perception of subtle distinctions which a good classical education superadds, is an intellectual luxury that ought not to be despised, but may easily be overvalued.

We have now to consider whether, in the acquisition of linguistic and literary knowledge, and linguistic and literary dexterity, by the various processes that we have been considering, there is really given to all the mental faculties a most complete and harmonious training;—and, if not, where the training appears defective and one-sided, and what the natural supplement is. There can be no doubt, I think, that the training, as far as it goes, is strong and effective, and there is no doubt too, that it is much more varied than its depreciators are willing to allow. Indeed, it is curious, that so many men of science fail to perceive that the study of language up to a certain point is very analogous in its effect on the mind to the study of any of the natural history sciences. In either case, the memory has to be loaded with a mass of facts, which must remain to the student arbitrary and accidental facts, affording no scope to the faculties of judgment and generalization. This is the weak point of either study, regarded as an exercise of the reason, and makes it desirable that the initiation into either should take place early in life. But, as in natural science, so in language, there is a large amount of material, that not only exercises the memory, but enforces constant attention and perpetual close comparison: rules and generalizations have to be borne in mind, as well as isolated facts; habits of accuracy and quickness in applying them are rapidly developed, and the important faculty of judgment is perpetually educed, trained, and stimulated. And the remark I quoted from a French writer is most just, that the judgment is exercised "in all its forms, both logical and nonlogical." In applying each newly learnt rule, it acts at first deliberately, by an express process of reasoning, afterwards instinctively, by an implicit process. I think, however, the common statement, that in learning a language the mind is exercised in induction, requires much qualification. The mind of the matured, the professional scholar, is so exercised, because he stands on a level with the authors of his grammars and dictionaries, and from time to time observes new rules of usage which they have not noted. But the boy, or youth, learning his lesson with ample grammar and dictionaries, is not, or is very rarely, called upon to perform any such process. For each doubtful case that comes before him his books and memory combined soon furnish him with an abundance, a plethora of formulæ:[1] he has only to choose the right one. In making this choice, besides close attention and delicate discrimination, an unconscious tact, a trained instinct, combines to guide him, and, by applying a mental magnifying glass to this tact or instinct, we may discover in it rudimentary inductive processes; but we might find the same in the mental operations of every skilled artisan, and it is perhaps misleading to dignify them by the name. Besides this training of the cognitive faculties, the

---

[1] If a boy could be more debarred from grammars and dictionaries, there would naturally be more induction in the process of learning the language. But the efforts that have been made in this direction (though deserving of all attention) do not seem as yet to have been conspicuously successful.

creative are also, as we have seen, developed. In composition, the boy applies the same rules, by the aid of which he has analysed complex products of speech, to form similar products for himself; and as in the former case he acted under the guidance of a gradually developing scientific tact, so in this he works under the influence of a slowly educed æsthetic instinct. He is taught to make an effort to be an artist in a material hard to manipulate, and the benefit of this training will, it is presumed, abide with him in whatever material he has afterwards to work.

If, then, say the advocates of classics, we offer a study of literature which at the same time combines scientific and artistic training, why is not the completeness of our system admitted, and why are we asked to introduce any new element except for the vulgar reason that it would be more useful? Simply because each element of the training is not (at any rate taken alone) the best thing of its kind or the thing we most want. We may allow that the education is many-sided: still, if it is defective on each side, this many-sidedness will not count much in its favour. And the very fact that the same instrument is made to serve various educational purposes, which seems at first sight a very plausible argument in its favour, is really, for the majority of boys, a serious disadvantage. In the actual process of education one or other of the purposes is continually sacrificed. Some boys with strong taste for literature and natural power of expression, pass with moderate success through their classical work by means of their literary tact alone, and get, after the first rudiments of grammar are acquired, very little training in close observation or accurate reasoning. But with the greater number (especially of boys who do not go to the University) the case is reversed. The mind, exhausted with the labours of language, imbibes miserably little of the lessons of literature. And here I may observe that some educational reformers have committed a most disastrous error—an error that might have been fatal, if anything could be fatal, to their cause, in allowing the notion to become current, that there is a sort of antagonism between science and literature, that they are presented as alternative instruments of education, between which a choice has to be made. It is so evident that if one or other must be abandoned, if we must inevitably remain either comparatively ignorant of the external world, or comparatively ignorant of the products of the human mind, all but a few exceptional natures must choose that study which best fits them for communion with their fellow-men. But I absolutely deny this incompatibility: nor do I think it would ever have occurred to any one except for the strange illusion that in the age in which we live classics must *necessarily* be the "substratum," "basis," "backbone," (or whatever analogous metaphor is used) of a literary education: and that therefore we must leave on one side every other form of literature with the view of imparting as much classics as possible. The consequence is that half the undergraduates at our Universities, and a larger proportion of the boys at all (except perhaps one or two) of our public schools, if they have received a literary education at all, have got it for themselves: the fragments of Greek and Latin that they have struggled through have not given it them. If so many of our most expensively educated youth regard athletic sports as the one conceivable mode of enjoying leisure : if so many professional persons confine their extra-professional reading to the newspapers and novels : if the middle-class Englishman (as he is continually told) is narrow, unrefined, conventional, ignorant of what is really good and really evil in human life ; if (as an uncompromising writer[1] says) " he is the tool of bigotry, the echo of stereotyped opinions, the victim of class prejudices, the great stumbling-block in the way of a general diffusion of higher cultivation in this country"—it is not because these persons have had a literary education, which their "invincible brutality" has rendered inefficacious : it is because the education has not been (to them) literary : their minds have been simply put through various unmeaning linguistic exercises. It is not surprising that simple-minded people have thought that since a complete study of Latin and Greek was felt by some[2] of those who had successfully pursued it to have been (along with the other reading that they had spontaneously absorbed) a fine literary education, therefore half as much as Latin and Greek ought to produce about half as much of the same kind of effect ; and that when they see the education on the whole to be a failure, instead of demanding more literature as well as more science, they cry for less literature. But the time seems to have come for us to discern and repair this natural mistake. Let us demand instead that all boys, whatever be their special bent and destination, be really taught

[1] Dr. Donaldson.
[2] I say advisedly "some." Many successfully trained scholars feel very differently with regard to their training.

literature : so that as far as is possible, they may learn to enjoy intelligently poetry and eloquence ; that their interest in history may be awakened, stimulated, guided ; that their views and sympathies may be enlarged and expanded by apprehending noble, subtle, and profound thoughts, refined and lofty feelings : that some comprehension of the varied development of human nature may ever after abide with them, the source and essence of a truly humanizing culture. Thus in the prosecution of their special study or function, while their energy will be even stimulated, their views and aims will be more intelligent, more central ; and therefore their work, if less absorbing, not less effective.

If this be done, it is a subordinate question what particular languages we learn. We must allow all weight to the advantages which a dead and difficult language has, as an instrument of training, over a modern and easy one.[1] But we must remember that it is a point of capital importance that instruction in any language should be carried to the point at which it really throws open a literature : while it is not a point of capital importance that any particular literature should be so thrown open.

[1] I think there would be a great advantage in combining a difficult with an easy language. The more facile conquest a boy would make over one, might encourage him in his harder struggle. Of course, for this, or any other valuable result to be attained, the easy language must be studied with as much attention and respect as the hard one. This is one of the numerous reasons for selecting French and Latin as the languages to be taught in early education. Another reason for teaching them together, is their relation to each other, and to English. (See Professor M. Müller's Evidence before the Public Schools Commission, vol. iv. p. 396). This eminent scholar there illustrates the way in which the rudiments of Comparative Philology might be taught by comparing words in the three languages, and ventures to assert, that an " an hour a-week so spent, would save ten hours in teaching French and Latin."

The defects of the usual exercises in Greek and Latin composition, as an artistic training, have been incidentally noticed; and the disadvantages of verse composition in particular, are pointed out elsewhere in this volume. We must not forget, however, that the place which these exercises fill in education must be filled in some way or other; the boy must be taught to exercise his productive faculty, and to exercise it in a regulated, methodical manner. In the later stage of education, when discursive thought on general and abstract themes may properly be demanded, essays and careful answers to comprehensive questions seem to constitute the best mode of developing this faculty, as attention may thus be paid to style and substance at the same time. In the earlier stages we require easier exercises in English prose, such as narratives and descriptions, drawn from experience or imagination, or freely compiled from authors read; the teaching of physical science would give occasion to descriptions of a different kind; the history lesson would suggest orations and declamations at appropriate points, so that rhythm and melody might be naturally taught. It is a doubtful point whether all boys should be exercised in producing poetry; it is hardly doubtful that they should be exercised, if at all, in a material less difficult than Latin or Greek is, up to a very advanced stage of its acquisition. Perhaps translations into English poetry of fine passages in foreign authors might be occasionally required from all; and original poetry, encouraged only by prizes. If, too, it is once admitted that production of the kind that develops the æsthetic faculty is to be encouraged, if the boy is to be stimulated to produce beautiful things, there seems no adequate reason why the brain alone should be exercised in such production; the training of the hand and eye which drawing affords is probably desirable for all boys up to a certain point; while after this point, boys who are absolutely unproductive in language, may develop their sense of beauty in pictorial art.

Then remains the training of the cognitive faculties which the process of mastering the classical languages supplies. We have seen that this training is in many respects very efficacious, and that it (unlike many supposed utilities of classics) is really given, to some extent, to most boys.[1] As I have said, it appears to me very similar to that which would be supplied by one or more of the physical sciences, carefully selected, limited, and arranged for educational purposes. It is clear that this latter study develops memory (both in extent and accuracy), close attention, delicate discrimination, judgment, both instinctive and deliberate, the faculty of rapidly applying the right general formula to the solution of any particular problem. I am not in a position to institute a close comparison of the efficacy of the two kinds of study in educating those faculties of the mind which both in common call into exercise.[2] But the study of language seems to have certain distinct ad-

---

[1] If the pernicious influence of Bohn's Library could be entirely excluded, this might be stated more strongly. But it must never be forgotten in discussing this question, that the training afforded by classics read with translations is very different from that afforded by classics read without them.

[2] It is much to be wished, that some competent person, equally acquainted with languages and science, and with equal experience in teaching the rudiments of both, would carefully make such a comparison. At present, the best exponents of the effect of either study generally speak of the other with comparative ignorance. It is, perhaps, an indirect testimony to the advantages of scientific education, that this ignorance is more frequently combined with contemptuous dogmatism in the case of the classical advocate.

vantages. In the first place, the materials here supplied to the student are ready to hand in inexhaustible abundance and diversity. Any page of any ancient author forms for the young student a string of problems sufficiently complex and diverse to exercise his memory and judgment in a great variety of ways. Again, from the exclusion of the distractions of the external senses, from the simplicity and definiteness of the classification which the student has to apply, from the distinctness and obviousness of the points that he is called on to observe, it seems probable that this study calls forth (especially in young boys) a more concentrated exercise of the faculties it does develop than any other could easily do. If *both* the classical languages were to cease to be taught in early education, valuable machinery would, I think, be lost, for which it would be somewhat difficult to provide a perfect substitute.

But the very exclusions and limitations that make the study of language a better gymnastic than physical science, make it, on the other hand, so obviously inferior as a preparation for the business of life, that its present position in education seems, on this ground alone, absolutely untenable. The proof of this I cannot attempt adequately to develop; but it seems appropriate to indicate the more obvious reasons, as they are still ignored by many intelligent persons. One point the advocates of the classical system sometimes admit by saying "that it does not develop the faculties of external observation;" and the more open-minded of them would desire that these faculties should be somehow or other exercised, without interfering with the "more important part of education." But this is a most inadequate view of the question. It is not enough that the intelligence should be trained at one time and in one way, and the senses exercised separately; we require that the intelligence should be taught to exercise the important functions of which we have spoken in combination with the senses; and we require this, because this is the normal mode of the action of the intelligence in human life. It is not enough that we should learn to see things as they are, important as this is: we must also train the memory to record accurately, and the imagination to represent faithfully, the facts observed: we must learn to exercise the judgment and apply general formulæ to particular phenomena, not only when these phenomena are broadly and clearly marked out (as they are when we come armed with complete grammars and dictionaries to the interpretation of foreign speech), but also when they are obscure, hard to detect, "embedded in matter," mixed up with a mass of other phenomena, unimportant for our purpose, which we have to learn to neglect. The materials on which our intelligence has ordinarily to act, even when we are thinking, and not observing, are ideas of the external world, mixed products of our mind and senses: and it must never be forgotten that the training of the eye and hand given by the various branches of physical science, the development of our sense of form, colour, weight, &c. is not merely a training of these external organs, but of our imaginative and conceptive faculties also, and will inevitably make our thinking more clear and effective. Similarly, the training in classification which most immediately fits us for life, is that which the natural history sciences afford. In learning them the student is taught not only how to apply a classification ready made, but also, to some extent, how to make a classification. He is taught to deal with a system where the classes merge by fine gradations into one another, and where the boundaries are often hard to mark; a system that is progressive, and therefore in some points rudimentary, shifting, liable to continual modification; along with the immense value of a carefully framed technical phraseology he is also taught the inevitable inadequacy of such a phraseology to represent the variety of nature; and these are just the lessons that he requires to bear in mind in applying method and arrangement to any part of the business of life.[1] And finally, above all, the study of language does not in the least tend to impart the most valuable and important of all the habits that we combine under the conception of scientific training: the habit, as is generally said, "of reasoning from effects to causes, and from causes to effects;" it might be more distinctly defined as the habit of correctly combining in imagination absent phenomena (whether antecedent or consequent) with phenomena present in perception. Physics and Chemistry are the most natural and efficacious way of teaching boys from some part of any of the invariable series of nature to infer and supply the rest; their place could not be adequately occupied by History and Literature, if ever so philosophically

---

[1] Cuvier, speaking of his own study, says:—"Every discussion which supposes a classification of facts, every research which requires a distribution of matters, is performed after the same manner; and he who has cultivated this science merely for amusement, is surprised at the facilities it affords for disentangling all kinds of affairs."

I do not think a student of languages could honestly claim an analogous advantage for his own pursuit.

taught; as History and Literature are taught at present, this training is simply absent from the classical curriculum.

Again, the advantage that the minds of the educated might obtain from a sufficient variety of exercise, is lost under the present exclusive system. This absence of variety is indeed sometimes claimed as a gain; we are solemnly warned of the paramount necessity of studying one thing well. And certainly the encyclopædic courses of study which some theorists have sketched out have given practical men an easy victory over them: it is so easy to show that this encyclopædic instruction would impart a great deal of verbal, but very little real, knowledge. But "est quadam prodire tenus, si non datur ultra." No doubt the studies of boyhood must be carefully limited and selected; but they may be representative of the diversity of the intellectual world in which men live. A boy must not be overwhelmed in a mass of details: he ought to be forced by all possible educational artifices to apprehend facts and not to repeat words; but in order that he may attain a thoroughly cultivated judgment according to the standard of our age, his education must be many-sided, he must be initiated into a variety of methods.[1] And it may be

---

[1] When people talk of "training the memory, judgment," &c., they often ignore the difference between a general and special development of these faculties. There is great danger lest, if trained to a pitch in one material only, they will not work very well in any other material. "The mind requires," as Mr. Faraday says, "a certain bent and tendency, a desire and willingness to accept ideas of a certain kind," while it becomes slow and languid in dealing with ideas of a different kind. Mr. Faraday's evidence of the inferiority of educated men to children in apprehending scientific ideas, is very interesting and impressive. (See Report of Public Schools Commission, vol. iv. p. 377.)

observed that under the present system, neither the advantages of concentration, nor the advantages of variety, are gained. A boy, in passing from Greek and Latin, has not sufficient change to give any relief to his faculties, but he has sufficient to prevent him from making as rapid progress in either language as he would make if he studied either alone. The transition from the study of language to the study of external nature would give so much relief, that it would be possible for a boy to spend more time in his studies on the whole, without danger of injurious fatigue. A still more important advantage of variety of studies is its certain effect in diminishing the number of boys who take no interest in their school-work: a net is spread that catches more; and it is generally found that if a boy becomes interested, and therefore successful, in one part of his work, a stimulus is felt throughout the whole range of his intellectual efforts.

In general the advocates of classical education, while they rightly insist that educational studies should be capable of disciplining the mind, forget that it is equally desirable that they should be capable of stimulating it. The extreme ascetics among them even deny this. Thus Mr. Clark[1] says, " it is a strong recommendation to any subject to affirm that it is dry and distasteful." I cannot help thinking that there is some confusion here between " dry " and " hard." No doubt the faculties both of mind and body must be kept a sufficient time in strong tension in order to grow to their full strength: but we find in the development of the body that this tension can be longest and most healthily

[1] Cambridge Essays, 1855.

maintained, by means of exercises that are sought with avidity.[1] Those who have argued that the pursuit of knowledge might be made agreeable to boys, have been somewhat misunderstood by the apologists of existing institutions. They never meant that it could be made pleasant to him as gingerbread is pleasant, but as a football match in the rain, or any other form of violent exercise under difficulties. The "gaudia" of the pursuit of knowledge are necessarily "severa:" but there seems to be no reason why the relish for them should not be imparted as early as possible. The universality and intensity of the charms of science for boys have been sometimes stated, I admit, with almost comical exaggeration. But it will not be denied that the study of the external world does, on the whole, excite youthful curiosity much more than the study of language. The intellectual advantage of this ought to be set against whatever disciplinary superiority we may attribute to the latter instrument. On the moral advantage of substituting, as far as possible, the love of knowledge, as a nobler and purer motive, for emulation and the fear of punishment, I have not space to dilate : but it seems difficult to exaggerate the importance, though we may easily over-estimate the possibility, of developing this sentiment.

And the superior efficacy of natural science in evoking curiosity is not due entirely, though it is due partly, to the exercise it gives to the external senses as well as the brain. It is due also to the fact that educa-

---

[1] It is curious, in contemplating English school life as a whole, to reflect how thoroughly we believe in natural exercises for the body, and artificial exercises for the mind.

tion in physical science is (in the sense in which I have previously used the word) a *natural* education in the present age. The book which it opens to the student is not one which he will ever shut up and put by: it is not one that he could easily have ignored. In the age in which we live the external world forces itself in every way, directly and indirectly, upon our observation; we cannot fail to pick up scraps of what is known about it: sciolism is inevitable to us, unless we avoid it by becoming more than sciolists. The boy's instinct feels this: so that, besides the obvious and primary advantages that a natural system of education has over an artificial one, there is this in addition: it not only teaches what the pupil will afterwards be more glad to know, but what he is at present more willing to learn. We may admit that a knowledge of the processes and results of Physical science does not by itself constitute culture: we may admit that an appreciative acquaintance with literature, a grasp of the method as well as the facts of history, is a more important element, and should be more prominent in thoughts of educators; and yet feel that culture, without the former element, is now shallow and incomplete. Physical science is now so bound up with all the interests of mankind, from the lowest and most material to the loftiest and most profound: it is so engrossing in its infinite detail, so exciting in its progress and promise, so fascinating in the varied beauty of its revelations: that it draws to itself an ever increasing amount of intellectual energy; so that the intellectual man who has been trained without it must feel at every turn his inability to comprehend thoroughly the present phase of the progress of humanity, and his limited sympathy with the thoughts and feelings, labours and aspirations, of his fellow-men. And if there be any who believe that the summit of a liberal education, the crown of the highest culture, is Philosophy—meaning by Philosophy the sustained effort, if it be no more than an effort, to frame a complete and reasoned synthesis of the facts of the universe,—on them it may be especially urged how poorly equipped a man comes to such a study, however competent he may be to interpret the thoughts of ancient thinkers, if he has not qualified himself to examine, comprehensively and closely, the wonderful scale of methods by which the human mind has achieved its various degrees of conquest over the world of sense. When the most fascinating of ancient philosophers taught, but the first step of this conquest had been attained. We are told that Plato wrote over the door of his school, " Let no one who is without geometry enter here." In all seriousness we may ask the thoughtful men, who believe that Philosophy can still be best learnt by the study of the Greek masters, to consider what the inscription over the door should be in the nineteenth century of the Christian era.

In conclusion, it seems desirable to sum up briefly the practical changes (whether of omission or supplement) which have been suggested from time to time by a detailed examination of the arguments for the existing system; and at the same time to add one suggestion which, if I do not over-estimate its practical value, will very much facilitate the introduction of such other changes as I desire. I think that a course of instruction in our own language and literature, and a course of instruction in natural science, ought to form recognised and substantive parts of our school system. I do not venture to estimate the amount of time that ought to be apportioned to these subjects, but I think that they ought to be taught to all, and taught with as much serious effort as anything else. I think also that, partly for reasons which I have indicated and partly with a view to practical advantages, more stress ought to be laid on the study of French. While advocating these new elements, I feel most strongly the great peril of overburdening the minds of youth, to their intellectual or physical detriment, or both. From Germany, where the system is now more comprehensive than ours, we hear complaints which show that this evil has arisen. I do not know which is its worst form, that the brains of boys should be perpetually overstrained, or that a number of things should be taught, all inadequately and superficially, so that verbal memory is substituted for real apprehension. A certain amount of time will be gained by the omission of verses as a general branch of education, (so that only the few who have a special capacity for such exercises be encouraged to pursue them). But I do not think the time thus gained will suffice; especially as it is desirable that the study of every language that is studied should be made more complete than it is now. I have before hinted at what appears to me the obvious remedy for the evil I dread—namely, to exclude Greek from the regular curriculum, at least in its earlier stage. The one thing to be set against the many reasons that exist for choosing Latin (if a choice between the two languages is, as I think, inevitable) is the greater intrinsic interest of Greek literature. But I do not think that, if this change were made, Greek literature would be thrown really open to fewer boys. I think that if Latin (along with French and English) was carefully taught up to the age of sixteen (speaking roughly), a grasp of Greek, sufficient for literary purposes, might be attained afterwards much more easily than is supposed; particularly if at that period (when in the case of all schoolboys the stringency of the general curriculum ought to be considerably relaxed) a proper concentration of energy were insured in the first assault on the rudiments of the language. It is supposed that there is a saving of time in beginning the elements of Greek early. I am inclined to think that very much the reverse is the case, and that if several languages have to be learnt, much time is gained by untying the fagot and breaking them separately. There are two classes for whom the present system of education is more or less natural,—the clergy, and persons with a literary bias, and the prospect of sufficient leisure to indulge it amply. The former ought to read Greek literature as a part of their professional training, the latter as a part of a comprehensive study of literary history. Boys with such prospects, and a careful previous training of the kind I advocate, would on the average, feel, as they approached the last stage of their school life, an interest in Greek strong enough to make them take it in very rapidly. I believe there are one or two living instances of eminent Greek scholars who have begun to learn the language even later than the time I mention. The experience of students for the Indian Civil Service shows how quickly under a stimulus strong enough to produce the requisite concentration, languages may be acquired more remote from Greek and Latin than Greek is from Latin. The advantage that young children have over even young men in catching a spoken language, has led some to infer that they have an equal superiority in learning to read a language that they do not hear spoken: an inference which, I think, is contrary to experience.

Of the benefit of such a change to all other boys now taught in our public and grammar schools, I need say no more than I have said already. Without such a change their interests, (even if the recommendations of the Public School Commissioners be carried into effect generally,) will still be sacrificed to the supposed interests of the future clergy and literary men—a great clear loss for a very illusory gain.

III.

LIBERAL EDUCATION IN UNIVERSITIES.

BY PROFESSOR SEELEY, M.A.

"In Würtemberg wird locirt bis in's Mannes alter hinein. Ausser China wird in keinem Lande so viel examinirt und locirt, als in diesem. Die Locationen werden gedruckt; sie sind der Maasstab bei den späteren Anstellungen. Nach seinem Locus misst man den Mann."—"*Life of Hegel,*" by *Rosenkranz.*

"In Würtemburg they arrange in order of merit even grown men. In no country but China is there so much examining and *placing* as in this. The lists are printed; they regulate the subsequent appointments. A man is estimated according to his place."

THE state of the English Universities is a subject sufficiently important in itself, but it is discussed here mainly on account of its intimate connexion with the state of English schools. In the leading schools it does not rest simply with the Head-master to decide what the higher forms shall study. The College authorities at Oxford and Cambridge take this question very much out of his hands by their examinations for entrance exhibitions, and the University authorities by their degree examinations. In the second place, the Universities are practically our Normal Schools, the places where our schoolmasters are trained. It is not, to be sure, a methodical training, but it is the only training they receive. The opinions about education which they imbibe there are the opinions upon which they act, so far as they act freely, in the work of education. The subjects they will consider most important in education will be, as a rule, the subjects which were most in repute at College when they were there; and they will commonly teach by the same methods by which they themselves were taught. The experience of teaching may afterwards modify their views, but it is less likely to do so in respect of the subjects than of the methods. A schoolmaster may discover by trial a better way of teaching a subject than the way he began with, but it will not so readily occur to him to doubt the expediency of teaching a particular subject at all. A master's faith in the Eton Grammar breaks down long before his faith in Latin itself is even shaken, and this profound faith in Latin depends ultimately upon the value which is attached to it at the Universities. In the third place, it is to be noticed that the Universities have lately, with much spirit, taken upon themselves the function of directing education even in those schools which do not send their boys to them. By the Middle Class Examinations a number of schools were brought under the control of a common system, which before had had neither control nor system. This was a great step; but at the same time it greatly increased the influence of Universities over Schools, and made the nature of that influence a more serious question.

Education, in fact, in England is what the Universities choose to make it. This seems to me too great a power to be possessed by two corporations, however venerable and illustrious, especially since we know them to have grown up under very peculiar circumstances, and to be fortified by endowments against all modern influences, good or bad. I wish we had several more Universities; I mean teaching as well as examining Universities. I hope that the scheme which was announced some time ago, of creating a University for Manchester, will not be allowed to sleep. I should like to see similar schemes started in three or four more centres of population and industry. Could any investment of money in philanthropy be less questionable at this time? Is there anything more undeniable than that our material progress has outrun our intellectual,—that we want more cultivation, more of the higher education, more ideas?

But in the meanwhile, since Education in England is, in the main, what Oxford and Cambridge make it, how important is it that Oxford and Cambridge should disseminate just and profound views on education! There is no greater or deeper subject: there is no subject which demands more comprehensive knowledge or more fresh observation. There are general principles to be grasped, and there are particular circumstances of age and country to be noted, by the men who would legislate for the education of a nation. Oxford and Cambridge legislate for us, and we may be sure that if those Universities labour at present under any serious defect of system, the whole education of the country will suffer for it: our schoolmasters will want just views of their duty, and they will also be fettered in the performance of it.

The remarks which follow refer principally to Cambridge, the University I know best. They endeavour to point out a serious defect, which has the effect of lowering the whole intellectual tone of the University. If I can make my case good, I may expect to be pardoned, even though I venture to criticise an institution to which personally I owe much: if I do not succeed in convincing the reader, then he is likely to think my language ungracious, and I can only defend myself by assuring him that I echo the thoughts of very many who have had experience of the system, and also that, serious as we think the evil, we none of us doubt that both Universities are doing much faithful and valuable work.

Oxford and Cambridge, then, are just now in low repute upon the Continent, and it is common with foreigners to remark that they have made few contributions of late to science and scholarship. Whatever it may be possible to urge on the other side, it is at least undeniable that original research is not prosecuted so methodically, so habitually, nor by so many people at Oxford or Cambridge as at Berlin or Leipzig. We may have isolated celebrities equal to the greatest of Germany, but we have not anything like the number of students engaged, each in his own department, upon original and fundamental inquiry. This will hardly be disputed; and, taken by itself, it is a fact which every one would deplore. But some regard it as inevitable, and as arising from an inherent inferiority of the English character to the German in intellectual industry; while others consider that the energy withdrawn from original study at our universities is given to the instruction of the undergraduates, and that this is a better application of it. The theory of radical inferiority will certainly not bear examination. There is plenty of industry at Cambridge; among the undergraduates a good deal of over-work; and among the graduates a considerable class whose intellectual industry is incessant and would not bear much increase. The other explanation is obviously to a certain extent true. The industry, for example, of the class just mentioned is absorbed in tuition. They are the private tutors whose services are in so much request at Cambridge. Though they are generally the most distinguished men of their respective years, they are unable to pursue their studies further because they are engaged for eight or ten hours of every day with their pupils. The college lecturers, if they formed a distinct class, would have the necessary leisure, but they are commonly private tutors at the same time. There remain the professors. These, as they are in the position most favourable to production, do actually produce the most. But how small is their number, compared with that of the men equally well circumstanced in a German university!

There are, however, other impediments besides want of leisure. As the habit and fashion of original production has long gone out; as no one beyond the handful of professors regards it as lying within his functions to extend the bounds of knowledge, all the arrangements which might facilitate production are neglected. This is seen particularly in the case of the college lecturers. Why are not these more productive? They form a considerable band. When they can resist the temptation to waste their leisure in private tuition, they have the first condition of production—leisure, and also the second condition—a prescribed task. What more do they need? In the first place they need a subject carefully limited, so that they may hope to master it thoroughly. For example, if you make a man lecturer on classics, you spoil him for the purposes of original production. The subject is too wide. If he is required to lecture one term on a Dialogue of Plato, the next on an Oration of Cicero, and the next on Theocritus, he will lecture at best in a second-rate manner upon each. And if he hold such a lectureship for ten years, he will not, at the end of it, be necessarily much more learned than when he began. On the other hand, if an able man lecture on Aristotle for ten years, his lectures will soon become first-rate instead of second-rate, and he himself will hardly fail to become an accomplished Aristotelian. Now, this condition of production is neglected at Cambridge, and the consequence is that a college lecturer who was promising at twenty-two is often no nearer to performance at thirty.

Again, in this great band of college lecturers, there is scarcely any division of labour. As each college thinks it necessary to furnish all the needful instruction to its students, and admits to its lecture-rooms only its own students, the same subjects are lectured upon at the same time in all the colleges. In the German Universities the whole field of knowledge is elaborately divided, and assigned in lots to different lecturers. In a prospectus of Heidelberg University, I count about sixty, each lecturing on his own peculiar subject; at Cambridge scarcely anything but classics and mathematics is lectured on in the colleges at all, and at every college the lectures are substantially the same.

In Germany, every lecture-room being open to the whole university, the size of a lecturer's class bears some proportion to his merits. At Cambridge the best lecturer is no better attended than the worst, and not only his salary, but also his reputation, is hardly at all affected by the merit of his lectures.

Again, not only do good lectures attract no more attention than bad ones, but neither good nor bad lectures attract any attention worth speaking of. The attendance in most cases is compulsory, and purely formal.

Once more, the college lecturers being commonly chosen from the Fellows, and the Fellows not from the University at large but from the students of each college, though they can never be incompetent or fall below a certain level of ability, yet they are not by any means invariably the most competent men.

In fact, if the conditions of original research are leisure and ability, a limited field, a sense of duty, and rewards in reputation and money proportionate to exertion, there is no class at Cambridge, except the professors, that possess them in any moderate degree. And, these conditions failing, another condition, also important, fails with them—the stimulus of the success of others in such research, and of a public opinion demanding it. There is no occasion, therefore, to suppose any natural inaptitude for original study in the Englishman; the present insignificance of our Universities in the world of science and scholarship explains itself very naturally by the system pursued in them. I am not at this moment considering whether that system is good or bad; I am only remarking that it has quite a different object from the advance of knowledge, and therefore, naturally enough, does not favour the advance of knowledge.

There are persons who, acknowledging all this, maintain that it is not to be regretted. Their position is, that a university may exist for one of two objects—either for the cultivation of science, as the German Universities, or for the education of youth, as the English ones; but that it is impossible to attain both these objects at once; that a choice must be made between them; and that if we have definitively chosen the former, and therefore to a considerable extent sacrificed the latter, it is equally true that the Germans have purchased the learning of their professors at the expense of the education of their young men. This is a perfectly logical position, and if we were really driven to make such a choice I should admit that something might be said for education as against learning. Only if Oxford and Cambridge devote themselves to education, we ought to have other universities that will devote themselves to learning. Or is the country already so impregnated with ideas that we can afford to sacrifice, without equivalent, our two principal nurseries of thought? Perhaps philosophy will grow of itself in England; perhaps every Englishman's head is such a hotbed of generalizations that it is unnecessary here, as in every other country in Europe, to encourage thought and study by special arrangements!

But I will endeavour to show that we are not driven to make such a choice. I will maintain that the two things help each other; that where the spirit of original inquiry is most active among the teachers, there the teaching is best; and on the other hand, that where it is languid or dormant, the teaching, however assiduous or conscientious, is degraded in character, and that such a university tends to become a mere school.

It will be admitted that teaching boys is very different from teaching men. If we inquire in what the difference consists, we find that the boy requires to be constantly supplied with motives for working, while the man brings these with him. On the other hand, the man needs above all things learned and profound instruction, which is less necessary for the half-formed mind of the boy. It is by no means necessary that the masters of a school should be deeply learned. If they have tact, firmness, and a lively way of teaching, with competent knowledge, they will do all that can be done in a school. Moderate learning will be sufficient to command the respect and stimulate the minds of boys. The qualifications most important to a lecturer are quite different. The liveliness and attractiveness which interest boys are not required in teaching young men. Manner is here much less important, and matter much more. The lecturer deals with a riper stage of intellect. In order to be a useful guide to the cleverest young men at their most impressionable age, he must be before all things a man of power and learning. In short, the success of a schoolmaster depends mainly upon his force of character, the success of a college lecturer mainly upon his force and ripeness of intellect.

For this reason I maintain that in a university education and learning can only flourish together, or in other words, that even if university teachers devote themselves absolutely to the work of education, they will find that the way to influence the students most powerfully is by becoming as learned as possible. I beg the reader to observe that this position is not the same as that which is often maintained by the same arguments. I do not assert that the professorial system ought to be revived and made to supersede the tutorial. The professorial system, as commonly understood, differs from the tutorial in two points, and it is only in one that I think it superior. Greater concentration upon his subject, and within the limits of it greater learning than the college tutor commonly has, I think all-important; but I do not advocate the rhetorical method of instruction which belongs to the professor as better than the catechetical method of the tutor.

The existing system of moderately learned college lecturers and over-worked private tutors—in short, of teachers who are not at the same time students—defends itself not so much on abstract grounds as on the ground of the present exigencies of the University. The argument runs as follows: The undergraduates are reading for triposes; upon their success in these triposes depend their chances of a fellowship, their chances of success in the scholastic profession, and to a considerable extent their chances of success in life generally. The teachers' business is to conform himself to these triposes, and to give such instruction as will give his student success in them. Now it is not practically found that this is best done by the man of great learning and original research. On the contrary, it is found that such men generally fail, and that the most successful teacher is the man who devotes himself most exclusively to his pupils, who considers most carefully their wants and what is likely to be set; in short, who trains them most diligently for the race. It follows that the interests of education and learning, whatever they may theoretically be, are not practically

the same, but conflicting. To this we might reply,
"But perhaps it is *not* the teacher's business to conform
himself to the triposes. Perhaps the influence of the
triposes is not beneficial, or only partially beneficial, or
only beneficial to some students. In these cases would
it not be the teacher's business to dissuade his pupils, or
some of them, from reading for the triposes, or to warn
them that success in a tripos is not the ultimate end of
education, nor an infallible test?" What answer would
be given to this? Some would answer very simply,
"We do not think so. We are convinced that the best
thing a student can do is to devote himself to a tripos,
and to measure himself by his success in it. The simple
contrivance of a tripos cures all freakishness of mind,
absolutely identifies interest and duty both for teacher
and taught, and renders moral considerations in education
once for all superfluous." *O fortunatos nimium*, those
who have found out how to do their duty by machinery!
But a larger class would urge very plausibly, "Whether
they will or not, the teachers *must* conform themselves
to the triposes. If they do not, if they teach what they
themselves hold to be important, without considering
whether it will pay, their pupils will simply refuse to
listen to them, and nothing will be learnt at all." There
is no doubt that this is in a great degree true, and it
brings to light another great impediment to learning
which exists at the English universities. We have seen
that there exists no class there which has at the same
time leisure and a strong motive for profound study.
We now see that the triposes act powerfully upon the
teaching class, and draw them by motives of interest, and what almost seems duty, into a method of

instruction which makes profound study unnecessary and scarcely possible.

The question then rises, is the machinery of triposes actually so admirable for purposes of education? Is it the best way of educating a young man to place before him the prospect of a great race, for which he is to train himself through a series of years? If so, his teachers will do their work best by becoming trainers; for this purpose they will have to sacrifice original study, and it will be necessary to admit that the interests of education are irreconcilable in a university with the interests of learning. I fully recognise the use of a system of rigorous examination, and the advantage of sifting the men to some extent, and arranging them with some reference to merit. But I do earnestly maintain that when this examining and placing are made the principal thing, and when the tripos is made the heart of the whole system, the great central pump which propels the lifeblood through all the arteries of the university, it becomes mischievous, and lowers the whole tone of education.

Let me point out the mischievous consequences of the system.

The object of a tripos is to discriminate accurately the merit of the students. Now it is found that the difficulty of doing this varies very much with the subject of the examination. There are some subjects upon which it is hardly possible to gauge a man's real knowledge by any set of questions that can be devised. There are other subjects upon which it is much more easy to do so. And unfortunately the suitableness of a subject for the purposes of examination is not at all in proportion to the importance of the subject in education. Whatever theory of university education you may adopt; whether you hold that it should aim at a complete training of the faculties, or that it should prepare the student for the pursuits of later life, it is evident that the curriculum ought to be determined by other considerations than the convenience of examination. To be able accurately to measure the amount of knowledge a student has acquired may be important; but it is infinitely more important that the knowledge be valuable. Yet, when a tripos is made the principal thing, this very obvious fact is apt to be forgotten. The imparting of knowledge begins to be regarded as less important than the testing or gauging of knowledge. Then subjects in which attainments can be accurately tested come to take precedence of subjects in which they cannot. These latter, however important they may be, gradually cease to be valued or taught or learned, while the former come into repute and acquire an artificial value. This cannot take place without an extraordinary perversion of views both in the taught and the teachers. They learn to weigh the sciences in a perfectly new scale, and one which gives perfectly new results. They reject, as worthless for educational purposes, the greatest questions which can occupy the human mind and attach unbounded importance to some of the least. Philosophy, for example, is in little repute at Cambridge. The subjects it deals with may be of vast importance, the study of them may be most improving and stimulating. But the fatal objection to philosophy is that you cannot satisfactorily examine in it; you cannot say confidently, as the result of an examination in it, A is better than B, or B is better than A. The consequence is that a student may run a most distinguished career and finish his education in utter ignorance of philosophy. Meanwhile the whole mind of a large section of the university is occupied by the grammar of the classical languages, simply because it is found possible to examine in this; and lads are taught to be ashamed of falling short of perfect knowledge in the genders of Latin nouns, which involve no principle at all, and in which a minute accuracy can hardly be attained without a certain frivolity or eccentricity of memory!

No one will deny the importance of rigorously testing knowledge. A student will often suppose himself to understand a proof or a principle; but, if he is required to write the proof out, or to do some exercise involving the principle, he shows by his failure that his knowledge was superficial, incomplete, or even imaginary. And it is true that the student who studies for a long time without ever undergoing strict examination, fills his mind with these vague and imperfect conceptions, and if he have at the same time a gift of ready expression, is in danger of becoming a rank impostor. It is also a useful thing that the men should be arranged in groups, so that a man may know of himself, and others may know of him, whether he is to pass in a particular department as a first-rate, or second-rate, or third-rate man. All this is very valuable; but there is much to be said on the other side. In the first place this testing is much more necessary to bad men than to good. It should, in fact, be comparatively little needed at a university. With a rigorous examination-system at schools the better men might form the habit of exact thought before going up to college, they might learn to criticise themselves, and might be fit, as indeed many are fit, to leave prizes and examinations behind them at school with the other toys and trammels of boyhood. And though it be useful to classify men, yet as soon as the classification pretends to be exact it becomes delusive. A difference of twenty places commonly has meaning ; but a difference of four or five places has not necessarily any meaning. And if it had, what is gained by such accurate discrimination ? Who is the better for learning that of two good men one is slightly better than the other ? I can imagine no useful result that is gained by all the conscientious care that is bestowed by examiners upon these nice determinations. In this case, at least, the result seems to me none the better for being quantitative. To act upon it—to give, for example, an appointment to the man who was fourth rather than to the man who was eighth,—is, I am sure, a folly. And to many such follies and injustices does this system of placing men practically lead.

Meanwhile the state of mind which is produced in the student by his perpetual preparation for the tripos is far from wholesome. In saying this I am confident I speak the sentiments of many who have had opportunities of observing it. I do not now speak of cramming. It is true that at Cambridge, by great care in the conduct of the examination, but still more by the summary process of eliminating out of education all subjects, important or unimportant, that can be crammed, cramming, in the ordinary sense, is rendered almost impossible. What I complain of is the vulgarizing of the student's mind. Surely nothing is more important at a university than to keep up the dignity of learning. Nothing surely is more indispensable than an intellectual tone, a sense of the value of knowledge, a respect for ideas and for culture, a scholarly and scientific enthusiasm, or what Wordsworth calls a strong book-mindedness. Now the spirit of competition, when too far indulged, is distinctly antagonistic to all this. In the case of boys I suppose it must be called in, because boys have not yet felt the higher motive to study. But it vulgarizes a mind capable of this higher motive to apply to it the lower motive in overwhelming force. Students at the university are no longer boys. They differ from boys principally in this, that they are old enough to form an opinion of the value of their studies. And that they should form such an opinion is most desirable; it is, in fact, one of the principal things they have to do. The student should be always considering what subjects it is most important for him to study, what knowledges and acquirements his after-life is likely to demand, what his own intellectual powers and defects are, and in what way he may best develop the one and correct the other. His mind should be intent upon his future life, his ambitions should anticipate his mature manhood. Now in this matter the business of the university is by a quiet guidance to give these ambitions a liberal and elevated turn. All the influences of the place and of the teachers should lead the student to form a high conception of success in life. They should accustom him to despise mere getting on and surpassing rivals in comparison with internal progress in enlightenment, and they should teach him to look further forward than he might of himself be disposed to do, and to desire slow and permanent results rather than immediate and glittering ones. Now I say that intense competition vulgarizes, because, instead of having this tendency, it has a tendency precisely contrary. Instead of enlarging the range of the student's anticipations it narrows them. It makes him careless of his future life, regardless of his higher interests, and concentrates all his thoughts upon the paltry examination upon which perhaps a fellowship depends, or success in some profession is supposed to depend. It is well understood that the examination demands this concentration. It is well known that the man who hesitates is lost; that any one who asks himself the question, "Is this course of study good for me? does it favour my real progress, my ultimate success?" is not fit for the tripos. Thinking of any kind is regarded as dangerous: it is the well-known saying of a Cambridge private tutor, "If So-and-so did not *think* so much he might do very well." The tutor in question probably defended what sounds so startling by arguing that it is really wise not to indulge the power of discursive thinking too soon, or with too little restraint. I am not now concerned with this, and may content myself with remarking that the particular student who *did* think too much, and who, perhaps as a consequence, was beaten in the tripos, now stands in scientific reputation above all his contemporaries. But whether or no such self-restraint be wholesome in itself, it is vulgarizing to those who practise it as a means of success in the examination. It is a violence done to all the better nature of the student. He does not inquire whether it is wholesome or not; the process of reasoning which goes on in his mind, and which you may hear avowed in his conversation, is this, "I know what I should like to be doing; I know what seems to do my mind good; I know what I shall study as soon as I am at liberty, if my taste for study lives as long; but at the same time I know what will procure me marks, what will procure me a fellowship; and it is my business now to narrow my mind, and for three years"—three of the most progressive years of a man's life—" to consider not what is true, but what will be set; not Newton or Aristotle, but papers in Newton or papers in Aristotle, and to prepare, not for life, but solely and simply for the Senate House." It is only persons ignorant of the facts who will consider this description exaggerated. And the worst is that this vulgarity in study infects not, as might be supposed, only an inferior class of men, but the men of the greatest ability and promise—so diligently have the glories of the tripos been trumpeted. I knew a man who had an almost unprecedented career of success at Cambridge, who had so completely made success of this sort his end, that when he had exhausted the prizes of the University he confessed that he did not know what next to do, or how to employ himself. Another Alexander!

Yet is even this quite the worst? I think it is worse still that the teaching should be vulgarized as well as the learning. It is bad enough that our youth should resort to the shades of Academe simply to seek marks, but it is worse still that the Platos of Academe should teach and earnestly preach that marks are the *summum bonum*. I can only wonder at the blindness of those teachers who do so under the belief that marks are the symbol of sound and accurate knowledge. Can they not see every year high places becoming the reward of schoolboy abilities and schoolboy knowledge? I can quite understand that others may be carried away by the torrent, and may think that it is useless to struggle against an influence which is overwhelming, and which at the same time is not purely bad. But, whatever may be the cause, I think it the greatest misfortune in a university that success in an examination should be held up by the teaching class in general as the principal object of study.

There are some who think that the principle of competition should not be introduced into education at all, and that there are better ways of teaching industry even to children. This may be an extreme view; but I am sure that competition is a dangerous principle, and one the working of which ought to be most jealously watched. It becomes more dangerous the older the pupil is, and therefore it is most dangerous in Universities. It becomes more dangerous the more energetically and skilfully it is applied. At Cambridge it is wonderful to see the power with which it works, and the unlimited dominion which is given to it. And therefore here it produces most visibly its natural effects,—discontent in study, feverish and abortive industry, mechanical and spiritless teaching, general bewilderment both of teacher and taught as to the object at which they are aiming. The all-worshipped Tripos produces, in fact, what may be called a universal suspension of the work of education. Cambridge is like a country invaded by the Sphinx. To answer the monster's conundrums has become the one absorbing occupation. All other pursuits are suspended, everything less urgent seems unimportant and fantastic; the learner ridicules the love of knowledge, and the teacher with more or less misgiving gradually acquiesces; there is something more necessary, more indispensable, something that cannot so well wait,—

ἡ ποικιλῳδὸς Σφίγξ τὰ πρὸς ποσὶ σκοπεῖν
μεθέντας ἡμᾶς τἀφανῆ προσήγετο—

I hold, then, that the influence of competition at Cambridge has increased, is increasing, and ought to be diminished; that the teaching class should set their faces against it, and study to use every means by which it may be moderated. If, therefore, it appears that one main reason why learning does not flourish is that education, depending mainly on the examination system, does not require learning, I consider that education itself suffers from this system. I would deliver education from its dependence, and, without renouncing the undeniable advantages of strict and well-conducted examinations, I would use them as little as possible for the motive or incentive to study. I would appeal directly to the students' love of knowledge, I would endeavour in all ways to kindle it, but especially by improving the quality of the teaching, and, even if the result were some diminution of industry, I should find full consolation in the improvement of tone.

But those who maintain that the interests of learning and education in a university are conflicting have still another argument. They say that the German system, which favours learning, leaves the student entirely without personal care or moral discipline; that it simply provides him with food for the understanding, but takes no pains to preserve him from vice or bad habits. The English system, they say, provides moral and religious instruction, and attaches greater importance to this than to the imparting of mere knowledge. It is thus driven to make certain arrangements which, as it happens, are not favourable to learning. No doubt the college system makes the great difference between an English and foreign university. Instead of leaving our students to live as they please in the town, we have established large boarding-houses, in which the students live under a certain discipline, and with a certain family life. It is very plausibly maintained that here the English system is superior to the German, and that for this superiority we may be content to sacrifice something in learning. It is certainly true that the college system keeps down the character of the teaching-class. I have already pointed out that, the lecturers being chosen from the fellows, and the fellows as a general rule from the students of the particular college, it may easily happen that a man may rise to be a lecturer, without any particular merit, through happening to be the best man at a small college. I have also remarked that, as each college undertakes to give its students a complete training, the lecturers are required to lecture on too many subjects, and so prevented from that concentration which is a condition of profound learning. But are these evils inseparable from the college system? Is it not possible to give the students family life and discipline in a boarding-house without at the same time undertaking their whole education? And, again, is it necessary that having lived in a particular boarding-house should confer a claim to the greatest reward of merit that is known to the University, a fellowship?

But what are the definite changes for which I plead? I plead for much more than an alteration in machinery;

still there are two or three changes[1] which I regard as essential. These are as follows :—

1. Let the fellowships at every college be thrown open to the whole University. In other words, let the greatest rewards of learning, and the position of teachers, be given to the ablest men and best teachers. This requires, I believe, no change in the statutes of any college. It requires simply a change of practice. Now why do the colleges make a general practice of giving their fellowships to their own men? Without denying that they may be partly influenced by the consideration that they know their own men best, and have had better opportunities of testing their worth, we may safely affirm that their principal motive is different. Their object undeniably is to attract students. A college is considered attractive where the fellowships are good and the competition is not excessive; in other words, where a little merit gets a great reward. It is surely unnecessary to use arguments in order to show that it is not for the interests of the public that there should exist this protection for mediocrity. The colleges might come to consider it not less opposed to their own interests, if they would cease to pride themselves upon the number of wranglerships, Porson prizes, &c. carried off by their undergraduates, and begin to place their pride in the number of learned and distinguished men they could assemble in their Combination-Room.

[1] I confine myself here to such changes as the colleges may make for themselves. It seems to me possible in the way here indicated to bring the University back to a healthy state without any new legislation. If Parliament were called in, another way of attaining the same end would more naturally be adopted, some such way as that sketched out in the evidence given by Professor Jowett and Mr. Fowler before Mr. Ewart's Committee.

2. Let the instruction given in the University be made altogether independent of the college system. That is to say, let the lectures at every college be open to the whole university; let it no longer be considered necessary for each college to furnish a complete course of instruction; and let each lecturer be directly interested in increasing the numbers of his class. In other words, remove the protection which is now given to second-rate lecturing by the college system. The existing abuse is obvious. It is not possible that the staff of a small college should, as a rule, furnish lectures equal to those given, for example, in Trinity. Even a small college man must allow the rule, though he may remember distinguished exceptions. Yet Trinity refuses to let the men of other colleges attend its good lectures, and the small college refuses to excuse its own students from attending its own inferior lectures. The system of private tuition is applied as a rough remedy, but it is a remedy which is scarcely better than the disease. If, on the other hand, all the lecture-rooms were open, and each lecturer received a capitation fee for each attendant in his lecture-room, there would spring up a competition among lecturers which would at once inspire life into a dying organization, and the private tutor would almost disappear. Nor is it to be supposed that the effect of such a change would be to crowd the lecture-rooms of Trinity and St. John's, and to empty those of the small colleges. The small colleges are not so completely inferior, and their inferiority would be removed by the throwing open of their fellowships. Their character would perhaps be changed. Instead of being copies of each other, they might find it advisable

to give themselves a more individual character, and to devote themselves to special studies. One might make itself a school of law, another of theology, another of natural science. But the proper character of the college, as exerting control and enforcing discipline, would remain what it is. The tutor would, just as much as now, require attendance at a given number of lectures, only they would not necessarily be lectures within the college.

The college organization might also be very serviceable in providing for the wants of the poll-men. There are at Cambridge a vast number of students who want either abilities or inclination for serious study, or both, or whose education has through special circumstances been neglected. There are also a certain number of considerable intelligence and cultivation who come to the University rather for the sake of the society than with the intention of going through any regular course of study. These two classes of men are very different; but they are alike in this, that it is not for them that the University exists, and that they are there by a kind of sufferance. It has even been questioned whether such sufferance should be extended to the former class, and it is certain that their preponderance in lecture-rooms is a perpetual discouragement to lecturers; and their preponderance in society, if it adds a certain vivacity to university life, lowers the intellectual tone and makes it more difficult to maintain discipline. In this Essay I have left them entirely out of consideration, and have throughout regarded the undergraduate as advanced intellectually a stage before the sixth-form schoolboy, though I well know that he is often several stages behind. I have done so because it seems to me clear that this intellectual element, whether or no it be tolerated at Cambridge, ought never to be allowed to interfere with the proper work of the place, and must be entirely neglected when we are considering how the studies of the University should be arranged. But we may make it welcome to any surplus power and any accidental conveniences we may find at our disposal. Now as every college must have a staff of officers who are much occupied in the mere management of the institution, and are thus unable to concentrate themselves, as I wish to see university teachers doing, upon a special department of learning, but who are learned men and not without leisure time, it would seem that we have here the surplus power required. Besides affording to genuine students accommodation and discipline, which they do not much need, and the society of mature and enlightened men, which they need above all things, the colleges may undertake to supply an inferior kind of instruction in separate classes, conducted by a different set of teachers to those various descriptions of the intellectually indigent that make up a large proportion of the poll.

3. But these changes would not by themselves give the teaching a high quality, though they would make it effective for its purpose. So long as the tripos dominates, the teachers will always be trainers, though they may be good trainers. This evil is chiefly felt at Cambridge, and the way to remove, or at least diminish, it, without losing the advantages of the examination system, is pointed out by Oxford. Let the names in each class of every tripos be arranged alphabetically. This simple change would, I think, at once clear away all

that vulgarity of competition of which I have spoken. The abler men would feel just so much restraint in the necessity of securing their first as would keep them sober in their studies; but within these limits they would be free. They would have leisure to look around them and before them, without fancying an examiner in every bush. They would begin to use their minds naturally, instead of warping and straining them to suit an artificial model. They would sometimes indulge, instead of habitually stifling, intellectual curiosity, and they would not accustom themselves to dismiss every thing new or original in thought as being certain not to be *set*. By the same change the teacher also would be set free. He would no longer feel it almost a duty to be common-place. He would no longer be afraid of making the pupil think lest thought should damage his chance in the examination. The *frigida curarum fomenta* would be left behind, and the intercourse of teacher and pupil would become intellectual, elevating, fruitful to both.

It is to be hoped, at the same time, that the triposes may become smaller. Competition will be less stimulated by the chance of being high in a list of twenty or thirty men than in a list of ninety or a hundred. And this result may be obtained by means which will at the same time benefit the University by encouraging variety of study. By fostering as much as possible the smaller triposes, and by constantly recommending students to take up some branch of moral or natural science, we should at last obtain a number of triposes all held in nearly equal respect, and all of moderate size. Besides the allaying of the competitive fever, which would follow, I think this change would operate beneficially upon the tone of undergraduate society. The intellectual part of the conversation of undergraduates must be mainly furnished, however morbidly unwilling they may be to *talk shop*, by their studies, and if these studies were made more various there would be more intellectual unlikeness, more ideas to be communicated, and conversation would become richer.

It may be urged that a new difficulty will be created by introducing the alphabetical order into the triposes at the same time that the fellowships are thrown open to the University. In this system it may be said, how are the fellowships to be awarded? It will not then be possible, as it is now, to determine the comparative merit of two candidates by simple reference to the Calendar. It will be necessary to introduce fellowship examinations held by the colleges, which will produce just as much competition as the present tripos, and which will not be regarded with so much respect or deference. The university examination, it is said, is entirely above all suspicion of corruption, and is also most searching. A college examination would of necessity be less searching and less free from suspicion. You would abolish a perfectly satisfactory method of awarding fellowships and introduce a very unsatisfactory one. I grant that the tripos does, on the whole, very satisfactorily test the merit of the students in special departments. Mischievous as I believe it to be in its indirect influence through attempting too much, I do not deny that its decisions on the whole and roughly are correct. It would be very unreasonable for the colleges to set them aside and supersede them by private decisions of their own, which would neither receive nor deserve half so much respect. But to admit this is not to admit that fellowships ought to be awarded by a simple reference to the calendar. The calendar can only prove that a candidate is good and sound in some special branch of study. Everyone will admit that a fellow should be such a person, but it is quite another thing to affirm that such a person has a right to be a fellow. A fellow of a college is a member of a learned society, of a society that exists for the purpose of promoting science and scholarship, and that is occupied in education. Now, it may easily happen that a high wrangler or a high first-class man has very little pretensions to be a member of such a society. The wrangler may chance to be totally without what we have learnt lately to call "cultivation." He may, in fact, be for all the ordinary purposes of life an entirely uneducated and ignorant man. He must, indeed, possess a considerable power of consecutive thought and considerable industry. But there is no necessity whatever that he should be in any sense of the word intellectual, or that he should take any pleasure even in his own special pursuit. It is not to be imagined that he is always a man with a natural taste for science. He is often merely a shrewd man of business, who has seen his way through mathematical study to a pension of two or three hundred a year. The same shrewdness which procured him the pension is likely to reveal to him the inutility of pursuing his studies after it is won. If the high wrangler may easily be uncultivated, the high classic may just as easily be a dilettante. A little natural taste for literature, a good memory, and a good school suffice to place many in the first class of the classical tripos, though their reasoning powers are very slightly trained, their range of information very narrow, and though they have not even formed, what the mathematical man has formed, the habit of industry.

In short, the merit of the tripos as a standard for fellowships is merely negative. It is a serviceable means of preventing thoroughly bad elections. But for this purpose it is not necessary that the men should be placed. It might be an understanding in the colleges that no one could sit for a fellowship who had not taken a first in some tripos. If this rule were adopted, no gross corruption would be possible. The only question is, how would you compare two men who had both taken a first? Now, for this purpose the placing is assuredly of no great use. The two men often belong to different years or went out in different triposes, in which cases they cannot be compared at all. Even when their names appeared in the same list the comparison between them is perfectly nugatory. For it is only their acquirements in one department that are compared, whereas the fellowship should be a reward of general intellectual merit. On this system a tenth wrangler, grossly ignorant of all ancient and modern literature, may be preferred to a twentieth wrangler who reads Goethe. It seems to me that the difficulty would be best solved by requiring all the candidates assumed to be first-class men to write an English essay upon one of several subjects put before them. In this way you might discover whether the classical man had any power of thought and the mathematician any power of language. The mere classic would be detected by his reasoning, and the mere mathematician by his spelling; and in this way you would readily distinguish the truly intellectual man from the highly-trained schoolboy.

The reader will see that my object is not merely to alter the machinery of the University, though I think some alterations in the machinery most important, but to recommend quite a different conception of what a university education should be. He will see my drift clearly by considering education under three heads: the motive to study, the instruction, the examination or test. Of these three parts, Cambridge regards the last, that is the test, as all-important, and it finds that it is possible to combine with a very accurate system of examination an exceedingly powerful motive, viz. competition. In this plan the second part, that is the instruction, becomes dependent on examination and competition. Nothing is taught with any care, but what is likely to be set in the examination, and nothing is learnt except with a view to success in it. In place of this I recommend a plan which has the instruction as its focus. I would have the instruction made at all costs the best possible, and every means taken, first to procure the ablest teachers, and next to enable them to cultivate their powers to the utmost. For the motive I would trust mainly to the stimulating power of good instruction. I allow that this motive would be less powerful than competition over the average man, but I maintain that it would be a purer and wholesomer motive; and that it would exercise a ripening instead of a retarding influence upon the character. It would produce moderate industry continued through life and producing great results, whereas the present system produces overwork, followed by listlessness and achieving nothing. Moreover it would be reinforced by a rational and manly ambition—an ambition for the great prizes of life, honour or fortune or station, an ambition for success according as each man conceives success; whereas the present system drops a curtain over the coming life, consigns the student blindfold to his private tutor, and expects him to take for granted that these same marks, the currency of the University, if a man can hoard up a sufficient fund of them, are legal tender for everything that human beings covet.

I will conclude by briefly enumerating the advantages of what I may call the teaching system over the examining system.

First, it is incomparably better for the teachers. The present system does not consider the interest of the teacher at all. It is wonderful how much interest is taken in the student until he takes his degree, and how little afterwards. It is of course quite right that control and supervision should cease, but it seems to me most important that in assigning the duties of the younger lecturers, pains should be taken to give them as much opportunity and as much inducement as possible to prosecute their studies further. I have no doubt that this is often done as far as the system permits; it is not the men that are in fault; it is the examination-system, which makes learning in the teacher superfluous, and the college system, which puts the good and bad lecturer upon the same footing. The result is, that there is a perpetual difficulty in prevailing upon the abler men to stay at Cambridge; and various methods have been proposed for bribing them to remain and devote themselves to teaching. You could bribe them if you offered them a career. Many men who are driven to the bar would be contented with a moderate income that they might increase by their own exertions, leisure to follow their tastes, a position of real influence, and an opportunity of rising to distinction.

The influence of the teaching system upon the reading-man I have already discussed. His studies would be made more manly and free: he would pass rapidly out of the school-boy stage, instead of being artificially detained in it. But there is a further advantage of which I have not spoken. It is often said, in arguing against the professorial system, that, after all, the student only gets from a professor what he might get as well from a book. This is true of a professor who merely delivers formal harangues and then disappears. But it is one of the greatest advantages of the system of learned lecturers which I have advocated, that it gives the reading-man the society, and to some extent friendship, of a man who is an authority on his subject. It is deceptive to compare him to a book. In the first place he is a great number of books; next, he is a book that can be questioned; and a book that can put questions; and a book that can recommend other books; and, last not least, he is a book in English. As a rule, good books are in German, and it may happen that the student does not read German.

Next, the teaching system would be most beneficial to that class of students who, without being in the strict sense reading-men, are intelligent, and can take an interest in literature, science, and scholarship. Upon this class the general cultivation of a country depends, as its eminence in the commonwealth of learning depends upon the reading-men. The present system, with its monotonous drill, its sedulous elaboration of minute details, is not calculated for them. What they want, and what is really best for them, is general views, and these the reading-men also cannot dispense with. A good course of lectures would offer such general views, and the class I speak of, the dilettanti of the lecture-room, would be infinitely the better for them.

Lastly, the teaching system would be beneficial to the whole country. Those who propose to sacrifice learning for what they consider the good of the students, do not seem to me distinctly to conceive the magnitude of the sacrifice they propose. They propose to sacrifice the intellectual rank and character of the country, which is left to chance when the universities renounce learning. Private thinkers and amateur writers may by accident rise to support our credit, just as, if we should disband our army, volunteers might succeed in defending the coasts. But how much we all lose, nay, how much we have already lost, by our strange system, may be judged by any one who will consider what has been done by university professors in the countries where the professorial system is adopted. If we take the single department of philosophy, is it not evident that, if the English system had been followed in the Scotch Universities, there would have been no Scotch school of philosophy? And has not the German school sprung entirely from the Universities? Were not Kant, Fichte, Schelling, and Hegel, without exception, university professors? That barrenness in ideas, that contempt for principles, that Philistinism which we hardly deny to be an English characteristic now, was not always so. In the seventeenth century, the author of "Argenis" considered the principal fault of English people to be their reckless hardihood in speculation, their love of everything new and untried. In the eighteenth century, Montesquieu called us the philosophic nation; and at the same date, Holberg, the Dane—to mention one more among many instances—describes England as the land of heroes and philosophers. It is not then the English character which is averse to thought; we are not naturally the plain practical people that we sometimes boast, and sometimes blush, to be. If in the present century we have fallen somewhat behind, and instead of overrunning the continent with our ideas, as in the days of Locke, Newton, and Bentley, have suffered in our own island the invasion of French and German philosophies, it is assuredly from no inherent weakness. We must seek for other causes, and among them we shall find this, that in the warfare of thought we have hoped to resist regular troops with volunteers.

IV.

ON TEACHING BY MEANS OF GRAMMAR.

BY E. E. BOWEN, M.A.

It may be useful to all persons who are disposed to take a conservative view of any disputed question, to point out that one of two charges may on all occasions be brought against an argument for reform. All topics, except metaphysical ones, have a theoretical and a practical side; and a writer cannot easily discuss both at one and the same time. Nothing then can be simpler than to urge in favour of an existing system, that the theoretical objections to it are not practical, and that the practical objections are not profound. But it is sometimes forgotten that a system may be bad both in theory and in practice at once; or, which is another way of stating the case, the way in which it is worked may be wrong, and the reasons for establishing it at all may be wrong also. Those who desire in great measure to remodel English education have, for the most part, views not only as to the substance but as to the manner of teaching; and these views are fairly separable. The present Essay will relate almost entirely to method. It will assume that other things have at least as much right as the classical languages to form the basis of modern training, and that it is desirable nevertheless that at some age and to some persons classics should still be taught. The question which it will discuss is whether the mode of teaching classics by a laborious preliminary instruction in Grammar is the best mode possible.

Pedantry is not only the commonest vice, and the worst vice, of schoolmasters, but it is one towards which every one who has engaged in the work of teaching must have repeatedly been conscious of a tendency. The work of every profession no doubt takes an undue importance in the eyes of men who devote themselves to it laboriously: but that of a teacher is peculiarly favourable to the development of crotchets. Let a clever man study assiduously the properties of a Greek particle or the ramifications of a theorem in mathematics, and he will be sure to find out some things which have not been found out before, to trace connexions which no one has yet thought of tracing, to illuminate his subject by the relation which he will find it bear to other branches of knowledge. There may be much good in what he does: but he will be more than human if he can help regarding his work as exceptionally interesting and valuable. He will find it fill much of his mind, and thrust itself in front of other branches of study which in reality have equal value: he will give to it a natural emphasis in his own thoughts, and an artificial prominence in the culture which he urges upon others. A kind of paternal solicitude will at any rate add weight to his favourite topic, and personal vanity will not impossibly help it. Now in most other professions a man deals with his equals, sees things in constant varying lights, rubs off his intellectual as well as his social angles. But a teacher is without this advantage. He is not under immediate control; public opinion acts upon him only indirectly and at a long interval of time; he is not at the mercy of those with whom he is brought into contact, and his results are seldom so patent that the connexion of cause and effect can be traced with much precision. There arises as the consequence of this a fixed impression that his own work is the best possible, simply because it has been the most fruitful to himself; an impression not so much irrational as unreasoning. The belief is not necessarily untrue, but the chances are greatly against it. At any rate it can hardly fail to be narrow and illiberal. Ask a disciple of Porson whether it is really the case that the chief object of examining the language of the classical writers is that one may know what the writers have got to say, and he will admit the proposition with so many limitations and modifications as to make it obvious that he hardly admits it at all.

It is quite certain, indeed, that the object which is now intended in the teaching of Latin and Greek must be different from what it was in the days of Queen Elizabeth. At that time, schools and universities made boys learn those languages in order that they might have some acquaintance with the authors who wrote in them. No sane man can assert that the same object is pursued at present, unless he is prepared to allow that it is sought at the avowed cost of sacrificing the many to the few. It is the evident failure to carry out the original intention of classical studies, which has made it necessary to bring more prominently forward the supposed advantages of grammar. If boys, it is felt, cannot in general be brought to get any good from the thoughts of Plato and Homer by their study of the tongue in which they wrote, at all events they will have the advantage of studying the words and constructions which they used. Without altogether denying the truth of this assertion, it is well to remember the position which it takes in the argument. No pleas are more open to suspicion than those which are urged in support of a falling cause. When we have to invent some new doctrine to prop up an institution which originally existed in virtue of a doctrine wholly different, we feel that we are treading at once on treacherous ground. The view that is promulgated may have its merits, but they are not generally found to be the precise merits which suffice to bear up the fabric. When paganism was seen to be untrue, it was said that at all events it was useful. When rotten boroughs were found to interfere with the representation of the country, it was pleaded that at any rate they produced Lord Macaulay. As regards the teaching of Grammar, it sometimes seems as if it would be a good thing to attempt to express distinctly, after the manner of Mr. Charles Buxton in his "Ideas of the Day," the grounds upon which it is based in the minds of those who assert its importance. They seem to fall under three heads: there is the idea that Grammar is useful for the sake of teaching the language; the idea that its difficulties are useful as a moral training; and the idea that it is a desirable object of study for its own sake. We may consider these as being the only ideas generally entertained; for the view, which was expressed last year in a pamphlet by an eminent composer of a School Grammar, to the effect that Grammar and Religion are so closely connected that uniformity in the one is the first step to uniformity in the other, has not been accepted so widely that we need stop to discuss it here. The ideas just mentioned we may proceed to consider in detail.

I. The first of them we will meet with a direct negative. By Grammar is, of course, meant a formal analysis of usage, in respect of inflexion and syntax. Can it be said that this system of teaching by means of Grammar is the most successful now? It will be remembered that the only question for the moment is how a language may be most quickly learnt. The problem is solved every day by grown up men and women. There is not an Englishman in the country who, if he wanted to learn French, would begin by committing to memory a whole volume of rules and formulæ. By doing so, he would certainly succeed in the end; but he would know that it would be a waste of time and labour. What does the captain of a boat-club at the Universities do, if he wants to teach a man to row? Does he keep him practising, on dry land, the motions which he will have to perform, and fixing in his memory the laws which are to guide him when he enters upon work at last? Nothing of the kind. If you wish to make a man row, you will give him an oar and show him how. You will make him feel what it is like; you will make him sit behind a good pattern of the art; you will give him the advice, just as you see that he needs it. There is nothing in the whole world which is not learnt best by trying. "*Per parlare bene,*" says the old Italian proverb, "*bisogne parlare male.*" No doubt, there is necessary for all practice some rudimentary conception of what the work is likely to be. A man must know which end of the oar he is to hold in his hand, and which to dip in the water. A child cannot do much in the classics till a few simple declensions have been taught him. But the sooner he can begin to "pick up" the language, the better. Let him get familiar with the commonest words, and know what they mean in English. Let him translate and retranslate the easiest possible sentences with no grammatical analysis in his head; let certain words in Latin correspond to certain others in English. He will see, as a matter of course, that a nominative comes syntactically before a verb; and he will see it far more clearly and truly than if he knew the fact from having learnt it in the form of a rule. If we have once made sure that a boy considers the expression "us are going out," as absurd and grotesque, he not only knows, with regard to the subject of a simple sentence, enough to enable him to learn Latin and Greek without any further teaching on this head; but it may be a question whether he does not know all that there is to be said on the subject. The study of language is, at the present day, the only kind of study which deliberately professes to advance in a direction exactly the reverse of every other branch of human progress. In every other fruitful inquiry, we ascend from phenomena to principles. In classical study alone, we profess to learn principles first, and then advance to facts.

It will be remembered that we are not undervaluing the benefit that the mind may receive from understanding grammatical principles. The question is temporarily narrowed; we are asking only how a language may be most quickly learnt: and we are insisting in reply that it is by cultivating, as soon as possible, a familiarity with its words and sentences, rather than with the principles upon which these are framed and joined. It is a truly painful sight to see a boy sit down to master a set of clumsy rules, of which he will never use the half, and never understand the quarter. He is, as almost all boys are, willing to be taught. He is, as very many are, prepared to submit to a reasonable amount of drudgery. He is, we will say, of average ability and endurance. Of such a boy, we will confidently assert that, for the purpose of learning the language to the extent to which he will probably be able to carry it at school and college, the greater part of what he has to learn in most grammars is wholly useless. His time, his temper, his docility, his confidence in his teachers, his desire to improve—all these are sacrificed in order that some analyst, for whose peculiar powers of mind the compilation of his grammar may have been a charming exercise, may not have written in vain. Pedantry gains, and English education suffers.

How then ought a set of boys to be trained, supposing that our immediate object is to make them understand a Latin writer? Plunge them, we answer, at once into the delectus. Let them begin the translation of easy sentences even before they know the declensions by heart. Never give a rule of any kind unless it is one which is clearly and obviously founded upon a collection of instances. Get the meaning accurately, and the grammar may follow as its handmaid. Never let time be wasted at a difficulty: if, when fairly coped with, it is insuperable, give quick and willing help. Be ready to tell liberally, aim at quantity as well as quality; treat inflexions invariably in connexion with their meanings. Make your accidence and syntax a result instead of a basis. So far from believing that "nil desperandum," be ready to despair very often—give up, that is, an attempt to force intelligence beyond its natural limits. The construction of relatives, for example, is a difficult subject to very young boys. If so, let it wait till they have read more, and added some hundred or so of examples to their store. In short, working always by means of reference to English, advancing regularly from known to unknown, never once allowing a statement to be taken on trust, or an abstract principle to precede its concrete illustration, train boys to know many things which they cannot hope to understand, but never to hope to understand a thing which they have not learnt to know.

In a Greek text-book, which is learnt by most English schoolboys, there occurs, as the introduction to an elaborate system of tense-forming, the following statement,— "Præsens medium et passivum formatur a præsente activo mutando ω in ομαι, ut τύπτω, τύπτομαι." This rule is supposed to be learnt by young boys in order that they may the better understand the Greek language. Now, in the first place, the statement is, as so many other rules of the same kind, absolutely false. The present passive was never yet formed from a verb in ω. The comparatively simple form in ομαι was in existence long before the contracted termination of the active. But, a grammarian may say, the pupil who has the active before him will now be able to form the passive for himself. Did any pupil ever do so since the world began? Why, he has just been learning the inflexion of τύπτομαι in his very last lesson. As a matter of fact, school-boys know very well that, when they want to think of a rule for the formation of a tense, they have to think first what the word is, and then what is the best way to get it. Their instinct reverses the illogical order which the grammar has tried to force upon them. Monstrous as these arbitrary rules are, they are but a sample of the substance of which grammars are generally full; and they are expressed in a language which the boys, however much they may translate it, can never at this period understand and make their own. It has sometimes occurred to us to fancy—but that the thing can hardly be fancied—a teacher of some other department of study attempting to succeed by the same means as those which we have described. We will suppose that a professor of Chemistry is beginning work with his class. Proceeding upon the classical principles, he will first commit the whole of his knowledge to a volume, which he will draw up in a dry and technical style, and if possible, in a dead language. Of this, he will ask his class to learn a certain portion every day, and to believe the time may come when they may want it. He will perform a few experiments, every detail of which he will refer to their position in the book. He will urge as carefully as he can that the phosphorus takes fire, not because chemical force is set at liberty, but because the book says that it shall. He will introduce into his book-lessons the rarest metals and the most elaborate combinations, not because the pupils will commonly use them in the laboratory, but because his system is not complete without them. And when he finds that his disciples hate their work, and, in practice, hardly know an acid from a base, he will believe that the fault lies not in his mode of teaching, but in the unfortunate incompleteness of his book.

Waste of time and waste of energy generally go together. The perpetual routine of text-books wearies, distresses, dissipates. That one method of study is more pleasant than another is no small argument in its favour, if this pleasure mainly consists in a rapid process of the intellect. Lexicons, by what we have said, are to beginners almost as noxious as grammars. Every one who knows Greek in the end, must remember well how dreary have been the hours which he has spent upon the simply mechanical exercise of turning over leaves, with his eye fixed upon the heading of the page. It is monotonous, it is unintellectual, it is distasteful in the highest degree; and there is not a public schoolmaster in the kingdom who has the courage and the benevolence to dispense with it. Lexicons must no doubt exist, for they are needed in many ways; but there is no worse way of discovering the English equivalent of a simple word than looking it out in a dictionary. It is better to have a glossary; it is better to ask a teacher; it is better even to have a literal translation: better, simply because these methods do not waste the time of the learner, and do not spoil his temper. In his first book of Homer, an average boy will look out somewhere between two and three thousand words in his lexicon, and spend, on a moderate computation, from forty to fifty hours in the search. Grievous, however, as his waste of time in this direction is, it is work of the fingers alone; the lessons of Grammar that he learns will torture his brains as much, and will not even give him the satisfaction of feeling in the end that he has gained his grain of knowledge. He will have done something, it is true; he will not have been idle; he will have done as hard work as people do who turn a treadmill. The use of Grammar has been defended on the score that it, after all, does give something for dull boys to do. The argument is perfectly clear. It is upheld as being, after all, an excellent substitute for education.

Hitherto we have considered Grammar as a help to the knowledge of Greek and Latin; and from the idea of Grammar we exclude a few simple paradigms, and all kind of oral explanation. We assert that systematic Grammar, complete, technical, printed in a book, for the purpose of learning the dead languages, is more an encumbrance than a help. The value of Grammar itself, we have not for a moment denied.

III. But it is as an end, not as a means, that it is valuable. When once a language has been mastered, there are few uses to which the knowledge can be more appropriately turned, than that of obtaining some insight into its organism. One student may care chiefly to investigate the history of its inflexions and the architecture of its words; another may find more interest in analysing their mutual connexion. Both paths of study are worth pursuing for their own sake, and some steps may be made towards both, even while the language itself is being learnt. Only let it be accepted as a cardinal law of education, that before it can do any profitable work, the mind must have material to work upon. The study of Logic presents a close parallel to the study of Grammar. It would be possible to conceive a boy taught to argue from first principles. If, by enormous labour, he could instil into his mind the various rules of Aldrich, and regard them as a code of laws which he was bound to obey whenever a sequence of propositions presented itself to his mind, it is conceivable that he might produce the requisite conclusion from the premises before him, though he had never conducted an argument before in his life. Supposing that a system of this kind existed at our English schools, it is more than likely that a great deal would be urged in its favour. It is necessary, it would be said, to imbue the mind with true and proper rules, in order that it may be prepared to use them when the time comes. To argue, we should be told, is nothing, unless one argues from a comprehension of the rules of argument. The defenders of this system would be no more driven from their position by the fact that many people are logical without having been to Oxford, than the Grammar writers of the present day are confounded by the circumstance that Euripides wrote excellent Greek without having ever heard of an optative mood.

Putting aside that part of Grammar which depends on memory, the rest is simply a logical training. It would be hard to find a better practising-ground than Grammar for the logical studies of manhood or even of adolescence, simply because it is so copious and ready to hand. Once given that the subject can be fairly grasped, and it is one which repays a liberal expenditure of time. But it is curious that it should be regarded at schools as the only vehicle through which logical ideas should be instilled. Not till after many years of Latin and Greek does a boy really come face to face with the thoughts which the grammars put before him; while considerations about all men being animals, but all animals not being men, are so simple that boys of fifteen might well sit down to attack them. "The dative," say the grammars, "is the case of the remoter object." Nothing could be simpler to the understanding of any of us who write or who read this volume. We have a clear, an educated comprehension of the remoter object; the notion is something more to us than a mere form of words. But an average boy does not, will not, cannot actually get at it. He can be taught to know a remoter object when he sees it in print; he will say to himself that it is a kind of thing which won't do for an accusative, and yet comes in and seems to make sense. He knows it as it were on the outside; he knows it as he knows a word that is put in italics. Give him time, make him familiar with dative constructions, let his mind get strength and flexibility, and these grammatical conceptions will come to have a meaning to him; but tell him at the outset of his studies (as the grammars do) that the Latin dative means the case of the remoter object, and you will merely add another grain to that heap of evidence which is slowly accumulating in his mind that learning is a thing unsuited for a young person of sense and spirit. Yet easy logical exercises would be a pleasant task for the same intellect which rejected the definition of the dative. The grammar-book—the scientific part of it—is simply too hard. High Grammar is fit to range with high astronomy or metaphysics. One actual teacher of boys, at all events, will hereby venture to question whether the meaning of an aorist is really ever grasped by any one below the age of twenty. He has found boys interested and intelligent when the nature of a syllogism or the fallacy of a proverb are explained to them; he doubts whether he has ever thoroughly conveyed to the mind of any one pupil the difference between οὐ and μή.

Let it be observed how naturally our view agrees with the practical demands of education. It is confessed that most boys gain very little from the knowledge of Greek and Latin that they pick up at school; and even if (which is devoutly to be wished) those only pursued the study of language who were likely to make some progress in it, still, at the best, it would be but a few who would be in at the death when it came to the dissection of the particles. In a word, very many learners can never master Grammar to any real purpose. The order of instruction which we claim as natural would then be also the most convenient. The mass will be able, when they cease their education, to know something of what the Greek and Latin writers said; the select few will have found their way on to the secondary goal, which but few of the writers themselves ever reached, that of understanding the exact physiology of their language. True, the study which we speak of as second in point of time will practically follow along with the mere parlance in the case of a clever boy. One group of phenomena in language well perceived, the synthesis and comparison and arrangement of these and other groups will not be an affair of difficulty. It is not to be supposed that the acquaintance with the speech itself must be perfect before the other study commences. This is not the way in which any branch of knowledge subordinates itself to another; but the first may be, and ought to be, the measure of the second. Let things be known in the rough, before they are polished into shape. A grain of showing is worth a bushel of telling, whether the topic be a handicraft or a virtue, the performance of a trick of cards or the construction of an infinitive mood.

We are by no means inclined, indeed, to make immoderate concessions, or regard the final attainment of grammatical principles as among the loftiest achievements of the mind. What, after all, is this "scholarship," upon the possession of which so many of us, with more or less reason, are in the habit of priding ourselves? A man is a fine scholar, a beautiful scholar, a finished scholar. What does this mean? It is simply that he remembers accurately the words and phrases that each particular Greek or Latin author was most in the habit of using—or, it may happen, of abusing. He knows exactly how often this trick of language occurs in Pindar, and within what limits that turn of a sentence is capable of being employed by Ovid. How far in intellectual growth has such an accomplishment brought him? Why, it is a knowledge which we should almost blush to possess in regard of Addison and Macaulay. Exactly so far as it makes us understand Greek thought better, it is worth having; but how miserably incommensurate are the means with the end. In Greek tragedy, a woman, when she speaks of herself in the plural, uses the masculine gender; and when she speaks of herself in the masculine, uses the plural. Here is a piece of knowledge, perfectly true, laboriously proved, necessary for writing Greek iambics; and most of us who profess to know the classical languages, would be ashamed of being without it. Well, how far does it go? Probably—though not certainly, for there is the widely reaching element of chance, seldom sufficiently recognised in philology—probably this practice corresponds, if we could only see it, to some sentiment lurking in the Athenian mind. The person who knows thoroughly half a hundred of such canons, will have a better equipment for ransacking and mastering Greek ideas than another who does not. That is to say, a minute acquaintance with words and phrases does in the end, and through much patience, help the clever man to place himself more fully at the point of view of an Athenian.

Let this be granted; and now let us glance at the result. Is it generally the case, that the "beautiful scholar" is the man who brings out most treasures from the chambers the dim light of which is clearer to him than to others? Is it not more often found that his long toil has made him confound the means with the end, and value his scholarship in regard of itself alone? The main object of seeing distinctly what Plato and Cicero thought, is that one may be able to look on all questions not only on the side which they now present, but on that also which they turned to observers long ago; to gain, as it were, a kind of intellectual parallax in contemplating the problems of life. Can it be fairly claimed, that high scholarship, the higher it reaches, attains more completely this object? The reverse notoriously is the case. We know well enough what becomes of the man who gives up his time to particles. He is not the man to whom, in nine cases out of ten, his generation turns for help. There grows upon a society of "beautiful scholars" a distaste for things in which taste and refinement have little room for display, and in which breadth is more important than accuracy; and the result is a lack of sympathy with human struggles and cares. Let some social or political movement arise, in which a man of real intellectual power, real eloquence, and evident sincerity aspires, in spite of ignorance of the classics, to take a leading part. He will find favour with but a minority of the writers of dictionaries and grammars. One will see narrowness of mind, another will insist on discovering vulgarity of tone. With some he will be too base in thought, with others coarse in manner. But all will be down upon his language. A man of classical education, we shall hear, would never have spoken of the "works" of Thucydides; a man of real culture could never value the penny press as a means of popular instruction. He mispronounced an English word last session; he did not understand when an allusion was made to Patroclus; to save his life he could not cap a line in the second book of the Æneid.

"Et les moindres défauts de ce grossier génie
Sont ou le pléonasme, ou la cacophonie."

How much better to be able to set a common room right upon some mystic conceit of Æschylus, or correct a class of boys (out of their Primer) on the gender of *clunis* and *splen*.

It is not, however, the object of this Essay to disparage the knowledge of Latin and Greek. They may be purchased, and often are, at too high a price; but those who have gained them most easily will be least likely to hold them too dear. Montaigne was not a man disposed to shut his eyes to the world around him, because he had learnt to speak Latin before he was able to write French. The advocates of a natural and easy method of classical teaching are sometimes challenged to give instances of the success of their system. It is certainly not easy to do so, for of late years the grammar writers have had it all their own way, and the one German apostle of a natural mode of teaching finished his career in prison; but the results of the teaching of Jacotot in France and Belgium are such as have never been surpassed, and it will be time enough to pronounce a system impossible, when in learning any modern language we cease to practise it ourselves. At any rate, there is good enough authority for learning Latin in this way. Milton distinctly urges it, and Locke in substance; but it is older than either. "Our most noble Queen Elizabeth," says Roger Ascham, "never yet took Greek nor Latin grammar in her hand after the first declining of a noun and a verb." In a year or two, by copious translation and retranslation, she learnt both languages well. It was with Lilly's Grammar that the more pedantic system came in; and that grammar, as its preface shows, was never originally intended to be learnt consecutively or by rote.

It has been said, with some degree of truth, that learning by heart is the great intellectual vice of boys. Perhaps it would be fairer to say that the tendency is so strong that it is almost certain to be misapplied. With boys of good or average memory—and none others ought to learn classics—the tendency will be directed rightly if they are made to learn examples of construction by heart, and carefully prevented from embodying the doctrines taught them in any set form of words. In

the Primer which has lately been put into the hands of
the boys at most of the public schools, the first two
pages of syntax consist of words of an *average* length of
about three syllables each. Now there is no doubt that
a boy of good memory will learn these, in time, to
whatever degree of perfection his masters care to enforce;
and if they were written backwards he would learn them
almost as easily. But the idea that a young boy will
ever *think* in polysyllables is almost humorous. The
better he knows the words, indeed, the less will be, in
many cases, his attempt to attach a meaning to them.
The parrot does not only not think, but it even prevents
itself from thinking. The pupil who is reading his
Euclid will know it less well, for purposes of culture,
if he attempts to commit it to memory. What is the
reason that we have given up the notion of enforcing the
duties of morality upon the rising generation by means
of memorial precepts in English or Latin prose? It is
not that the ideas of duty which they would convey are
less likely than in former times to meet with illustrations
in common life. It is simply because the duty is in
most cases not a matter of formula; and even when it
is so, the words of a formula have a tendency to remain
in the corner of the memory where they have been
placed. The same is true of Latin composition. A very
few memorial rules are useful in cases where usage alone
is a guide to what is correct; but even these have no
educational value whatever, and any other than these
absolutely interfere with the right understanding of
a principle.

There has been some discussion during the past year
with regard to the introduction into the chief public

schools of Dr. Kennedy's Public School Primer. Into the merits of the book itself it is not necessary now to enter, because, in the first place, it is irrevocably accepted at the nine public schools; and, in the second place, the general opinion of persons interested in education has already condemned the work. But, independently of its merits or demerits, the introduction of a universal text-book is distinctly a retrograde step in education. It was clearly felt to be so not long ago in Germany; and the idea, which had been mooted a few years back, was dropped by general consent. It is with us much as if the study of Aristotle were imposed once more by the authority of the Church, or an adherence to the unities by that of the managers of the London theatres. It implies the belief, which will at once be recognised as an heresy, that there are such things as eternal and immutable rules of language; that a Latin grammar is to be considered not as an interpreter of Latin, but as it were its authorized legislator. What is meant by a declension? Is it a division which the language consciously employed? Is it one which is certain, and beyond the domain of controversy? Has it any claim to be regarded as the embodiment of a law in the sense in which the word is used in science? Not at all. Distributing words into declensions is simply the best means that we can contrive for organizing them in a way which shall appear to the memory as symmetrical. The analysis of words was pushed very far among the Romans, and yet Quintilian wrote a chapter on grammar without ever mentioning the classes of declensions at all. What is to be inferred is, not that declensions are not useful, but that the division is an arbitrary one; and that any plan of education can have but little confidence in its teaching which will bind itself for the next twenty or thirty years to believe in five declensions rather than in eight or ten. No reason can be given for the compulsory uniformity of English Schools in their method of teaching the analysis of the Latin language, which would not equally tend to show that the Universities of Oxford and Cambridge are bound to adopt the same text-book of algebra for continuous use. This might easily be done, and an inferior book be stereotyped for a long time to come. As it is, fresh books supersede one another as the methods of algebraical working improve, and the reign of a single author at Cambridge lasts sometimes two years, sometimes twenty. In the teaching of languages, as a matter of fact, one good teacher will have one way of instructing, and another another. Common sense points out that if a boy only learns a thing well, it matters little in what way he has reached his knowledge. As for bad teachers, they will simply save their credit and their labour by teaching the primer straight through by heart.

One is driven, sometimes, in thinking of these and similar mistakes, to the verge of asserting that books are the great obstacle to education. Whether this be too audacious a paradox or not, our teaching wants sadly to be humanised. There will be some gain, no doubt, when it is once clearly understood that there is no absolute connexion between riches and the dead languages, and that a boy need not in every case be set down to a course of study for which he may be wholly unfit, just because his parents or guardians happen to be able to pay for it. But is it too much to hope that the classical teaching itself may some day cease to be the dull routine which it now so often is? It may have been remarked that in considering the reasons for which grammar may be taught, we have omitted the second of our three ideas—the one which considers that the difficulties in a course of study ought to be left there as introducing a moral education in the struggle which is necessary for overcoming them. A person who will assert this is beyond the pale of argument. It is not worth while to discuss whether a method ought to be easy or hard. But we should even go on to say that it is the duty of a teacher not to rest as long as any difficulty exists which by any change of method can be removed. Involuntary learning is of as little use to the mind as involuntary exercise to the body.

Now it is certain that a large proportion of boys dislike the work which they have to do. Some like it; some are indifferent; a great many simply hate it. We maintain that an educator of boys has no business to be satisfied as long as this is the case. A very few may dislike all intellectual labour, just as a very few men dislike it; but these cases are as rare with boys as with men. The great mass of human beings, whether young or old, have appetites for mental food of some kind, and the reason that so many turn away from it is, that what is given them is not what they can digest. There is a sort of incongruity, which falls little short of injustice, in punishing a boy for being idle, when we know that the work which the system of his school exacts is as cramping and distorting to his mind as an ill-fitting boot to the foot. No one would claim indeed that every pupil shall have his tastes suited with minute accuracy; and the energy of a boy, if he is in good health, and otherwise happy, will carry him through minor difficulties. But no young boy since the world began has liked a Latin syntax, or a "formation of tenses," or felt anything in them for his mind to fasten upon and care for. Consider the case of a stupid boy, or an unclassical boy, at school, and the load of repulsive labour which we lay upon him. For many hours every day we expect him to devote himself, without hope of distinction or reward, to a subject which he dislikes and fears. He has no interest in it; he has no expectation of being the better for it; he never does well; he rarely escapes doing ill. He is sometimes treated with strictness for faults to which the successful among his neighbours have no temptation; and, when he is not visited with punishment, he at least is often regarded with contempt. He may be full of lively sympathies, eager after things that interest him, willing even to sacrifice something for the sake of becoming wiser; but all that he gets in the way of intellectual education is a closer familiarity with a jargon the existence of which in the world seems to him to controvert the Argument from Design, and the chance scraps of historical and literary knowledge which fall from the lips of his routine-bound master. If only it could be regarded as an established truth that the office of a teacher is, more than anything else, to educate his pupils; to cause their minds to grow and work, rather than simply to induce them to receive;

to look to labour rather than to weigh specific results; to make sure at the end of a school-half that each one of those entrusted to him has had something to interest him, quicken him, cause him to believe in knowledge, rather than simply to repeat certain pages of a book without a mistake,—then we might begin to fancy the golden time was near at hand, when boys will come up to their lessons, as they surely ought, with as little hesitation and repugnance as that with which a man sits down to his work.

This is indeed something worth being enthusiastic for. To convince boys that intellectual growth is noble, and intellectual labour happy, that they are travelling on no purposeless errand, mounting higher every step of the way, and may as truly enjoy the toil that lifts them above their former selves, as they enjoy a race or a climb; to help the culture of their minds by every faculty of moral force, of physical vigour, of memory, of fancy, of humour, of pathos, of banter, that we have ourselves, and lead them to trust in knowledge, to hope for it, to cherish it; this, succeed as it may here and fail there, quickened as it may be by health and sympathy, or deadened by fatigue or disappointment, is a work which has in it most of the elements which life needs to give it zest. It is not to be done by putting books before boys, and hearing them so much at a time; or by offering prizes and punishments; or by assuring them that every English gentleman knows Horace. It is by making it certain to the understanding of every one that we think the knowledge worth having ourselves, and mean in every possible way, by versatile oral teaching, by patient guidance, by tone and manner and look, by anger and pity, by determination even to amuse, by frank allowance for dulness and even for indolence, to help them to attain a little of what gives us such pleasure. A man, or an older pupil, can find this help in books; a young boy needs it from the words and gestures of a teacher. There is no fear of loss of dignity. The work of teaching will be respected when the things that are taught begin to deserve respect.

Above all, the work must be easy. Few boys are ever losers from finding their task too simple, for they can always aspire to learning what is harder; many have had their school career ruined from being set to attack what was too hard. It may be said, perhaps, that what was easy enough for past generations, ought to be easy enough for the present. Those who urge this view, may simply be asked whether they are satisfied with the working of the classical education that exists. We are not bound to depend upon Dr. Liddell's testimony, that public schoolmen are generally ignorant of Greek and Latin, for there are obvious reasons which would prevent the Dean of Christchurch from forming a satisfactory opinion on the subject; but, taking those who go to the University with those who do not, can the education that is given be said to be the best which modern ingenuity can contrive? Allowing that the very best scholars can assimilate anything whatever, and that with the very worst it is next to useless to try at all, is it true to say that the average boys have a fair chance of making the most of their powers? If not, there are two resources before the teacher. He can, as is elsewhere pointed out, vary and enlarge the basis of education ; he can also, as we have ventured in this Essay to urge, teach classics so as to include more that is of rational interest, and less that is of pedantic routine.

V.

OF GREEK AND LATIN VERSE-COMPOSITION AS A GENERAL BRANCH OF EDUCATION.

BY THE REV. F. W. FARRAR, M.A. F.R.S.

" . . . . le triste rôle d'imitateurs, et celui non moins triste de créateurs de choses parfaitement inutiles."—NISARD, *Poètes de la Décadence*, i. 334.

THE belief in a system of education exclusively classical is an "idol of the theatre," which will not easily be obliterated from the enchanted glass of the public judgment. Its defenders have been numerous and energetic; nor have they been slow to retaliate upon their opponents the language of criticism. For many years, they have spoken of educational reformers as "mechanical" and "utilitarian;"—in fact, as mere "Philistines," incapable of forming any high conception of the ends and aim of intellectual culture. All such compliments may be accepted at present with that good-humoured indifference which naturally results from the consciousness of a victorious cause. The roots of the fabled mandrake were said to shriek when it was pulled up from the ground, and the inveterate prejudices of many classical teachers will do the same. There are, however, some stock objections against all criticism of our existing system which will not be applicable to the present Essay. It has been asserted that the critics of "classical education" have generally been men without that experience which is deemed essential to a true insight into the nature of teaching; that they have been cautious enough to refrain from any attempt at reconstructing the edifice which they tried to destroy; and that their complaints have been of so vague and general a nature as to deprive them of all practical importance. Now, although it will not be my present business to attempt any redistribution of those hours which I consider to be wasted—and often worse than wasted—in the ordinary course of a Public School education, the other objections, at any rate, must be laid aside in any attempt to refute what is here advanced. Although I cannot, indeed, pretend to re-echo the exultant cry of the mystæ,[1] yet, I have been duly initiated into the mysteries. In other words, I speak of things which I know; I come forward with a precise object and a definite proposition: that proposition is one of an eminently practical character; and it is one to which, in spite of powerful tradition and natural prejudice, I have been gradually driven by long years of laborious experience. I am so desirous to speak on this subject with perfect candour and unreserve that, at the risk of startling on the threshold those readers whom it is my earnest desire to convince, I will say at once that the reform which will here be advocated is the immediate and total abandonment of Greek and Latin verse-writing as a *necessary or general* element in liberal education, and the large diminution of the extravagant

[1] ἔφυγον κακόν, εὗρον ἄμεινον.

estimation in which this accomplishment has hitherto been held.

It is, of course, an obvious corollary to my proposition that the hours now devoted to "composition" should be assigned to other studies of the highest value, which have hitherto been very partially recognised or very openly ignored. Among these studies are Comparative Philology, History, Modern languages, the Hebrew language, and the language and literature of our own country; but foremost in the weight of its claims is the study of Science—a study so invaluable as a means of intellectual training, and so infinitely important in the results at which it arrives, that the long neglect and strange suspicion with which it has hitherto been treated can only be regarded as a fatal error and a national misfortune.

It is not, however, my present purpose to add anything to the arguments which have been urged elsewhere, respecting the irrefragable claims of some of these studies to demand a place in our curriculum. The question of what ought to be introduced as an essential element in every liberal education is indeed closely connected with the question of what ought to be abandoned. But the labours and reasonings of the last few years have not been fruitless, and it may now be definitely assumed that our course *must* henceforth be a broader one, and indeed so much broader that many teachers will assert that it must also, as a necessary consequence, be discursive and superficial. I do not here mean to refute this assertion, but I should be sorry even for a moment to seem to give it my assent. For if, without entering on argument, I may venture to assume that *some* value, however slight, will be attached to an opinion founded upon experience, I will beg leave to declare my profound and earnest conviction that, by the frank adoption of wiser and better methods than those which we now employ, we shall be able to teach much more in other subjects without teaching one whit less in those with which we have hitherto been exclusively occupied. At present we send forth a few fine scholars and a multitude of ignorant men : I am convinced we might send forth the same number of scholars, and a large number of men who, while they would know as much or *more* Latin and Greek than the paltry minimum to which they now attain, should not at the same time startle and shock the world by the unnatural profundity of their ignorance respecting all other subjects in heaven and earth. Such a result is neither "Utopian" nor "Quixotic," although, indeed, the first lesson which every reformer should learn is to feel perfectly invulnerable to the censure of those miserable words. But to produce such a result does not rest with schoolmasters alone ; it demands the cordial co-operation of parents, and it demands a modification of our present methods and traditions, more sweeping and more unselfish than is immediately probable or perhaps even attainable. Assuming, however, that the hour is ripe for *some* economy of time and method in learning the two ancient languages, it is obvious that one very facile and important means of economy presents itself by the curtailment in some cases,—the total abandonment in a vastly greater number,—of the hours at present squandered over Greek and Latin verse.

The desirability then, nay the imperative necessity, of such a change, is the narrow limit of the question immediately before us; and it is a change which the most enthusiastic advocates of classical education may well dispassionately consider. For composition is a branch of "classics" in which many scholars, otherwise eminent, have but very partially succeeded; to which of all civilized nations England alone attaches any extraordinary importance; which, if it be a very showy, is also a very fallacious test of solid scholarship; which is capable of co-existing with a complete absence of all that makes classical training most valuable; and, lastly, which has tended more than any single cause, perhaps more than all other causes put together, to create that profound public dissatisfaction which has brought our entire system into discredit and contempt. It is certain that classical education will soon wither away under the dislike, or be torn up root and branch by the zeal of its opponents, unless our Public School authorities are content to lop away with their own hands these diseased branches which only injure and disfigure a noble tree.

If prejudice were less tenacious, and habit less invincible,—if it were not a common experience that the members of a profession are always the last to welcome necessary innovations, — one would feel amazed that there are learned and able men who still cling to a system of verse-teaching which bears to so many minds the stamp of demonstrable absurdity. Verse-making has been adopted as the best method of teaching Greek and Latin, and has never been systematically applied to the teaching of any other language under the sun. Regarded as an end it is confessedly insignificant; regarded as a means it is notoriously unsuccessful.[1] It has

[1] *Vide* the Report of the Public School Commission, *passim*.

been condemned alike by the learned and by the ignorant, by men of letters and by men of science, by poets and by dullards, by the grave decision of philosophers and by the general voice of the public. Names of the most splendid eminence over a space of two centuries can be quoted in its condemnation; barely one single poor authority can be adduced in its favour. Cowley, Milton, Bacon, Locke, Coleridge, Wordsworth, Macaulay, Thirlwall, Ruskin, Mill,—some of our most learned poets, some of our deepest metaphysicians, some of our most classical historians, some of our most brilliant scholars,—are unanimous in speaking of it with indifference or with contempt. Few even of second-rate or mere professional eminence have ventured to uphold it. To this day many bewail the time they frittered away over it, while scarcely any one is found to express the faintest gratitude for any supposed benefit which he has acquired from its compulsory practice.

It is not, however, by the overwhelming force of *à priori* considerations, or external testimonies, that I have long been led to desire the annihilation of verse composition as a general or necessary element in the teaching of our schools. The force of habit, the natural reluctance to be convinced of the futility of an accomplishment, to the acquisition of which so large a part of my own time had been sacrificed, long enabled me to fight against the weight of condemnatory evidence. It was simple experience, it was constant observation of the system in its actual working, backed by the astounding revelations of the Public School Commissioners, which first revolutionised my own feelings respecting it, and forced me, three years ago, to denounce it before the

British Association as a huge gilt wooden idol for whose overthrow I longed. This fact will prove, I trust, that there is nothing rash or unreasonable in my present opposition, and will exonerate me from all appearance of wishing to throw blame or ridicule on those who still hold an opinion which for many years I held myself. If in any part of this Essay I appear to use strong language, let me frankly ask pardon for it beforehand, as having sprung from the pent-up bitterness of twelve years' experience. Those who know what leisure is, and who can afford to while it away in writing Latin Verse, are apt in the beauty of the exotic to forget its costliness. They forget that they are admiring the flowers —and after all they are but fruitless flowers!—of the one productive seed which has here and there survived its countless abortive brethren. The aspect of Latin Verse to the classical scholar who recurs to it as the light amusement of his manhood, is very different from that which it wears to the weary teacher, who has wasted so many of his own and his pupils' precious hours in the hopeless task of attempting to make poets of the many.

Let me premise that I have in view the case, not of the brilliant few, but of the mediocre multitude; and then I will proceed to describe the system as I have seen it actually worked by eminent masters, and as I know it to be still worked in a very large majority of English Public and Private Schools. The system which I choose for description is the one most commonly in use, but by far the larger part of what I have to say will apply equally well to any system whatever.

A parent, applying to enter his son at a Public School, is informed, with much *empressement*, that one of the chief and most important subjects of the entrance examination is LATIN VERSE, both ELEGIACS and LYRICS, and that some knowledge of at least the former is essential to the boy's attaining any but the very lowest position. The same information is duly reverberated on all the teachers of preparatory schools; and they, knowing the difficulty of the accomplishment—an accomplishment which in many cases they themselves have wholly failed to acquire—are driven by necessity to initiate their young recruits as early as possible into the mysteries of the dreadful drill. About the dreary iteration of those preliminary years, I only know by dim report,—by the groans of "grinders" during the period of their labour, and their exclamations of unfeigned delight when the era of their emancipation appeared to be approaching. But at the age of thirteen or fourteen the little victims, duly instructed in LATIN VERSE, make their appearance. The large majority of them—and with them at present it is my sole object to deal—know as well as we know, that they *have* not succeeded, and never, by any possibility, *can* succeed in acquiring the mysterious art. Without a conception of rhythm, without a gleam of imagination, without a touch of fancy, they have been set down to write verses; and these verses are to be in an unknown tongue, in which they scarcely possess a germ of the scantiest vocabulary, or a mastery of the most simple construction; and, further, it is to be in strict imitation of poets, of whom at the best they have only read a few score of lines. English passages of varying difficulty, but to them for the most part hopeless, are then placed in their unresisting hands, accompanied by dictionaries mainly intended for use in *prose* composition, and by those extraordinary herbaria of cut and dried "poetical" phrases, known by the ironical title of *Gradus ad Parnassum*. The bricks are to be made, and such is the straw of which to make them. And since the construction of the verse often depends on the knowledge of phrases or constructions which a boy either never knew, or is unable to apply, what wonder that in the "Latin," which he endeavours to torture into rhythm, "changes of seasons" takes the form of "*condimentorum mutationes*," and "the sunbeams" are metamorphosed into "*Phœbi trabes?*" Over such materials the unfortunate lad will sit glowering in dim perplexity, if he be diligent, or vaguely trifling, if he be idle, ready with the indisputable defence of "I can't do the verse," when the *Deus ex machinâ* appears in the shape of some weary and worried tutor.

In the natural course of things, a boy, long before he has mastered these elementary difficulties, will be promoted into a higher form, and presented with a more difficult phase of work. This is very frequently embodied in verse books consisting of old prize-exercises, baldly re-translated into English, of which some portion is withheld in every line, until, towards the end of the book, a word or two stands for an entire period. In these narrow grooves the boy's imagination is forced to run. He is required, under all the inexorable exigencies of metre, to reproduce in artificial and phraseological Latin the highly elaborate thoughts of grown men, to piece their mutilated fancies, and reproduce their fragmentary conceits. In most cases the very possibility of doing so depends on his hitting upon a particular epithet, which presents the requisite combination of longs and shorts, or on his evolving some special and often recondite turn of thought or expression. Supposing, for instance (to take a very easy line, typical of many thousands of lines), he has to write as a pentameter—

"Where Acheron rolls waters,"

he will feel that his entire task is to write—

"Where *something* Acheron rolls *something* waters."

His one object is to get in the "something" which shall be of the right shape to screw into the line. The epithet may be ludicrous, it may be grotesque; but provided he can make his brick, he does not trouble himself about the quality of the straw, and it matters nothing to him if it be a brick such as could not by any possibility be used in any human building. It is a literal fact, that a boy very rarely reads through the English he is doing, or knows when it has been turned into Latin, what it is all about: hence, for the next year or two, his life resolves itself into a boundless hunt after epithets of the right shape to be screwed into the greatest number of places; a practice exactly analogous to the putting together of Chinese puzzles,[1] only producing a much less homogeneous and congruous result.

At the next stage of promotion, or often earlier, a boy is forced to begin a far more desolate and hunger-bitten search, for something, sarcastically denominated

---

[1] "The same instinct which guides the infant in putting his wooden bricks together, or a little girl in clothing her doll, lies at the bottom of verse-making." I take this sentence from a deliberate defence of the practice by one of the ablest of our modern classical scholars!

"ideas of his own," to clothe the skeleton, or the "vulgus," presented to him for his "copy of verses." Now, long and laborious as this course is, dreadful and unremitting as is the miserable drudgery which it entails upon the tutor, yet it is so universally unsuccessful, that by the time such a boy is required to do "originals," or to turn English poetry into Latin, he either succumbs in hopeless desperation, or only with cruel sweat of the brain succeeds in achieving a result which both he and his tutor equally despise. What wonder that many bright and promising boys, whose abilities do not lie in this direction, are either crushed under this worse than Egyptian bondage, or require the entire fortitude of their best principles of honour to abstain from using such means of deliverance as lie most easily within their reach. Many do not do so. I have known some who left school in sheer weariness and disgust, or deliberately chose one of the unlearned professions: some, who losing all ambition, and all regard for intellectual culture, contented themselves with the baldest and meanest minimum which would save them from positive disgrace; and many, who with few or no twinges of conscience, availed themselves of old vulguses, borrowed lines, rough copies, corrected copies, and every form of illicit aid, direct or indirect, which could get them, without detection and punishment, through a labour which they believed to be useless, and knew to be impossible.

It may, however, be hinted that I have been unlucky in my experience; and, therefore, as I take no sort of credit to myself for the result, let me be allowed to say that I have, on the contrary, been very far from unfortunate in the number of brilliant composers whom I have had the good fortune to call my pupils; and yet, out of reams and reams of verses which it has been my lot during the last twelve years to correct, I do not believe that there have been half a dozen which I should think worth preserving for their intrinsic merit. I have heard teachers of long standing express the most perfect contentment while admitting that they have never produced a single good composer; but if any one thinks that a tutor may fairly plume himself on the development, here and there, of a Porson prizeman or Camden medallist, he little knows the mysteries of our system! In it alone are things taught with no hope of their being learnt, and with no expectation of their being subsequently practised. In it alone no tutor is held responsible for the vast multitude who fail—the failure is due to innate incapacity; in it alone no tutor gets any credit for the few who succeed—the success is the result of heaven-born talents which would have been developed equally well by *any* teacher under *any* system! In a word, everybody seems to be content, though the thing nominally taught is but very rarely learnt, and though the tutor's failure on the one hand involves no discredit, and his success on the other earns no praise.

And what is the daily spectacle presented by the system?—hours upon hours spent by many boys in the moiling evolution of one or two wintry and wooden elegiacs, consisting of halting hexameters and hypermetric pentameters; boys whose utter inability might have been predicted at thirteen, kept at the same galley-work up to eighteen and nineteen, as unprogressive as the seamen who plied the oar on land; and a multitude of

Englishmen bitterly regretful, or good-humouredly contemptuous, at the unpractical and fantastic character of their youthful instruction. When we consider how little, at the end, our schoolboys know, and how vast are the regions of science with which they are wholly unacquainted; how valueless is much of their little knowledge, how dangerous is the nature of their ignorance; and, above all, how rich in fruit might have been those many barren hours which have been lavished on the impotent effort to acquire a merely elegant accomplishment, —then I confess that my regret deepens into sorrow, indignation, and shame. Is it pleasant to know that the first thing of which an old pupil may think, when he meets us in after life, is the little intellectual cause he has for gratitude towards men who occupied his boyhood by teaching him that which he has not only long forgotten, but to reach which he would not now take the trouble to raise his little finger?[1] Knowing this, I cannot but disregard the charges of injustice and exaggeration which have been brought against my exposure of such a system, and I rejoice that a serious effort is now being made to emancipate English boys from a yoke whose "cruel absurdity"[2] neither they nor their fathers have been able to bear. I feel sure that the whole nugatory system will soon totter to its fall. Our sons will know nothing of compulsory verse-making; they will smile at our disproportionate admiration of a petty knack; they will satirize a curriculum of education which proudly vaunted its stigma of inutility, and which frequently produced a profound self-confidence in combination with a very

[1] See Inaugural Address at St. Andrews, by M. E. Grant-Duff, Esq. M.P.
[2] Bishop Thirlwall.

empty mind. In the next generation, at any rate, tutors will not be degraded from powerful intellectual guides into the mechanical encouragers of mere imitation; forced to pay far more attention to words, and phrases, and turns of expression, and tricks of rhetoric, than to solid information and manly thought. Nor will a deadly discouragement be dealt to our faith in boys, and (which is worse) to their own confidence in themselves, by a study in which the powers requisite for success are neither the noblest nor the best powers, so that those who succeed are, in not a few instances, incomparably inferior in all true ability to those who fail.

And even now the English nation has surely a right to demand, that in sending its sons to Public Schools it shall not *necessarily* be dooming them to seven or eight years of this weary mill-wheel. At least, let them ask those headmasters who still believe that this is a good way to learn Greek and Latin, to demonstrate its usefulness by themselves acquiring some other language—say Persian or Sanskrit—in the same way. When they know a dozen or two Persian and Sanskrit words, and have laboriously toiled through, say a hundred lines of Firdausi or the Hitopadésa, let them be set down for five or six hours every week for some years to produce epic lines in the style of the Sháh-námah, or love poems, in the S'loka or Indra-vajrá metres. Probably, before their demonstration is complete, this astonishing theory of education will have perished in the unspeakable weariness which will be caused by its practical application.

But as there are men who find *something* to urge on behalf of everything which exists, let us now proceed to consider the arguments put forward in defence of these "habits of composition" into which we have supinely drifted. Let people judge of the system from the calibre of the only arguments adduced in its favour. For myself, I can only say that, after years of familiarity with the subject, I have been unable to get straightforward answers even to questions so simple as these:—Are Greek and Latin verses taught in order that they may be learnt, or that something else may be learnt by their means? Is the end in view in any way homologous to the process adopted? And if so, is that end produced in the many who, being taught verses, never learn them, or in the very few who do?

I. First, it is argued, that the Schools must follow the direction of the Universities, and that they must continue to teach Latin verse so long as the Universities reward, with their most splendid and considerable prizes, the accomplishment of producing them.

This may be regarded as the strongest temporary argument in favour of retaining verses,—and astonishingly weak it is. In the first place, the rapid changes which are going on have rendered it but partially true. In the second place, it simply amounts to a reciprocal abnegation of responsibility, since the University professes to reward because the Schools teach, and the Schools to teach because the University rewards. And, thirdly, three-fifths of our boys no longer proceed to the university at all; of the remaining two-fifths not one half ever think of touching verses again; of the small remainder but few gain any university distinction by their means; and even out of the last insignificant residuum, some, as I shall prove hereafter, are rather injured than aided by the entire process. Our plan, therefore, has been justly compared to that of the ostrich, which is said to assist the incubation of the few eggs which it intends to hatch, by heaping up around them a larger number which it intends to addle. How long are we to suffer nine-tenths of our boys to be addled, because it is thought necessary to put them all through a process which shall hatch out of their entire number a few Senior Classics or Craven scholars?

II. But next it is asserted, and I suppose in all seriousness, that verse writing is a good way of learning Greek and Latin!

If so, why is it that no one, either in or out of his senses, ever thinks of learning any other language by a similar process? Even to Greek the practice is applied with a timidity which shows the incipient triumph of common sense; for Greek verses, though begun far too early, are still postponed to a much later period than Latin, and yet our Greek scholarship is beyond all comparison superior to anything which we have attained in the sister tongue. And a method so entirely unique ought at least to produce the evidence of magical success; yet, it is admitted on all hands to end, as regards the mass, in signal failure. Certain it is that in continental schools, where verses are either very slightly practised, or not at all, I have not only heard boys converse in Latin with perfect fluency—an accomplishment in which even our best scholars are needlessly deficient—but even turn into good classical Latin long German sentences, which would have surpassed the powers of English boys far older than themselves. I shall not readily forget the quickness and accuracy with which the boys at the

Schulpforta—the Eton of Prussia—rendered into Latin, *vivâ voce*, involved periods with which I should never have dreamt of testing the attainments of English boys in a corresponding division of the school. In short, that Latin verse writing is a valuable or expeditious method of teaching Latin to miscellaneous groups of boys, is a fallacy which ought long to have been exploded from the minds of all observant and unprejudiced men.

III. But composition teaches the quantity of words, and furnishes the best means of acquiring taste and style.

Of *quantity* I need hardly speak. It can be *amply* taught by reading aloud. That years of drill in verses should be deemed necessary to teach it, only proves the extent to which an unreasoning pedantry—a pedantry of the worst and most objectionable kind—has affected our entire conception of the relative proportion of things. I cannot pretend to share in the traditional horror of a false quantity. I have long sincerely repented for having despised a dissenting minister who talked to me as a boy about the "gravămen" of an offence. It is deplorable to hear a petty scholar triumphing with all the airs of conscious superiority over some great man who has substituted a long for a short, or a short for a long. I cannot affect to think one atom the worse of Burke's imperial genius, because he said "vectĭgal" in the House of Commons; or of the Duke of Wellington's intellect because he turned round, when reading his Chancellor's address at Oxford, to whisper, "I say, is it Jacŏbus or Jacōbus?" I was taught as a schoolboy that a false quantity makes a man ridiculous, and sticks to him for life; and the dictum reminds me of St. Augustine's disdainful remark that the Sophists of *his* time thought it as disgraceful to drop the aspirate in *homo* as to hate a man. Considering that our entire method of pronouncing Greek and Latin is radically wrong, I cannot pretend to regard a false quantity in some rare word as otherwise than an entirely venial error, and one of infinitely less consequence than a mis-translation in the rendering of a passage. Those people may hold the reverse who think it worth while to learn Classics in order to understand "graceful quotations from Virgil and Horace" in a House where it would be considered "very bad taste" to quote St. Paul! The death-knell of all such fastidious littleness will be the birth-peal of a nobler and manlier tone of thought.

But into the subject of taste and style it is necessary to enter more at length, because I believe that the fallacy of supposing that they are cultivated by "composition" lies at the root of half the countenance which that practice still receives. Even if the assumption were true, I should say that "taste" is a kind of sensibility which is purchased at a fearful cost if long time and labour be spent in its acquisition. If by "taste" be meant a fine sense of beauty and propriety, *that* is only attainable by moral culture, and by a constant familiarity with what is great in conduct and pure in thought. It is a gift partly due to a certain natural and inborn nobility, and partly to be evolved and fostered by familiarising the mind with all that is lofty and of good report. *This* kind of taste, these fine harmonies in the music of the mind and soul, are certainly not to be won—although I believe that they may be irretrievably lost—by grinding boys into a laborious imitation of Propertian prettinesses and Ovidian conceits. But by "taste" something widely different from this is generally implied; viz., a certain delicate fastidiousness, a finical fine-ladyism of the intellect, which I hold to be essentially pernicious. It is an exotic which flourishes most luxuriantly in the thin artificial soil of vain and second-rate minds. It cannot co-exist with robust manliness of conviction or of utterance. It is the disproportionate intellectualism which rejoices in paltry accuracies, while it can condone mighty wrongs. It prizes rhetoric above eloquence; it values manner more than matter. It can pore over an intaglio, but has no eye for a Gothic cathedral. It is the shrinking enemy of all untutored force and irresistible enthusiasm. It is the enthronement of conventionality, the apotheosis of self-satisfaction. "I want you to see," says Felix Holt, "that the creature who has the sensibilities which you call taste, and not the sensibilities which you call opinions, is simply a lower, pettier, sort of being—an insect that notices the shaking of the table, but never notices the thunder." Perhaps Greek and Latin verse writing *does* tend to foster—and that too in a wholly disproportionate degree—this petty kind of taste and finish, and it is one of the reasons why I for one wish to see the practice abolished and condemned.

And as for style—to *whom* does it teach style? Is it to that vast majority who can show no tangible result from years of teaching beyond the ability, after infinite labour, to torture good English into an execrably bad semblance of Latin and Greek? Or does it teach style to a handful who become good scholars? I cannot admit even the latter assertion. Certainly no argument in its favour can be drawn from induction. Some of our very worst writers have been splendid scholars; some of our very best writers have been no scholars at all. The Latin of even a Dante is bad and unidiomatic,[1] and Milton's magnificent prose constantly disgusts the "nice" taste of a Ciceronian Pharisee. Is there any human being who prefers the turgid tautologies of Dr. Johnson and the windy pedantic bombast of Dr. Parr, to the despatches of the "ignorant" Wellington, or the homeliness of the "unclassical" Cobbett? Is style—which should be the intensest expression of an author's individuality—to be best learnt by conscious imitation of foreign writers? and is originality of expression likely to result from ingenious centos of borrowed phrases, which, although I have known them to gain the highest prizes and the warmest applause of both Universities, recal the very meanest remains of late Roman poets in their most degraded compositions?[1] The greatest masters of all style were the Greeks, who knew no word of any language but their own. The Roman writers, in exact proportion to their study of Greek, paralysed some of the finest powers of their own language, and produced a literature which, in its uninterrupted decadence, became more and more deficient in originality and in worth. It is a remark as old as Cicero that women, from being accustomed solely to their native tongue, usually speak it with a grace and purity surpassing that of men. Our own poets and philosophers—who have certainly a pre-eminent right to speak on matters of style—unite

[1] Sperone, in his Dialogues on Latin and Italian, said, "It was the general opinion that no one could write Italian who could write Latin." See Hallam, *Lit. of Europe*, i. 445.

[2] I am not aware of any cento earlier than Ausonius. Yet I have seen university prize-verses handed round for admiration, in which line for line and word for word were nothing in the world but Virgilian tags.

in denouncing or depreciating the practice of composing in foreign idioms. Keats, the most thoroughly classical of all our writers—Keats, of whom Byron said that " he was a Greek himself,"—could not read a line of the Greek language. Milton, the greatest scholar among poets, and one of the few poets whose originality has survived their scholarship, discarded the practice from his own ideal system, and speaks of it, as we all know, with intense and undisguised contempt.[1]

And indeed the study of Greek and Latin composition has distinctly injured our own English language, and done mischief to some of our great writers. Milton himself did not escape the taint.[2] To it are due such sentences as " The summer following, *Titus then Emperor*, Agricola continually with inroads disquieted the enemy;" and such lines as—

> " with keen despatch
> Of real hunger and concoctive haste
> To transubstantiate ; what redounds transpires
> Through spirits with ease;"

which go far to justify Dryden's complaint that " Milton Romanised our language without complying with its idioms." To it we owe a multitude of "inkhorn terms," which are now fortunately as dead as the rootless flowers stuck in a child's garden. To it we owe that

> " Babylonish dialect
> Which learned pedants most affect ;
> 'Twas English cut on Greek and Latin,
> Like fustian heretofore on satin."

---

[1] Macaulay considers that Milton's success in Latin verse adds greatly to our astonishment that he should have been able to write the Paradise Lost.

[2] See "Studies in English," by Dr. C. Schele de Vere. But in referring to Dr. de Vere I must add my regret that he should so frequently borrow from others without the least acknowledgment.

It had its share in producing the feeble voice of the Elizabethan euphuism, with its falsetto tones and vaporous inanities. In fact, from this cause, our language once ran no little risk of being fairly buried under the Greek and Latin scoriæ flung up by the volcanic enthusiasm of the Revival of Letters. "And indeed," complacently observes Sir Thomas Browne, whose stately and sesquipedalian rhetoric is nearly ruined by his unpardonable pedantry, "if elegancy still proceedeth, and English pens maintain that stream which we have of late observed to flow from many, we shall within few years be compelled to learn Latin to understand English, and a work will prove of equal facility in either." Happily the masculine good sense of the nation saved it from so miserable an atrophy; but the dangerous influences long remained at work. It was especially to the patronage of Latin verse that we owe the "poetic phraseology," that is, the gaudy and artificial inaccuracy, of such passages as Dryden's once famous, now justly ridiculed description of night. To this, more than to any other cause, no less an authority than Wordsworth attributed the monotonous conventionality of the school inaugurated by Pope. To it we owe the meaningless ornamentation which spoils the poetry of Gray, and which produced such lines as—

"And reddening Phœbus lifts his golden fires,"

a line which has in it a fine flavour of compulsory Latin verse writing. Coleridge well illustrates the "poésie épithétique," which is fostered by the practice, in his story about the line—

"Lactea purpureos interstrepit unda lapillos."

The first half of this line is a ludicrous and tasteless variation, and the last half, an open plagiarism of the line—

"Pura coloratos interstrepit unda lapillos;"

and such lines, half-tinsel, half-mosaic, *abound*, with many lines which are whole-plagiarism, in University exercises and similar compositions. All idiomatic freshness, all simple beauty, all nervous originality are, I feel convinced, obliterated rather than developed by rewarding an ingenuity so misplaced; while insincerity and incongruity in verse, and a "turgid and tumultuary style of sentence" in prose, are directly fostered. "Certain it is," says one of the great masters of our English language, "that our popular style has laboured with two faults that might have been thought incompatible: it has been artificial by *artifices peculiarly adapted to the powers of the Latin language*, and also, at the same time, careless and disordinate (inconditus)." Among our best and finest writers are those who have drunk simply and solely at "the pure wells of English undefiled." Is it conceivable that Shakspeare or Burns would have written as they have written, if they had been drilled for years in Latin verse? The best of all styles, and the best of all poems, have belonged generally to

"The days when mankind were but callans
At grammar, logic, and sic talen's,
They took nae pains their speech to balance,
    Nor rules to gie;
But spak their thoughts in plain braid lallans,
    Like you or me;—"

and some of the best in modern days have been written by men whose individual condition most resembled the age which Burns describes.

If then it be desirable to educate boys—not indeed in style, but in a power of expressing themselves in their own language—then, instead of encouraging verbal imitations, and cramming their memory with classic tags, let us adopt the incomparably truer and better method of requiring a careful description of natural phenomena and scientific experiments,—a process which, while it teaches them a terse and lucid use of their own language, will, at the same time, fire their imagination with some of the grandest and noblest objects of human thought. If taste and style be a fine appreciation, and a masterly power of producing beauty of form in the expression of thought, will it best be created by making boys write in languages which they do not know, about things for which they do not care, or by making them express carefully in their own language their natural observations and their genuine experience? With the examples before our eyes of scientific men who wrote as Sir Humphry Davy and Dr. Whewell wrote, or as Mr. Darwin and Professor Owen are writing now; and with men who speak with the power and eloquence of Professor Tyndall and Professor Huxley, we need have little fear that our boys will lose in "taste" or "style," by substituting a more solid and scientific training for the time which they are now wasting, or worse than wasting, over Greek and Latin verse.

IV. "But boys must be made to *produce* something original."

Argal, they must write Latin verses! Will not a moment's consideration show to any one that such reasoning involves an immense *non sequitur*? By "producing something" is meant, I suppose, that boys must give evidence of having thought for themselves. Now, without stopping to prove that few things have less claim to be called original than the *crambe repetita* of ordinary Latin verse, or that few exercises involve less thought as distinguished from mere memory and skill, I will ask whether it is seriously asserted that we can get no better evidence of a boy's having thought for himself than the limping and pitiable feebleness of an average copy of Latin verses? Such an assertion would only provoke from most thinkers an exclamation of "*Spectatum admissi . . . ?*" and would go far to prove that all which has been discovered and all that has been written on education since the days of Ascham and of Milton has been discovered and written quite in vain.

V. "But verse-making has a disciplinary value: it gives boys some occupation, and it enables a master to look over very quickly what boys have done very slowly; and it can be taught successfully" (for, strange to say, *this*, too, is an argument which I have heard deliberately and repeatedly advanced), "taught even by stupid men, who can teach nothing else."

Since these arguments seem to me to be abandonments of the question at issue, and mere confessions of defeat and weakness, I may be allowed to deal with them very summarily. Their truth is the worst condemnation of the whole system. They show how mechanical our teaching has become, and how completely it subordinates the interests of the pupil to the convenience of the tutor. And this low conception of what early education should be, involves its own Nemesis; for though little boys may be cheaply and easily kept out of mischief while they are thus being amused with a miserable semblance of production, they demand heavy arrears of labour from every conscientious tutor, when they have reached the higher forms.

And, as for the disciplinary value of verses, is it necessary that discipline should be so purely infructuous? Can we teach nothing in heaven and earth which shall be valuable as *an end*, no less than as *a means*? Is it not a sheer blasphemy against the majesty of knowledge to assert that there is nothing worth *teaching* which shall be also worth *knowing*? To walk on a treadmill, to dance on a tight-rope, to spin round and round like an Oriental dervish, may be practices which require skill, and involve healthy exercise; but are they preferable to good honest walking? We are told of a certain philanthropist that, when work was slack, he employed his labourers one day in dragging stones from one place to another, and the next day in dragging them back again. Well, he certainly kept them at work, and even such work is, I suppose, preferable to idleness. But would labourers, so occupied, be likely to conceive a high opinion either of the good sense of their employer, or of the high dignity of labour, and its infinite importance in the evolution of human progress? And was not such work a mere waste of organised frivolity? Now we have been exactly imitating this philanthropist by degrading education into a mere discipline, and thus teaching our boys to disbelieve that *anything* was worth knowing, since the immediate end set before them was, to the majority, alike unattainable and valueless. What wonder is it that so many of them have grown up to despise culture, and to disbelieve in the necessity for any kind of intellectual effort?

On the very day on which I am writing these words, it has been my fortune to meet in succession three old Public School boys, two of whom had been pupils of my own. Nothing could be more widely diverse than the general character of their lives; yet each of them possessed different ability, and each of them had worked with special diligence. One of them, formerly a lieutenant in the army, had emigrated to South America, and had just returned from his home on one of the central Pampas of the Argentine Confederation. The second was a young Oxonian of private fortune, and distinguished talents, who, after winning the highest honours of his University, was devoting himself to the careful cultivation of his intellectual gifts. The third was a writer of rank and reputation, a poet, a critic, and a man of many accomplishments, familiar with every phase of English and continental thought. One and all they lamented the hours fruitlessly squandered over Latin verse. The young sheep-farmer of the Pampas groaned with good-humoured despair over the continuous misery they had caused him. The Oxford First Class man, though he had cultivated composition with taste and success, declared, after deliberate thought, that he could not attribute to the time spent over it, a single intellectual advantage. The man of letters expressed himself in language so forcible and decided, that I thought it worth while to quote his testimony *verbatim :*—" I was," he says, " at three private schools before going to ——, where I had the advantage of the private tuition of an able, accomplished, and most assiduous teacher, besides all the other appliances and means, to boot, of the school, at a time when it was generally regarded as a model Public

School. And yet, through all those years, *I learnt nothing whatever but a general disinclination to learn anything, and a special loathing for Latin verse.* Nothing of the simplest elements of a single science,— nothing of my own language — nothing even which tended to facilitate the subsequent learning of what was *not* learnt then,—nothing which has been of the slightest use to me in after life—no accomplishment which added to the enjoyment, and no knowledge which has enlarged the utility or diminished the difficulties of life by so much as one inch. But the new comers will be better off than their predecessors. I hear that something of music, something of botany, and of other sciences, is now taught at ——— . . . . I am sincerely thankful for this for my boy's sake. It is all too late for me."

Familiar with such testimonies from constant experience, is it surprising that I have used my best efforts, (and mean to use them still), to shake to the ground the whole system of universal and compulsory verse manufacture; or that I regard the results which it produces with a sorrow which is not unmingled with disgust? One school at least,[1] has had the courage to be the first in rejecting for ever this pernicious absurdity; and I believe that thereby it has earned the gratitude of the present generation, and will deserve the yet warmer admiration of the future. But let me entreat the powerful aid of the Universities to help us in thus infusing fresh truth and vigour and reality into the education of England. Much they have already done; but they are liable to be misled by seeing the ships which reach the

[1] Harrow School.

port, and forgetting the numberless and melancholy wrecks which strew the shore. They cannot however any longer plead ignorance of the effect produced by their extravagant patronage of verse composition upon thousands of youths who are never destined to enter their walls. Let them by all means retain prizes to reward the ingenuity of a few advanced scholars; but, until they have ceased to render verses an essential requisite, either for entrance-scholarships or for their classical examinations,—until they at least counterbalance, by alternative papers, the immense preponderance which they have hitherto given to what has often been mere correct nullity, or imitative knack,— they are doing much to injure, in the opinion of many, (and those not the least entitled to be heard), that proud and legitimate position to which they should ever aspire of leading and moulding with a farsighted wisdom the higher education of that country to which they owe their splendid revenues and their elevated rank.

Let the Colleges, then, boldly loosen these gilded and fantastic chains which were forged in an age of logomachy, and tightened in an age of artificiality and retrogression. Let them determine more decidedly, and avow more distinctly, that verses are not essential for scholarships or for honours. When they have done so, we shall no longer hear of classical teaching degraded into recommendations to treasure up particular words and phrases "with a view to using them in your composition." Youths of robust minds will no longer be alienated from classical study, or diverted from good reading to bad writing; nor will they be forced to waste over Tibullus and Ovid the time which might have been devoted to

Plato and Thucydides. I have even heard of Cambridge scholars who toiled through Ausonius, Silius Italicus, *et tous ces garçons-là*, in the hope of picking up here and there some gaudy epithet, some sonorous combination, some rhetorical παρήχησις which might "pay" in a set of verses for the Tripos or for a Prize. I have known even boys who thought it necessary to bathe themselves, by daily repetition, with the soft atmosphere of the "Amores" in order to improve their Latin verse, even if it were at the expense of all simplicity and ingenuousness of mind. Some of them reaped their reward in University applause, and afterwards in the wanderings of an enervated imagination and in the over-refinement of an intellect at once fastidious and weak.

Could it be otherwise? I have been censured for saying that, in this elegant trifling, success was often more deplorable than failure; but what was derided as an epigram I most deliberately and determinately repeat as a truth of experience. I have known cases in which a fair intellect was visibly weakened and demoralised,—rendered visibly smaller and shallower,—by an excessive admiration for classical composition. But, as one may not quote individual cases, let us take *instantiæ ostensivæ* of the fact as illustrated by the tendency of three distinct periods of human history. For there *have* been periods ere now, in which verse-writing and style-polishing have formed the main part of youthful education, and by glancing at these periods we can see in large the natural effects which such an education is calculated to produce.

Take for instance the age of Nero, during which, in the countless schools of rhetoricians, Grammar and Philology were everything, Philosophy nothing. What was the result? Never since the world began was there less invention or more men who taught the art of inventing. Never was the style of even those writers who had the gift of genius more pedantic or more obscure. Never was the degradation of the literary character more pitiable or more complete. Occupied from childhood in the art of writing verses, in which they were forced to express emotions which they did not feel, and sentiments which they could not understand, what wonder that the poets ended by going off into emulous raptures at the beauty of lapdogs, and invocations of all the gods and goddesses to take charge of a minion's hair? What wonder that they hid the sterility of their ideas under the exuberance of their words, and mistook literary contortions for original achievements? When merely secondary and external facts of form and metre were thought to constitute the essence of verse, no wonder that "receipts for making poetry were given like receipts for making *Eau de Cologne*."[1] It was the age of τόποι and τρόποι, and *loci communes*; the universal triumph of barren platitude tricked out with affectation and grimace. The thoughts of the rising generation resolved themselves into a flux of words; and who shall tell us what single benefit the world has gained from whole ages of such empty talk,—from the "*calamistri*" of Mæcenas and the "*tinnitus*" of Gallio, down to the florid and tasteless declamations of a Libanius and a Julian?

But there was again another age which deliberately, and without any sense of absurdity, regarded the acqui-

[1] This whole subject has been admirably treated by M. Nisard, in his *Poètes de la Décadence*, from whom I have here borrowed a phrase.

sition of a Latin style as the main end of life. And, again I ask, what was the result? "It was," as Bacon says, "that men began to hunt more after words than after matter," falling into a vanity of which Pygmalion's frenzy is a good emblem. "But the excess of this," continues Bacon, in words to which I ask the earnest attention of our University authorities, "is so justly contemptible, that as Hercules, when he saw the image of Adonis, Venus's minion, in a temple, said in disdain, '*Nil sacri es;*' so there is none of Hercules's followers in learning, that is the more severe and laborious sort of inquirers into truth, *but will despise those delicacies and affectations as indeed capable of no divineness.*" The result, as regards style, was that "then grew the fluent and watery vein of Osorius, the Portuguese bishop, to be in price;" but what was the result on men's minds? I can only say that never was there a more pitiable group of pedants and sophisters than flourished in the "professor-ridden" world during the period of the Renaissance. Such were the brilliant Filelfo, gorged with conceit and bursting with petty spite; the erudite Poggio, author of the treatise "on the elegancies of the Latin tongue," whose books were a sink of abominations, abounding in vanity, arrogance and invective; Angelo Politian, whose manners, if fame says true, "were even uglier than his countenance;" Zacchario Ferrari, who tried to paganise even the Hymnarium and Liturgy; Sannazar, who surrounds the very cradle of Bethlehem with the prurient paganism of hamadryads and satyrs; the worldly and frivolous Bibbiena, the cardinal author of a questionable comedy; Pomponatus, the Paduan professor, who wrote to show that the "unreasonable" doctrine of the immortality of the soul did not rest on the authority of Aristotle, but "only" of the Scriptures; Bembo and Sadoletus, the first Latinists of their age, who turned with fine contempt from the "screams" of Isaiah, and the "barbarism" of St. Paul, and who could not even speak of the blessed influences of the Holy Spirit of God without introducing such sickening inanities as "the whisper of the Celestial Zephyr!" Such was the corrupt paganism, the self-sufficient half-learning, the meretricious eloquence, the inflated arrogant littleness, of minds trained from the cradle on the husk of words and metres—of minds which, turning from the divine brightness of truth and of nature, thrilled only to Ciceronianisms and tropes and idioms and locutions. And such minds were the legitimate outcome of an age which rewarded with its highest honours the empty-headed pedants and conceited rhetoricians who had eaten out all that was valuable in their lives in the successful attempt to acquire a Latin style!

Once more, and lastly—to what country does the reader suppose that we must look for the greatest outburst of fecundity and facility in the production of Latin Verse? Few, I suspect, would be likely to guess that the palm must undoubtedly be given to backward and superstitious Portugal. Yet so it is. Not even the "Musæ Etonenses," supplemented by all the other *nugæ canoræ* of the British Muse, can pretend to equal in bulk and magnificence the seven quarto volumes, published in Lisbon in 1745, which contain the mouldering remains of no less than fifty-nine illustrious Lusitanian poets! Alas that so many of these "illustrious" should be consigned to oblivion in the obscure limbo of a "corpus;" alas that the world of "taste" and "style" should be unconscious of what it owes to Mendez Vasconcellos, or to Diego Fayra de Andrada; alas that in its Philistine ingratitude it should have forgotten Figueira Duram, who was an epic poet at sixteen, and who improvised before his examiners "The Temple of Eternity;" or F. de Macedo, who poured forth *vivâ voce* 1,000 verses on the history of the Popes, and who tells us in his "Myrothecium Morale" that he had written 2,600 epic poems, 110 odes, 3,000 epigrams, 4 Latin comedies, and 150,000 impromptu Latin verses! How much was the world better for these Goliaths among modern Latin poets? And what benefit accrued to Portugal from its not very noble army of imitative versifiers? Why, a gain the *very reverse* to that which the arguments of our classical composers would have led us to expect, viz. a literature the poorest and the most jejune of any country in Europe! Their Latin Verse-writing was, it appears, as useless and deceptive as the iridescence on the surface of a very shallow and a very stagnant pool. It was (if I may borrow an expression from Guibert, the good and eminent abbot of Nogent sous Coucy, who in his autobiography has bewailed the manner in which he was led astray in his youth by the temptations incident to the study of Latin Verse) "a ridiculous vanity."

I do not for a moment mean to say that our age has run to the same ridiculous excess. Thank God, our modern education has involved many better and richer elements than this. But I do say that our extensive Latin Verse system is a useless and unfortunate relic of training of this sort. And training of this sort is, let us hope, irrevocably doomed. Those who now cling to it will sooner or later be *forced* to give it up. And if those of us who *have* given it up make some mistakes in our early attempts to substitute a better training in its place, we may at least console ourselves with the thought that, unless we are guilty of deliberate treachery, it is *impossible* for us to reproduce a system equally pernicious and equally infructuous. The social forces are all arrayed on our side. In this age, more perhaps than in any other, we have a right to demand as an essential element in the education of our youth something broader, deeper, more human, more useful, less selfish, less exclusive. We require the knowledge of *things* and not of *words*; of the truths which great men have to tell us, and not of the tricks or individualities of their style ; of that which shall add to the treasures of human knowledge, not of that which shall flatter its fastidiousness by frivolous attempts at reproducing its past elegancies of speech ; of that which is best for human souls, and which shall make them greater, wiser, better; not of that which is idly supposed to make them more tasteful, and refined.— Very soon we shall have seen and heard the last of this card-castle built upon the sands; let us strive in all earnest and thoughtful faith to rebuild, not on such weak foundations, but with broad bases and on the living rock, some great and solid structure of enduring masonry, which shall be hereafter among those things which cannot be shaken and shall remain.

VI.

ON TEACHING NATURAL SCIENCE IN SCHOOLS.

BY J. M. WILSON, M.A. F.G.S. F.R.A.S.

WHAT ought to be the relations of Science and Literature in liberal education, is one of the most important questions which come before those who reflect on the theory of education. It is only lately that the question has been distinctly stated. No complete answer can yet be given. It needs no proof that the present state of education into which we have drifted is not satisfactory, and among its most marked defects is the neglect of science. This is equally the opinion of the many and of the few; and lately some valuable contributions have been made to public opinion on this point by Mill, and Thirlwall, and others, to whom this neglect is a matter of astonishment and regret. I shall not attempt an essay on the relations of science and literature in human culture in general; nor discuss the processes by which truth is arrived at in the different natural sciences; nor the effect of scientific method on the minds of scientific men; nor can I touch on the proper position of these studies at the universities. It is with school education alone that I am concerned at present. I intend in the following pages to put forward some reflections on teaching natural science in schools that occur to me after having been occupied for eight years as a mathematical and natural science master at Rugby School. What I may have to say will not indeed come with the weight that attends the words of some previous writers on this subject, but it comes from an entirely different point of view, and from one who has at least honestly endeavoured to form his theories by experience and reflection, and to put his theories into practice.

I shall endeavour, therefore, to state distinctly some of the reasons why it is believed that the introduction of some teaching of science into schools is so very desirable as its advocates hold it to be; to meet some of the objections that are urged against it; to make some suggestions as to the spirit and method of the teaching of science at schools, a subject on which there is much misconception; and to add some reflections on the obstacles that retard improvement in school education, and the probable results of a more general cultivation of science.

Few will deny that the present results in our classical schools are not very satisfactory. The astonishing ignorance of Latin and Greek, or at least of all the finer part of this knowledge on which so much stress is laid; and the ignorance—which is less surprising, if not less lamentable—of everything else, with which so many boys leave most schools, has been dwelt on again and again. Is it remediable or is it not? Is it due to the carelessness and inability of masters; to the inherent unsuitability of the subjects taught; to neglected early education and bad preparatory schools; or to the illiterate tone of the society in which boys are brought up; to excessive novel reading and devotion to games, or to the great fact that the majority of the species are incapable of learning much? Partly perhaps to them all; certainly to an ill-advised course of study. For at present, literature, or the studies which are subordinate to it, has almost a monopoly: and on language the great majority of boys fail in getting much hold. The exclusive study of language at schools weakens the fibre of those who have genius for it, fails to educate to the best advantage the mass who have fairly good sense but no genius for anything, and obscures and depresses the few who have special abilities in other lines; and it precludes the possibility of learning much besides. So that even at a school where classics are well taught, where the masters are able and skilful, and the boys industrious, not very much is learnt. It was said of a Scotchman who enjoyed a cheap reputation for hospitality, "that he kept an excellent table, but put verra leetle upon it." This epitomizes the report of the Public Schools Commission: the schools are excellent, but they teach "verra leetle." And this is the less excusable because the experience of the best foreign schools is showing the advantage of introducing greater variety into the course of study. A wider net is cast; fewer minds repose in unstirred apathy; more varied abilities are recognised; there is less over-estimation of special branches of knowledge; and, what is of more importance, the variety seems itself to be a stimulus.

And if the extension of the school curriculum is not absolutely forbidden by an appeal to reason or to experience, the claims of science to become recognised as a branch of liberal education are exceedingly strong. For, in the first place, most boys show a degree of interest in their scientific work which is unmistakeably greater than in any other study. I am no advocate of a theory of education in which boys should learn nothing but what they show a taste for. I hold this to be a pestilent heresy. It would be worse than allowing children to eat whatever they pleased, because the mischief is more irreparable and the detection of it longer delayed. The thing that is valuable in all education is effort; and it is an advantage which science possesses that the interest that boys take in it induces them to make efforts in its study. If it were less interesting it would be right to teach it. I utterly repudiate the notion that a lecture ought to be made interesting, and merely observe that it happens to be so, and that it therefore secures an amount of attention and active thought which is very difficult to get in other subjects. The excitement, and interest, and competition in games make boys endure and enjoy an amount of fatigue and pain that they would naturally shrink from; and this fatigue and pain are the means by which they win the *corpus sanum*. The *mens sana* must be sought by similar efforts and pain; and if an interesting subject induces efforts, then, and then only, is its interest a merit. The temple of knowledge in the apologue had twelve gates, and the student had but one key given him to open them all. This master-key is the power of active thought. And it is perhaps worth remarking, that since the introduction, three years ago, of a little natural science into our school course at Rugby, there has already been noticed an increase generally of what is described by different and acute observers as docility, love of work, aptitude for attention, grasp, power of seeing the point, in the average material of which our classical forms are composed. It is in fact an increase of mental activity and logical power. This is due to three causes which simultaneously began to operate,—to our system of superannuation, which prevents the existence of aged ringleaders of idleness in the forms; to the entrance examinations, by which a few very idle boys are rejected who would in former times have been admitted; but it is also commonly and reasonably attributed in a still greater degree to the study of natural science, a new and positive influence which has begun to operate.

And again, there are mental instincts just as there are bodily instincts. The bodily instincts anticipate the experience of physicians and experiments of physiologists, and are their guide to the treatment of the body; but the mental instincts, which are even more important, are nevertheless almost ignored in the art of education. One of these instincts is curiosity. It is a mental phenomenon which the skilful master studies, a power which he turns to account in the education of the boy. It is the one principle that makes self-education possible. It is a form of the love of knowledge; and when it concerns natural objects we call it curiosity, and half despise it. That it is often weak and unaccompanied with effort, I admit. But it is often altogether repressed—"little boys should not be curious:" whereas it ought to be guided, stimulated, and strengthened. The guidance of curiosity is to lead a boy to observe more, to combine, to reason. The stimulation of it is to show how much more there is still to be learnt. The strengthening of it is to make it deep and lasting; to check the mere love of novelty, the idle discursiveness that asks disconnected questions, and forgets, even if it waits for, the answers; and to refuse information till the foundation is laid on which it can securely rest. Guidance often takes the form of repression. Curiosity is the ordinary form of activity in a young mind, and it is unnatural and foolish to ignore it as we do. There is a fine passage on this subject in Goethe's "Hermann and Dorothea," which I shall make no apology for quoting at length. If any one despise this power in a child's mind, I ask him to weigh these words. The village apothecary had been blaming the curiosity which led all the people out to see the sad procession of exiles pass near the town—

"Unverzeihlich find ich den Leichtsinn: doch liegt er im Menschen;"

and to him, the wise and intelligent pastor, experienced in life and well versed in learning, replied—

" . . . Ich tadle nicht gerne was immer dem Menschen
Für unschädliche Triebe die gute Mutter Natur gab;
Denn was Verstand und Vernunft nicht immer vermögen, vermag oft
Solch ein glücklicher Hang, der unwiderstehlich uns leitet.
Lockte die Neugier nicht den Menschen mit heftigen Reizen,
Sagt! erfuhr er wohl je, wie schön sich die weltlichen Dinge
Gegen einander verhalten? Denn erst verlangt er das Neue,
Suchet das Nützliche dann mit unermüdetem Fleisse;
Endlich begehrt er das Gute, das ihn erhebet und werth macht."

And where this curiosity exists in boys it is almost exclusively directed towards external objects, and may be best cherished and ennobled into a genuine love of knowledge by guiding it to find some food in natural history and science. How much better and more intelligent would early training be if curiosity were looked on as the store of force, the possible love of knowledge in embryo in the boy's mind, which in its later transformations is so highly valued. "For our incitement,—I say not our reward, for knowledge is its own reward,—herbs have their healing, stones their preciousness, stars their times."

And even if scientific knowledge were not selected by a boy's natural interest and curiosity, yet let us reflect for a moment on its dignity and grandeur. This is no mean, and peddling, and quibbling knowledge, as the ignorant believe; it is the key to the possession of the loftiest ideas. We count a man educated in proportion to the exactness, width, and nobleness of his ideas. What is needed to elevate a man's intellectual nature is not that he should be an encyclopædia, but that he should have great ideas. And these must be based on knowledge. They do not, indeed, always accompany knowledge. Great ideas may be got by various studies, and all studies may be pursued by men who fail to gain great ideas. I know men with a wide and microscopic knowledge of history who know nothing of the love of freedom, of national justice, of the progress of the world, of the power of genius and will;—men who are theologians by profession, whose thoughts still revolve in the narrowest circle of earthly prejudices;—scholars indifferent alike to literature and learning. And so there are scientific men who combine poverty of intellect with width of knowledge. A botanist may be as foolish as a crest collector; a geologist, and even an astronomer, may, perhaps, be a pedant not more ennobled by the sphere of his thoughts than a cathedral spider is affected by the majesty of his abode; but I will venture to assert, that the great thoughts and principles which are to be gained only by scientific knowledge are not only of a quality that increases the dignity of a man's mind, are not only intrinsically glorious and elevating, but are not inferior, whether we regard their effect on the intellect or on the imagination, to those which may be reached by other studies. And I am not speaking only of the discoverers in science. There is a special charm, indeed, and stimulating power in original research, in exploring new regions; but there are splendid ideas, magnificent points of view, which, though others have reached them before, yet to attain is a lifelong pleasure. The ordinary tourist may climb to some well-worn spot in the Alps, he may ascend by the beaten track, he may even be carried there, and yet he will be richly rewarded by the view that unfolds itself before his eyes. He may not feel the glow of health, the buoyant soul of the first mountaineer that stood there; but he will see what he will remember for ever; he will get more than a new sensation, he will have enlarged his soul. So to be the first to climb, as Newton did, with solitary steps to the untrodden heights from which he gazed on the solar system spread out at his feet, can never again be given to mortal man; but to attain the knowledge, to see the magnificent orderliness and progress, to be profoundly impressed with the infinities of space and time which it silently suggests, is to have gained a treasure that lasts as long as life will last. So also geology has a sublimity of its own, slowly reached by many steps and much toil. And, above all, the great ideas of natural law and harmonious adjustment can only be obtained by patient study in the fields of science; and are they not priceless to those who have in any degree won them? Who can contemplate our globe in this orderly system of the universe, with all the delicate adjustments that astronomy reveals, and all the splendid mechanism of the heavens—contemplate our atmosphere, with all its mechanical, chemical, and physical properties —the distant sun darting its light and heat and power on the globe, and fostering all the varied and beautiful animal and vegetable life, giving rise to winds and showers and fruitful seasons, and beauties of form and richness of colour, filling our hearts with food and gladness; who can know something of the inexorable sequences, see something of the felicitous combination of all the varied forces of nature that are employed,—and not feel impressed and awed by the view; not feel that he is in the presence of a Power and Wisdom that as far transcends the power and wisdom of man as the universe surpasses a watch in magnitude?

> " To see in part
> That all, as in some piece of art,
> Is toil, coöperant to an end"

is to see that which he who sees it not is as incapable of estimating as the deaf man is of judging of music, or the blind of enjoying the glories of a sunset. Such are some of the ideas which crown science, and it is not granted to us to attain them except by slow degrees. Step by step must the growing mind approach them; and to exclude from our schools the preliminary steps is to debar from the attainment of such ideas all whose leisure in after-life is so curtailed that they can never break ground in any fresh subject for thought or labour.

And, moreover, the kind of knowledge that science offers is not only wide, and interesting, and elevating, but it is also exact; and this exactness is a very great merit. It is a knowledge of things, and not of words. In the education of the upper classes there is too little of positive and exact knowledge, and too much of mere training and drill: we have too much distrusted the virtue of knowledge. In a purely classical education there is always something of the *bellè et probabiliter opinari* as opposed to the *certò et ostensivè scire* of Bacon. For the ultimate conceptions of grammar are by their nature only to be attained by self-analysis and metaphysical introspection; and though boys sometimes attain great knowledge of usage, yet it is empirical and not demonstrative. And natural science supplies this want of clearness and certitude better than arithmetic or geometry: its exactness amid its diversity serves as a kind of standard in the mind of what knowledge is. Arithmetic, geometry, and natural science represent positive knowledge in a boy's education; they have the 'know how' and the 'know why,' and this gives confidence and certainty.

But there is another and even a stronger ground for advocating the introduction of science as an element in all liberal education, and that is, its peculiar merit as a means of educating the mind. Science is not only knowledge, but it is also power. The mind is not only an instrument for advancing science, but, what is more to our present point, science is an instrument for advancing the mind. All that can be said on this point has been said over and over again, and I can contribute nothing except my daily experience that what is said is true.

Mill speaks of "the indispensable necessity of scientific instruction, for it is recommended by every consideration which pleads for any high order of intellectual education at all." Science is the best teacher of accurate, acute, and exhaustive observation of what is; it encourages the habit of mind which will rest on nothing but what is true; truth is the ultimate and only object, and there is the ever-recurring appeal to facts as the test of truth. And it is an excellent exercise of memory; not the verbal, formal memory, but the orderly, intelligent, connected, accurate storing up of knowledge. And of all processes of reasoning it stands alone as the exhaustive illustration. It is pre-eminently the study that illustrates the art of thinking. "The processes by which truth is attained," to quote again from Mill, "reasoning and observation, have been carried to their greatest known perfection in the physical sciences." In fact, the investigations and reasoning of science, advancing as it does from the study of simple phenomena to the analysis of complicated actions, form a model of precisely the kind of mental work which is the business of every man, from his cradle to his grave; and reasoning, like other arts, is best learnt by practice and familiarity with the highest models. Science teaches what the power and what the weakness of the senses is; what evidence is, and what proof is. There is no characteristic of an educated man so marked as his power of judging of evidence and proof. The precautions that are taken against misinterpretation of what is called the evidence of the senses, and against wrong reasoning, and tracing the thoughts backward down to the ground of belief; the constant verification of theories; the candid suspension of judgment where evidence is still wanting; that wedding of induction and deduction into a happy unity and completeness of proof, the mixture of observation and ratiocination — are precisely the mental processes which all men have to go through somehow or other in their daily business, and which every human being who is capable of forming an intelligent opinion on the subject sees would be better done if men had familiarised themselves with the models of these processes which are furnished by science. I do not mean that a boy knows he is doing all these things; but he *is* doing them visibly. And when he applies the analysis of logic to the processes of his mind, he will find that he has been thinking logically, though unconsciously so.

Thinking is learnt by thinking; and it is my strongest conviction, as it is my daily experience, that boys can and do learn to think,—learn all the varied operations of the mind we sum up in that word,—by the study of science. A more vigorous school of thought, and a habit of mind less inclined to the faults of dogmatism on the one side, and deference to authority on the other, with more reverence for truth, and more confidence in knowledge, is the natural product of scientific instruction.

And again, how perfectly does science illustrate what the attitude of the mind ought to be towards the unknown and unrevealed. It shows the methodical advance and conquest of knowledge over ignorance, and marks where there is uncertainty on the border ground between them; it exercises its judgment on the degree of uncertainty, and casts longing looks into the darkness beyond. But it never mistakes the penumbra of uncertainty for the full light of demonstration.

Moreover, taking education in its broad sense as the training of all the powers that go to make up the man, I would point out how much science contributes towards increasing the powers of the senses. All science is based, some one has said, on the fact that we have great curiosity, and very weak eyes; and science gives men a marvellous extension of the power and range of the acuteness of those eyes. "Eyes and no eyes" is the title of an old story; and it scarcely seems too strong a way of marking the difference between the powers of perception of a cultivated naturalist, and those of the ordinary gentleman ignorant of everything in nature. To the one the stars of heaven, and the stones on earth, the forms of the hills, and the flowers in the hedges, are a constant source of that great and peculiar pleasure derived from intelligence. And day by day do I see how boys increase their range of sight, and that not only of the things we teach them to see, but they outrun us, and discover for themselves. And the power, once gained, can never be lost. I know many instances of boys whose eyes were opened at school by the ordinary natural science lectures, who have since found great pleasure and constant occupation in some branch of scientific study.

And I would add that whatever may be the defects of a purely literary education, which I obviously do not intend to discuss, they cannot be remedied by mathematics alone. Mathematics are so often thought, by those who are ignorant of them, to be the key to all reasoning, and to be the perfection of training, and so often spoken of by proficients in them as mysteries that it is worth the labour of half a lifetime to understand, that it is worth while to remember that after all they are only compendious and very limited methods of applying deductive reasoning, assisted by symbols, to questions of which the data are, or are supposed to be, extremely precise. They no more *teach* reasoning in the ordinary sense of the word than travelling by railway fits a man for exploring in Central Africa. And hence, while I set a very high value on arithmetic and geometry in all education, it is not because they supply the place of science in any sense, but on entirely different grounds. They form the language of science, however and are indispensable to its study.[1]

It will be observed that in this sketch of the grounds on which I urge the claims of natural science to be admitted into the ordinary course of a school education, I have omitted some points which are obvious enough. There is for example the very great practical utility of the knowledge; and if boys cannot gain enough knowledge at school to enable them to solve the scientific problems that may meet them in their later life, yet it is something to know that they are scientific problems. It is something, to know enough to know that others know more; to be able to say that this must be referred to a chemist, and this to a geologist.

And again, there is the very great increase of interest

[1] It is singular that the Mathematical Tripos at Cambridge is so unscientific, and the Natural Science Tripos at Oxford so unmathematical. At Cambridge a man may get the highest honours in mathematics and natural philosophy and have never seen a crystal, a lens, an air pump, or a thermometer; and at Oxford a man may get his First in natural science without knowing the Binomial Theorem or the solution of a triangle. Surely these are mistakes.

that an acquaintance with the elements of science gives to an educated man. An age of progress is an age of exceeding interest to those who can follow it intelligently.

And it seems only reasonable that schools should at least have the power of discovering special abilities.

And the presence of science side by side with literature is a protest against the narrowness which overvalues one branch of learning and despises others. Co-operation is necessary to secure a happy co-existence of these studies. Each alone becomes conceited; and conceit is the most fatal enemy to progress.

The advance also of science depends to some extent on the number as well as the genius of its students. How many rare and precious fossils, how many singular phenomena have been lost to the world, seen by blind eyes! How many gas-lamps might have trembled at sounds before a Lecomte observed under what conditions the ball-room lights responded to the tones of a violoncello!

And the extent to which the methods of science have affected all other studies, the existence of social and economical *science*, and the relation of science to religious thought, make it absolutely necessary that it shall be no longer excluded from liberal education.

The narrow range (to recapitulate) of our existing curriculum invites extension, and natural and physical science claims admission on all grounds that render intellectual education in itself desirable. The natural interest boys take in it, and the effort it consequently induces them to make, the dignity of the ideas it unfolds, and the exactness of the knowledge that it is built upon; its value in practice and in philosophy; the extension it gives to the range of intellectual perception and consequent intellectual pleasure; the truth-seeking habit of mind, and the training for an intelligent contemplation of the world that it imparts; and above all the completeness of the illustrations and models of the art of thinking that it affords in a form that attracts and retains the attention, and almost unconsciously trains the student in habits of logical thought,—form a body of arguments that seem unanswerable for introducing science into our schools as a branch of liberal education.

There are several objections brought forward by those who think more or less on this matter, and they reduce themselves to three: which urge respectively the worthlessness, the inhumanity, and the discursiveness of the study of science.

All that may be said on the worthlessness of science as a means of education in schools is before the world in the evidence given by Dr. Moberly, of Winchester, before the Public Schools Commission; to which I refer the reader.

The inhumanity of science is urged by some who feel that in order to train men, education must deal mainly with the feelings, the history, the language of men; that our relation to men, past and present, is more intimate, more important, and more elevating than our relation to the objects and forces of nature. Granted; and it proves that an education in science alone would be not the highest; but it is really no argument against a proper and moderate use of science as a means of educating certain faculties, such as the logical, which are very important for a true study of men, and yet are not best trained by a study of language, and literature, and history. This, however, does not go to the bottom of the matter. Many men have a kind of instinctive fear, not so much of the inhumanity, as of the inhumanising influence of science. And this instinct has, I believe, a real foundation. It is not simply false, that there is an inhumanity about science. The vague impression that reverence, faith, belief in the unseen and the spiritual, and in truths derived from individual consciousness, are diminished, as superstitions are diminished, by the school of science, must not be met by an off-hand denial that there is any foundation for it; for constant dealing with nature and exercise of the intellect alone, as contrasted with humanity and the exercise of the moral feelings, unquestionably tend to exclude men from the highest thoughts. All that may be said about the dignity of the study of created things—and this is a truth that often needs to be enforced—must not make its advocates lose sight of the relation of this study to others. The wish of many men of science that it should form the staple of liberal education, if gratified, would probably lead to a loss of gracefulness and unconscious art in style, which characterises nations which study the classics, and moreover would produce a peculiar and dangerous one-sidedness, which may be distinctly seen in many individual cases. In such cases, their constant study of one kind of evidence raises a secret disinclination and real inaptitude, for the time being, to accept evidence of a different kind, and induces them openly, or tacitly, to depreciate and distrust it. They are constantly tempted to consider the finer mental and religious sensibilities as useless, and as if they proved nothing. They are facts, of course, but facts which verge on fancies; and they have acquired a distaste for this kind of reflection, and something of contempt for its value in others. They seem to have raised a wall between themselves and certain truths; to have dazzled their eyes by a study of the glaring truths of external nature, and to be for the time incapable of discerning the dimmer but nobler truths of the soul and its relations. They distrust what may not be referred to the mechanism of organization, and disbelieve that the reason alone can be the source of real truths. Yet all this does not tend to prove that science should be excluded from schools, but that it should not form the staple of our education.

Discursiveness is a real danger. To do one thing well does undeniably give the power of going on acquiring more knowledge, making it exact, and using it. And schools and universities must still aim at concentration and excellence if they are to turn out men of power. But this is not attained by an exclusive curriculum, but by a reasonably comprehensive and elastic one; by making it possible for more varied excellence to be attained. I hold that a boy is best educated by learning something of many things and much of something: and that a man of the highest education ought to know something of everything, and everything of something. And to avoid the distraction and dissipation of mind which is the result if too many things are being learnt at once, will require some care on the part of those who arrange work at schools. Leisure must not be cut away. Nothing refined and artistic in classics, nothing sound and progressive in mathematics, nothing masterly and philosophical in science is attained in a system where there is much hurry and little leisure. Hence the curriculum must be made to some extent elastic: it is perfectly easy to make it so in any school; to make some studies compulsory and some optional, throughout the whole course; to make others compulsory at one period and alternative at another. And where this is done with judgment, no fear of disorganising the school and causing idleness need be entertained. This will readily be granted; but when it is urged that science ought to be one of the compulsory subjects, for at least a part of the period spent at school, then the claim is disputed. We cannot look on science as a πάρεργον which may serve for the amusement of those who fail to be scholars, but as a frivolous pursuit for men of ability—the doctrine very generally held by classical scholars; on the contrary, we claim for it a position in the education of all on the ground of the advantages it possesses for this purpose. In a dialogue it is impossible to discuss this question; for sooner or later the classicist argues thus in fact: " Whatever the faults of an exclusively classical system may be, it turned me out as one of its results. Whatever the value of science, it is not indispensable, for I am wholly ignorant of it." " My dear sir," one longs to say, " you are the very man in whose interests I am arguing. It is you who would be so much wiser, so very much less conceited, so much more conscious of the limitations of your knowledge, if you had been scientifically educated. You are far from stupid, and not uncultivated; but you lack what I consider of great value. When I speak of philology as a *science*, and of comparative philology as a *science*, you imperfectly understand me; and your depreciation of these studies (the whole nation depreciates them) results from your want of proper education. You would have more power in your own subjects, and an infinitely wider range of ideas and interests, if your classical education had been less unmitigated than it seems to have been." It is not enough therefore only to provide at schools means of learning something of science, as one might demand for the flute; but it must be made one of the compulsory subjects.

It is time now to make some remarks on the introduction of science into practical school work. Every schoolmaster, and every one who looks at the subject of this Essay on its practical side, will wish to know exactly what the advocates of instruction in science want. Is it desired that science should be taught as a necessary subject to all boys through their whole education? or as an optional subject? How many hours a week ought to be given up to it? How can we spare them? What subjects ought to be taught? and how?

I will take these questions in order, and answer them to the best of my judgment; disclaiming, of course, entirely the position of spokesman for others. I will at once say that I do not think that science should be taught through the whole of a boy's education: we do not, I think, make our teaching in schools sufficiently progressive as it is; there is no difference between the subjects of the lower and higher teaching: in the Lower School and in the Sixth form, precisely the same things are done, if we except Greek composition. This is contrary to the judgment of many who have thought on the working of the system, and is contrary also to the system of the French and German schools. And science is one of those subjects which I would, on many grounds, not introduce into the lower part of the school at all, or at least only in a modified form, which will be explained hereafter. There, more arithmetic, more French, and some geometrical drawing might be taught with great advantage. Science should be introduced into a school beginning at the top, and going downwards gradually, to a point which will be indicated by experience. At this point it should become compulsory, and be necessarily learnt by a boy until he reaches the higher part of the school. Here Science may be made alternative with something else, and here also some small portion of classical work may be allowed to be commuted for further scientific work, such as chemical analysis, or higher physics and mathematics; and *vice versâ:* any of these being remitted on the understanding that the time so given is really devoted to some other study.

Then as to the time to be devoted to science. Two hours a week, with the same time for preparation out of school, is the time given at Rugby, and is as much as I would wish to see the subject started with. I do not doubt however that ultimately it will be thought better to increase this, in the upper part of the school, to three or four hours a week. This seems too little to ask, and the advocates of science outside schools will disallow so petty a claim. But there is very little experience of the working of scientific teaching in great schools; there is at present so slight a recognition of science in schools on the part of the Universities, that any public school which gave up much time to science, would be hopelessly out of the race at the Universities. And this would be suicidal. If the reform is on sound principles, let science gain a footing only, and a friendly struggle for existence will point out whether the foreigner can be naturalised, and flourish.

Next as to the parts of science to be taught, and the methods of teaching; and the discussion of these must be given at some length.

It is important to distinguish at once, and clearly, between *scientific information* and *training in science*. "In other words," to quote from the Report of the Committee appointed by the Council of the British Association to consider the best means for promoting Scientific Education in Schools, "between general literary acquaintance with scientific facts, and the more minute and accurate knowledge that may be gained by studying the facts and methods at first hand, under the guidance of a competent teacher. Both of these are valuable; it is very desirable, for example, that boys should have some general information about the ordinary phenomena of nature, such as the simple facts of Astronomy, of Geology, of Physical Geography, and of elementary Physiology. On the other hand, the scientific habit of mind, which is the principal benefit resulting from scientific training, and which is of incalculable value, whatever be the pursuits of after life, can better be attained by a thorough knowledge of the facts and principles of one science, than by a general acquaintance with what has been said or written about many. Both of these should co-exist, we think, at any school which professes to offer the highest liberal education."

With these remarks I need hardly say that I most heartily concur.

There may be used in the lower part of the school, some work on Physical Geography, embracing the elements of the subjects above-named; and it will be found extremely convenient to introduce short courses of lectures on such subjects as these, even in the higher parts of the school. For since new boys are perpetually coming, and it is impossible that a new course of lectures on Botany, or on Mechanics, should be started in every division of the school at the beginning of every term, without requiring the number of natural science masters to be almost indefinitely increased, there must be some collecting place, a class in which the new boys shall accumulate until they are numerous enough to form a body to enter on the regular course. This must be a class in which physical Geography, including if the master likes, the elements of Geology and Astronomy, is taught. In such classes as these the ideas of boys are expanded; fresh books are opened to them; and some will avail themselves of the opening, and learn a good deal about the subjects spoken of: but the value is more literary than scientific; and even after the most careful teaching will be found disappointing. In lecturing on such subjects as Geology, Astronomy, or Physical Geography, the master never can be sure that the ideas he has so clearly in his own mind are seized by all his boys. There seems to be a deficiency in powers of conception on the part of very many boys. Theorists may say what they please, but it is true that the act of the mind in forming a conception is difficult to excite. There is a marvellous, truly marvellous, want of imagination in many minds, a want of power to form and keep in view a distinct image of the thing reasoned or spoken about. It is not only want of attention, but there seems to be a total separation in some minds between words and things, perhaps the result, in part, of early teaching; so that the knowledge apparently gained is sometimes wholly unsound. I will instance what I mean. I once gave three lectures on coal, in such a course of Geology. During those three lectures, every individual in the class handled and examined some scores of specimens, to illustrate the vegetable origin of coal; and no part of the subject was left unillustrated. One, however, in an examination paper, in reply to a question about coal, answered exactly as follows : " Coal is supposed by some persons to be a kind of inflammable substance, and must therefore be classed among the igneous rocks." And another once told me that nummulitic limestone (after handling and examining it), was made by little fishes, who lived in the limestone and carried limestone to the mountains from the sea; and answers that show the same total want of conception are common. So it will be seen that something else is meant when men of science and writers on education urge, that instruction in science should form part of all liberal education.

The mental training to be got from the study of science is the main reason for its introduction into schools. It is with reference to this that the subjects of instruction, and the methods of instruction, must be chosen. It is important, therefore, that what is meant by *mental training* should be distinctly understood. Training is the cultivation bestowed on any set of faculties with the object of developing them. It is possible to train the body, and to train the mind, for a great variety of purposes, some very foolish ones. But in all cases the training consists in *doing*. If you wish to swim, you must go into the water and swim as best you can : if you wish to box, there is no way of learning but by boxing: if you wish to study music or drawing, you must play and sing or draw : and thus in educating others you must make them *do* whatever you intend them to learn to do, and select subjects and circumstances in which *doing* is most facilitated. Now, laying aside out of consideration the mere accumulation of statistical information, and all kinds of education except intellectual, it is clear that this ultimately divides itself into the training of the artistic and logical faculties. And the logical faculties are of two kinds. It is by a logical faculty that we are able to understand other men's thoughts and apprehend new ideas. The cultivated, intelligent, imaginative mind is one in which this receptive faculty is strong. Nothing so marks the uneducated man as his dulness, his incapacity, in understanding what you say to him, if you depart in the slightest degree from the range of his daily thoughts. For the ordinary intercourse of men of education, for the spread and fertility of active thought, this faculty of intelligence is invaluable. Again, it is by a logical faculty that the mind deals with things and the relations of things. The mind which is thoughtful rather than receptive or imaginative, which studies phenomena, be they in mental philosophy, in politics, or in natural science, with a view to elicit and establish the true relations that exist among these phenomena, is the type of the mind in which the logical faculty of investigation is well trained. Nothing so marks the imperfectly educated man as his helplessness when dealing with facts instead of men, and his insecurity both in arriving at truth from them, and in judging of the validity of the conclusions of others. For the advance of thought, on all subjects which require thought, this faculty of investigation is indispensable. Probably no study will cultivate one of these faculties and wholly neglect the others, but all studies aim principally at one or other of these. A study of the classical languages, for example, is an artistic exercise, and moreover it educates the receptive faculties in a manner in which no other study educates them. The study of a language and literature not our own is the best preparation for entering into the thoughts of others; but even when best taught and best learned it can only be a very imperfect exercise in logic, for it omits nearly the whole of the logic of induction. The study of science, on the other hand, while not without its influence on even the artistic powers, and exercising in a remarkable degree the powers of intelligence of a certain kind, deals mainly with the faculty of investigation, and trains the mind to ponder and reflect on the significance of facts. And the methods of these studies are in many respects precisely the same. Models and exercises are given by the one; models and exercises by the other. Thucydides must be read, and Latin prose must be written, by the student of form and style; and the man who would cultivate his powers of thought must read his Newton, and study Experimental Physics. And as the student of Thucydides and Plato is likely to gain in clearness and brilliance of expression, and an insight into history and humanity, in intelligent and ready apprehension of the thoughts of others, in versatility, and in polish ; so the student of natural science is likely to bring with him to the study of philosophy, or politics, or business, or his profession, whatever it may be, a more active and original mind, a sounder judgment and a clearer head, in consequence of his study. A good style perhaps may be got by reading and writing ; thinking is learnt by thinking. And therefore that method of giving scientific instruction is best which most stimulates *thought*; and those subjects which afford the best illustrations of the best method ought to be selected for instruction in schools.

Now there are two different methods of teaching science: one, the method of investigation; the other, the method of authority. The first starts with the concrete and works up to the abstract; starts with facts and ends with laws : begins with the known, and proceeds to the unknown; the second starts with what we call the principles of the science; announces laws and includes the facts under them : declares the unknown and applies it to the known. The first demands faith, the second criticism. Of the two, the latter is the easier, and the former by far the better. But the latter is seen in most text-books, and is the method on which many unscientific people ground their disapproval of science. What this former method is, and why it is the better, will be seen by the following remarks.

In the first place, then, *knowledge must precede science:* for science is nothing else but systematized experience and knowledge. In its extreme applications this principle is obvious enough : it would be absurd to teach boys classification from minerals, or the power of experimental science by an investigation into the organic bases. A certain broad array of facts must pre-exist before scientific methods can be applied.[1] This order cannot be reversed. And this is illustrated by the profound analogy that exists between the growth of scientific knowledge in an individual and in the world. Generation after generation of men passed away, and the world patiently accumulated experience and observation of facts ; and then there sprang up in the world the uncontrollable desire to ascertain the sequences in nature, and to penetrate to the deep-lying principles of natural philosophy. And the same desire is based in the individual on the same kind of experience. Where there is wide knowledge of facts, science of some kind is sure to spring up. After centuries of experience the *Philosophiæ naturalis principia* were published.

And, secondly, this knowledge must be homogeneous with pre-existing knowledge. It is of no use to supply purely foreign facts ; they must be such as the learner already knows something of, or be so similar in kind that his knowledge of them is equally secure : such that he can piece them in with his own fragmentary but widening experience. It is to his existing knowledge,

---

[1] This truth has been entirely lost sight of in teaching elementary geometry. The extreme repulsiveness of Euclid to almost every boy is a complete proof, if indeed other proofs were wanting, that the ordinary methods of studying geometry in use at preparatory and public schools are wholly erroneous. To this I can do no more than allude here, as being my conviction after considerable experience,—a conviction which has overcome every possible prejudice to the contrary. It is much to be hoped that before long the teaching of practical geometry will precede the teaching of the science of geometry.

and to that alone, that you must dig down to get a sure foundation. And the facts of your science must reach continuously down, and rest securely thereon. Otherwise you will be building a castle in the air. Hence the master's business is to take up the knowledge that already exists; to systematize and arrange it; to give it extension here, and accuracy there; to connect scraps of knowledge that seemed isolated; to point out where progress is stopped by ignorance of facts; and to show how to remedy the ignorance. Rapidly knowledge crystallizes round a solid nucleus; and anything the master gives that is suited to the existing knowledge is absorbed and assimilated into the growing mass: and if he is unwise and impatient enough (as I have been scores of times) to say something which is to him perhaps a truth most vivid and suggestive, but for which his boys are unripe, he will see them, if they are really well trained, reject it as the cock despised the diamond among the barley (and the cock was quite right), or still worse, less wise than the cock, swallow it whole as a dead and choking formula.

On these grounds then, in addition to other obvious ones, Botany and Experimental Physics claim to be the standard subjects for the scientific teaching at schools. In both there pre-exists some solid and familiar knowledge. Both can so be taught as to make the learner advance from the known to the unknown—from his observations and experiments to his generalizations and laws, and ascend by continuous steps from induction to induction, and never once feel that he is carried away by a stream of words, and is reasoning about words rather than things. The logical processes they involve are admirable and complete illustrations of universal logic, and yet are not too difficult. These considerations mark the inferiority, in this respect, of Geology and Physiology, in which the doctrines must far outrun the facts at a boy's command, and which require so much knowledge before the doctrines can be seen to be well founded. And these considerations exclude Chemistry, as an elementary subject at least, since there is so little pre-existing knowledge in the learner's mind on which the foundations can be laid. On all grounds the teaching of Chemistry should follow that of Experimental Physics. To this point, however, I shall have again occasion to refer.

Unless this method of investigation is followed, the teaching of science may degenerate, with an amazing rapidity, into cramming. To be crammed is to have words and formulæ given before the ideas and laws are realized. Geology and Chemistry are frightfully crammable. But Botany and Experimental Physics are by no means so easy to cram. What they might become with bad text-books and a bad teacher I cannot, indeed, say; but it is a very important consideration. For it is possible to teach even Botany and Experimental Physics with exquisite perverseness, so as to deprive them of all their singular advantages as subjects for elementary training in science. It is possible to compel the learning the names of the parts of a flower before the condition of existence of a name, viz. that it is seen to be wanted, is fulfilled; to cumber the learner with a terminology that is unspeakably repulsive when given too soon; given before the induction which justifies the name has been gone through; to give the principles of classification before a sufficient acquaintance with species has called out the ideas of resemblance and difference, and has shown the necessity of classification; to give theories of typical form when it seems a wild and grotesque romance; to teach, in fact, by the method of authority. And this may be done by truly scientific men, fully believing that this is the true and only method. Witness Adrien de Jussieu's " Botanique."

The true method is assuredly to begin by widening for your boys the basis of facts, and instantly to note uniformities of a low order, and let them hazard a few generalizations. The boys will far outrun their master. Their tendency to make generalizations of the most astounding kind is both amusing and instructive; it constantly reminds me of the ancient Greek Philosophy; it is the proof that there is both the power to be trained, and a need of the training. A theory is necessary to observation. Make them verify, and expurgate, and prune, and, if need be, reject their theories by a constant appeal to facts; sympathise with them in their search for truth, and so search for more facts and more accurate observations; and thus the crystal pyramid of their science grows, its base ever widening, its summit ever rising.

The art of the schoolmaster is a maieutic art now as it was in the days of Socrates; it is still his business[1] to make his boys bring their notions to the light of day, to the test of facts; constantly to require verification; but as often as possible to give them the pleasure of discovery. He may guide them to the treasure, but let him

---

[1] Βασανίζειν παντὶ τρόπῳ πότερον εἴδωλον καὶ ψεῦδος ἀποτίκτει τοῦ νεοῦ ἡ διάνοια, ἢ γόνιμόν τε καὶ ἀληθές.—Plato, Theætetus.

unselfishly give them the delight of at least thinking they have found it. This is the charm that tempts them on, and is the highest reward they can win. At first the seeming progress is slow, but it soon accelerates, and the avidity for learning soon compensates for the apparent poverty of the results at first.

I insist upon this point because I am convinced that it is very important, and very likely to be overlooked: and as Botany seems the best subject for beginning to train boys in scientific methods, and as no English work[1] is thoroughly to be recommended as a guide to botanical teaching, I shall devote a brief paragraph or two to the illustration from Botany of what I hold to be the true method of *beginning* to teach science. It is a subject, however, for an essay of itself.

Suppose then your class of thirty or forty boys before you, of ages from thirteen to sixteen, as they sit at their first botanical lesson; some curious to know what is going to happen, some resigned to anything; some convinced that it is all a folly. You hand round to each boy several specimens, say of the Herb Robert; and taking one of the flowers, you ask one of them to describe the parts of it. "Some pink leaves" is the reply. "How many?" "Five." "Any other parts?" "Some little things inside." "Anything outside?" "Some green leaves." "How many?" "Five." "Very good. Now pull off the five green leaves outside, and lay them side by side; next pull off the five pink leaves, and lay them side by side: and now examine the little things inside. What do you find?" "A lot of little stalks or things." "Pull them off and count them:" they find ten. Then show them the

---

[1] Oliver's Botany is the nearest approach to a good text-book.

little dust-bags at the top, and finally the curiously constructed central column, and the carefully concealed seeds. By this time all are on the alert. Then we resume: the parts in that flower are, outer green envelope, inner coloured envelope, the little stalks with dust bags, and the central column with the seeds. Then you give them all wall flowers: and they are to write down what they find: and you go round and see what they write down. Probably some one has found six "*storks*" inside his wall-flower, and you make him write on the black-board for the benefit of the class the curious discovery, charging them all to note any such accidental varieties in future; and you make them very minutely notice all the structure of the central column. Then you give them all the common pelargonium and treat it similarly; and by the end of the hour they have learnt one great lesson, the existence of the four floral whorls, though they have yet not heard the name.

Next lesson-time they come in looking more in earnest, and you give them single stocks and white alyssum, which they discover to be wonderfully like the wall flower; and you have a lot of flowers of vegetable marrow, some of which are being passed round while you draw two of them on the board. The difference is soon discovered; and you let them guess about the uses of the parts of the flower. The green outer leaves protect it in the bud; the central organ is for the seeds; but what is the use of the others. Then you relate stories of how it was found out what the use of the dust-bags is: how patient Germans lay in the sun all day to wait for the insects coming: and how the existence of a second rare specimen of some foreign tree was found out in Paris, by its long-widowed spouse in the Jardin des Plantes at last producing perfect seeds. A little talk about bees, and moths, and midges, and such creatures, finding out what they have seen, and your second lecture is over.

In the third lecture you take the garden geranium, and beg them to examine it very closely to see if it is symmetrical. Several will discover the unsymmetrical outer green leaves; one or two will discover the hollow back of the stem: then the pelargonium, and its more visible unsymmetry: then the common tropæolum: in each of which they find also the same parts, and count, and describe them: and lastly the tropæolum Canariense, with its grotesque irregularity: and they are startled to find that the curious-looking flower they know so well is constructed on the same type, and is called by the same name; and by the end of the lesson they have learned something of irregular flowers, as referred to regular types,—something of continuity in nature.

So in succession, for I cannot give more detail, you lead them through flowers where the parts cohere, as in the campanula, through plants deficient or odd, through roses, and mignonette, and honeysuckle, and all the simple flowers you can find; till they thoroughly know the scheme on which a simple flower is made. Then you challenge them to a dandelion or daisy: and each has to write down his ideas. Your one or two geniuses will hit it: some will be all wrong, without a shadow of doubt; the majority fairly puzzled. You give them no hint of the solution, tell them to lay it aside;

and you give them the little thrift, and challenge them to find its seeds, and how they are attached. This many will do, and pick out the little seed with its long thread of attachment, and then they will go back to their dandelions with the key to the structure; and find its seeds too, and be charmed to discover the remains of its poor outer green envelope, and even its little dust-bags. How proud they are of the discovery! they think they have the key of knowledge now. And then you begin a little terminology,—calyx and sepals, corolla and petals, stamens and pollen, pistil and stigma, and so on; and test their recollection of the forms of all the flowers they have examined. Then you notice the spiral arrangement of leaves on a twig of oak, or thorn, or willow, and the internodes; and the over-lapping of the sepals of the rose and Herb Robert; the alternance of the parts; and finally they work out the idea, that the floral whorls grow on the stem, and are a sort of depressed spiral of leaves with the internodes suppressed. A few monstrosities and pictures are shewn, and the grand generalization is made; the pistils are re-examined with fresh interest to test the theory; and all their old knowledge is raked up once more. Then, too, the value of the theory is criticised; and a lesson of caution is learnt.

Then a step forward is made towards classification, by cohesion and adhesion of parts; and the floral schedule is worked; and so step by step to fruits, and leaves, and stems, and roots, and the wondrous modifications of parts for special uses, as in climbing plants; and the orchids, which are a grand puzzle till a series of pictures from Darwin step in to explain the use of the parts and plan of the flower. Then some chemistry of the plant is introduced with some experiments, and the functions of all the organs are discussed. And lastly, strict descriptive terms are given, and the rest of the course is occupied by the history and the systems of classification, with constant reference however to the other conceptions that the class has gained.

Such a method as this has many advantages. It is thoroughly scientific, however irregular it may seem, and a professor of Botany may smile or shed tears over it for anything I care; and the knowledge is gained on a sound basis of original observation. Whatever flower a boy sees after a few lessons, he looks at with interest, as modifying the view of flowers he has attained to. He is tempted by his discoveries: he is on the verge of the unknown, and perpetually transferring to the known: all that he sees finds a place in his theories, and in turn reacts upon them, for his theories are growing. He is fairly committed to the struggle in the vast field of observation, and he learns that the test of a theory is its power of including facts. He learns that he must use his eyes, and his reason, and that then he is equipped with all that is necessary for discovering truth. He learns that he is capable of judging of other people's views, and of forming an opinion of his own. He learns that nothing in the plant, however minute, is unimportant; that he must observe truthfully and carefully; that he owes only temporary allegiance to the doctrines of his master, and not a perpetual faith. No wonder that Botany, so taught, is interesting: no wonder that M. Demogeot, who visited some English schools last year at the request of the French Emperor, expressed himself to me as charmed with the vivacity and intelligence of the botanical class of one of my colleagues.'

Very possibly a master might make his boys get up a book on Botany, and learn it in the order in which it stands in the book,—cellules and parenchyme, protoplasm and chlorophyll, stems and medullary rays, petioles and phyllodes, rhizomes and bulbs, hairs and glands, endosmose and exosmose, secretions and excretions, and so on, and so on; and ultimately come to the flower and fruit; and possibly a boy of good digestion might survive it and pass a respectable examination in a year's time. But this is not the aim. And even if in this way a greater number of facts could be learned, it would be far inferior to the method of investigation. A master must never forget that his power of teaching facts and principles is far inferior to a willing pupil's power of learning and mastering them. He must inspire his boys, and rely on them: nor will he be disappointed. Those who have in them anything of the naturalist will collect and become acquainted with a large number of species, and follow out the study with care and accuracy; and the mass, to whom an extensive knowledge of species is a very unimportant matter, but who can appreciate a sound method of investigation and proof, will have gained all that they can gain from botanical teaching. And it must be remembered by those who speak of teaching science, and yet have never tried it, that a method which would succeed with a few naturalists, might utterly fail with the mass.

There is a time in the growth of mind in which there

---

[1] The spirit of this method is admirably illustrated in Le Maoût's "Leçons élémentaires de Botanique, fondées sur l'Analyse de 50 Plantes vulgaires."

is considerable activity and considerable power of accumulation, but little power of method. And to insist at this stage on rigorous definitions, on sternest formality, is to forget the indications given by nature alike in the growth of the individual and of the world. In a boy's mind is only the dawning twilight of science, which brightens out slowly, if at all, into the perfect day.

A boy leaves the botanical class as a rustic leaves the militia after three months' drill. He has gained something: he is more awake, can listen and learn better, knows what he is about; in fact he has been drilled. Year after year I have had new boys and old in my classes, and always have been able to notice that at first the new boys seemed to be at a positive disadvantage in competing with the old, although the subject I was teaching had no reference to Botany.

The next training subject is unquestionably Experimental Physics. This term is used commonly to denote the sciences which can be studied experimentally, without an extensive knowledge of mathematics, and excludes Chemistry. Mechanics and Mechanism, Heat and Light, Electricity and Magnetism, Hydrostatics, Hydrodynamics, Pneumatics, and Acoustics are the principal branches of the subject. In selecting from them the subjects most fit for use at schools, and in choosing the order in which they should be taught, we must be guided by the principles already enunciated. We must proceed from the concrete to the abstract, from the familiar to the strange, from the science of masses to the science of molecules. Hence Mechanics and Mechanism must come first. In a year most boys are able to learn the great principles of Statics and Dynamics, and the elements of Mechanism, such as the ordinary methods of converting one kind of motion into another. They become tolerably familiar with the ideas of motion and space, and time, and form, in their exact numerical relations. Ignorance of arithmetic and the want of ideas in practical geometry are the main hindrances in their way; but even they are improved by the many illustrations of arithmetic and geometry that are afforded by Mechanics, and by the growth of exactness in all ideas of quantity and form as expressed by numbers. Arithmetic is too often the science of pounds, shillings, and pence alone; and by being so limited it loses in dignity and in interest, and in clearness. In Mechanics, also, the notion of force is constantly present in its commonest and simplest forms; and in this respect also this branch of science serves as the best introduction to the later branches.

Hydrostatics and Pneumatics, I do not doubt, are the best subjects to take next: the range of these subjects that could be taught at school is not great; and they may be learnt very thoroughly and exactly, and provide very good illustrations of the principles of the subjects that precede them. Hydrodynamics, Acoustics, and Geometrical Optics will be only studied profitably beyond the bare elements by those who have special talent for mathematical or experimental investigation, and should, I think, be in general reserved for University teaching. Physical Optics unquestionably should be excluded from school teaching.

The next year's course should be Heat and the elements of Electricity. By the time boys have reached this stage they are far more able to acquire new subjects than in the previous stages, and are fit to enter on these branches of physics, if they have studied the earlier subjects intelligently. And of all subjects of experimental investigation, Heat[1] seems to me the best for work at schools. Three times I have taken classes in Heat, and with more satisfactory results than in any other subject. The phenomena of Heat are so universal and so familiar; it has so central a position among the physical sciences; its experimental methods are so perfect; it affords such a variety of illustrations of logical processes; that it seems unrivalled as a subject for training in science. And allowing for seventy lectures in the year, it is clear that this year's course will allow of some time being given to Electricity. This may be made an enormous subject, but I apprehend that it will not be worth while to attempt its more difficult branches, but to reserve them for the University and for private study.

I will repeat, that a boy can learn, when he knows how to learn, far more than a master can teach; and it is at increasing the boy's power that the master must aim unweariedly. And by combining a voluntary and a compulsory system, giving opportunities for learning something of the higher branches, and insisting on a sound knowledge of the more elementary parts of Physics in which the teaching can be most stimulative and suggestive, all requirements will be met.

The methods of teaching Physics will be different in different hands; they will vary with the knowledge, the enthusiasm, the good sense, the good temper, the practical skill, and the object, of the teacher. If the thing to be aimed at is to make them pass a good examination as

---

[1] On this subject there is a very good text-book by Balfour Stewart.

soon as the subject is read, the best means will be to put a text-book into the hands of everyone, and require certain parts of it to be learnt, and to illustrate them in an experimental lecture with explanations. The lecture may be made very clear and good; and this will be an attractive and not difficult method of teaching, and will meet most of the requirements. It fails, however, in one. The boy is helped over all the difficulties; he is never brought face to face with nature and her problems; what cost the world centuries of thought is told him in a minute; his attention, clearness of understanding, and memory are all exercised; but the one power which the study of physical science ought pre-eminently to exercise, and almost to create, the power of bringing the mind into contact with facts, of seizing their relations, of eliminating the irrelevant by experiment and comparison, of groping after ideas and testing them by their adequacy—in a word, of exercising all the active faculties which are required for an investigation in any matter—these may lie dormant in the class while the most learned lecturer experiments with facility and explains with clearness.

Theory and experience alike convince me that the master who is teaching a class quite unfamiliar with scientific method, ought to make his class teach themselves, by thinking out the subject of the lecture with them, taking up their suggestions and illustrations, criticizing them, hunting them down, and proving a suggestion barren or an illustration inapt; starting them on a fresh scent when they are at fault, reminding them of some familiar fact they had overlooked, and so eliciting out of the chaos of vague notions that are afloat on the matter in hand, be it the laws of motion, the evaporation of water, or the origin of the drift, something of order, and concatenation, and interest, before the key to the mystery is given, even if after all it has to be given. Training to think, not to be a mechanic or surveyor, must be first and foremost as his object. So valuable are the subjects intrinsically, and such excellent models do they provide, that the most stupid and didactic teaching will not be useless; but it will not be the same source of power that "the method of investigation" will be in the hands of a good master. Some few will work out a logic of proof, and a logic of discovery, when the facts and laws that are discovered and proved have had time to lie and crystallize in their minds. But imbued with scientific method they scarcely will be, unless it springs up spontaneously in them.

For all classes, except those which are beginning, the union of the two methods is best. If they have once thoroughly learnt that the truths of science are to be got from what they see, and not from the assertions of a master or a text-book, they can never quite forget it, and allow their science to exist in a cloud-world apart from the earth. And undoubtedly the rigid and exact teaching from a book, insuring a complete and formularised and producible knowledge, is very valuable, especially with older classes.

The work out of school for a natural science lecture consists chiefly at first in writing notes on the previous lecture. When the lecture has been discursive, and the method hard to follow, some help may be given by a recapitulation; but in general it may be left to the boys. It is an admirable exercise in composition. To reduce to order the preliminary facts, to bring out the unity in them, to illustrate, to describe, to argue, and that about things in which they are interested, and for which they feel a match, are the very best exercises that can be put before boys. They begin with a helplessness and inanity almost incredible, improve constantly, and end generally by writing these notes very well. And in the higher classes the working of examples and problems may well be thrown in part on the out-of-school hours.

There are three other subjects on which a few words should be said. These are Chemistry, and Geology, and Physiology.

I am fully convinced, and could support my conviction by that of others, that Chemistry is not a good subject for lecture instruction to beginners in science. Laboratory work must precede, in order that a certain degree of familiarity with facts may be acquired before they are analysed and methodized scientifically. It can be taught, even to young boys, and so can anything else; and it has the advantage of being rather amusing; but as an exercise in reasoning it is very deficient. The notions of force, cause, composition of causes, are too abstruse in this subject for boys to get any hold of. Hence it is, as a matter of fact, accepted as a mass of authoritative dogmas. It is not the conclusiveness but the ingenuity of the proofs that is appreciated. It is of all subjects the most liable to cram, and the most useless, as a branch of training, when crammed. Most of it requires memory, and memory alone. The manufacture of alum, the sources of borax, and the properties of the oxides of nitrogen, are the kind of knowledge that is got by chemical lectures, and demanded in most examinations in

Chemistry. Now this is a part of the necessary knowledge of a chemist; and to one who has, by laboratory work and leisurely thought, arranged his knowledge, and digested it into science, it is valuable; but the acquisition of it is not a valuable process when it is got by lectures alone. And as laboratory work is not likely to form an integral part of school education, Chemistry ought not, I think, to take an early place in the scientific course. It it most desirable however that schools should possess laboratories, into which boys of some talent may be drafted, and there prepared for the profitable attendance on good chemical lectures in the higher part of the school.

Geology is a popular and attractive subject with boys, but it lies outside the subjects which best illustrate scientific method. The largeness of the ideas in it; the great inferences from little facts, as they seem to boys; the wide experience of scenery, and rocks, and fossils, and natural history, which it seems to require; the very unfinished condition of it; are all reasons which make its advocates enthusiastic, but unfit it for the staple of school teaching. Nevertheless, the value of it on other grounds, such as its interest, its bearing on all kinds of thought, its position as typical of Palætiological sciences, and the opportunities it offers for original investigations in most places, seems to me so high, that I think it ought to be introduced parenthetically into the course of instruction in whatever way or place may seem most convenient.

Physiology cannot be taught to classes at school. Nor ought it be learnt before Physics and Chemistry. A most enthusiastic advocate of Physiology at school talked over the subject with me at Rugby. Practical work, he admitted, was necessary; and that it was impossible. I could not give my class forty rats on Tuesday, at 9.15, to dissect for an hour, and then put them away till Saturday at the same hour. And the other subjects, if well taught, will have given boys a method and a knowledge which will fit them for acquiring, by reading alone, even if they cannot have practical work, some intelligent acquaintance with the doctrines and facts of Physiology.

Is education in natural science a panacea for stupid boys? Will it herald in the golden age to schoolmasters when all boys are to be industrious and intelligent? It will be found that first-rate ability is as rare in this as in anything else. All the different subjects have their stars at school, as in the great world. And great inability is rare also. The great majority display intelligent interest and power of learning which does not amount to original genius, of course, but is genuine intellectual work. The active thought of the master is contagious, for he is visibly thinking as he teaches. And science admits of having excellent questions asked about it. The Germans have a proverb, "Mit fragen wird man weise." And it is true in a double sense. To put a question well is no mean attainment. Many will be asked simply from muddleheadedness, and will answer themselves when a distinct statement is insisted on. I am sure that more is gained by insisting on good questions than by giving good answers. So therefore the effect on the whole is to make boys more intelligent, to widen their range of ideas, to make them more active-minded, more logical, less one-sided. But while it succeeds with the great majority in accomplishing this at least, still it is not a panacea. There are some whom science, like everything else, fails to educate. The author of "Daydreams of a Schoolmaster" has, indeed, said, that a physically healthy booby is as rare as a live Dodo. I do not agree with him. Boobies are not extinct: in the interests of science—say for preservation in the British Museum, or for dissection at the College of Surgeons—two or three very fine specimens might be procured in a certain great school. In young specimens, however, the species is almost as difficult to determine as it is in young ammonites ; and the old ones have a singular imitative instinct (apparently with a view to concealment from their natural foes), and externally resemble persons of intelligence.

The truth is, that there is no place like school for having notions of equality driven, by dire experience, out of one's head. There are scores and scores of boys whom you may educate how you will, and they will know very little when you have done, and know that little ill. There are boys of slipshod, unretentive, inactive minds, whom neither Greek grammar nor natural science, neither schoolmasters nor angels, could convert into active and cultivated men. They are, as one of our own poets has described them—

> ἀμελεῖς σοφίας, ἀμελεῖς δ' ἀρετῆς,
> ἀμελεῖς δὲ λόγου, πάντων δ' ἀμαθεῖς,
> περί τ' οὐρανίων κἀπιχθονίων,
> περί τε φθογγῶν ἑτερογλώσσων,
> βαρβαρόφωνοι, βυρβορόθυμοι,
> γράμμασιν ἐχθροί, συρφετὸς ἄλλως
> Ἀκαδημίας, ἄχθος ἀρούρας,
>   ὀκνηροὶ μὲν
> παῖδες, ἀχρεῖοι δὲ πολῖται.

and in most respects this description is true ; happily

not in all. Those who are ἀμελεῖς σοφίας are not necessarily ἀμελεῖς ἀρετῆς, and among the πάντων ἀμαθεῖς are those who, as experience teaches us, may become useful citizens.

There is no great mass of opinion unfavourable to making natural science a regular part of school instruction; and there is a large, and not very inactive mass of opinion favourable to it. But progress in this direction is not likely to be very rapid, as both the men and the machinery that are to work the subject have to be created. At present a Natural Science master is very hard to get. When the demand begins, doubtless more will qualify themselves. And most schools are unprovided with buildings and apparatus necessary for teaching science properly. These essentials cannot be supplied without considerable expense; that is, in general, without increasing the cost-price of education. And schools naturally hesitate before raising their terms with this object. They wait till they are sure that the opinion of their clientela will sanction both their object and their method of attaining it.

But more than all, the influence of the universities and colleges is on the whole unfavourable. The universities, by their Triposes and prizes, affect generally the studies in the colleges. But the colleges, by their scholarships, exhibitions, entrance examinations, prizes, and lectures, direct the studies of the schools throughout the kingdom. They do this to an extent of which they are, in general, unconscious. If the colleges, for example, ceased to demand Latin verses for their scholarships, Latin verse would almost die before the breath of their disfavour. If the colleges offered scholarships and exhibitions, to acknowledge and encourage the study of science at schools, then the teaching of science would at once be naturalized in most of the schools which contribute many men to the Universities. Up to the present time Oxford has taken the lead in this: Christchurch, Balliol, Merton, Magdalen, and New College all encourage natural science more or less. And their recognition of it, though very small, has been most useful. But at Cambridge very little is done by the colleges; and the two great colleges, Trinity and St. John's, have hitherto out of their large revenues, liberally expended for the encouragement of some other branches of learning, devoted literally nothing to reward the successful prosecution of natural science. Hence all the abler boys at school are in fact heavily bribed to study either classics or mathematics, even though their genius is for natural science. And from this want of recognition of science by the colleges generally, and from a belief that it is founded on a well-grounded disapproval of science as a part of early liberal education, and from some distrust of it as a possible disturber of classical tradition, schools naturally hang back from taking the step of incorporating natural science into their course of study.[1]

[1] This was written in April. Since that time Trinity College has appointed a Lecturer in Science, and St. John's College has made it known that an exhibition of 50*l*. a year, tenable for three years, will in future be offered in the spring for competition in natural and physical science. This is a great and important first step, and will doubtless soon be followed by further movement in the same direction. When some attainments in physical science are looked on as a necessary part of higher culture, as a means of forming a superior mind, the great colleges will not fail to encourage these attainments by a much more extensive recognition. The great colleges will remember that they have not only to train common minds for common professions, but to keep alive and advance all kinds of human culture, and knowledge, and

Cambridge, moreover, must undergo a great change of disposition, and therefore of its institutions, before science will flourish there. For science requires above all things the ardent and devoted love of knowledge: it requires enthusiasm for study: it cannot live where teaching has taken the place of learning; and where a nearly stationary unprogressive condition of learning is tolerated, and is supposed to be even favourable to the education of students. Whatever change is made for the revival of learning at Cambridge will be favourable to the cultivation of science there. Nothing, I believe, is of greater importance as affecting the progress of education in England than the reforms, now whispered, which must soon be made at Cambridge.

Besides the immediate results of the recognition of science as a part of the higher liberal education in improving the working of schools, there are other remoter effects of much greater importance. To them, in the concluding paragraphs of an essay already too long, it is not possible to do more than briefly allude. It is impossible not to feel that with the spread of scientific modes of thought are bound up all the highest interests of philosophy and religion. Much of modern logic, and philosophy, and thought is incomprehensible except to men trained in science. To any one tolerably conversant with the distressful state of mind of thoughtful men on some religious questions, most welcome will be any progress which may help to free our successors from the same partition of soul, the same divided allegiance, from which the present

philosophy. And in the present century physical science is perhaps the greatest school of philosophy.

generation suffers. It cannot long be possible for us to consent to turn out men into the world totally unprepared to meet the problems which will necessarily force themselves on their notice; to turn out men, professedly of the highest education, totally unfurnished with true scientific method and knowledge, totally unable to meet the shallowest arguments from a false philosophy of nature brought on the side of materialism or atheism; who will talk glibly of the supernatural, and yet be ignorant of the natural. Does it seem strange to hail as a friend to religion that scientific spirit so often denounced as hostile? Yet how can it be otherwise? "Are God and nature then at strife" indeed? At present there is secret, if not avowed, hostility between religion and science, or at any rate a distrustful toleration; nothing but active co-operation will permanently reconcile them. To endeavour not to see the results and tendencies of modern science is folly in the highest degree. The study and knowledge of the seen is sure to react on the study of the unseen; and he will entertain these studies in perfect harmony, and he only, in whom the scientific and religious ideas are allowed to grow up, not in antagonism, but fearlessly and freely, side by side, co-operating in the formation of a reverent, active, and independent mind, and well balanced judgment. To think otherwise is to think that half the world is God's and the other half the devil's.

We inherit a noble inheritance, the achievements of the intellectual giants of past ages carried forward by the intelligent sympathy of thousands of their fellows. It confers on its inheritors a calmness, and dignity, and confidence which will ever increase. For them no fear of to-morrow's discoveries breaks the night's rest: they utter no little shrieking cries of alarm: they are confident in the power and in the ultimate unity of truth. Not to any generation is it given to outstep its place in the history of philosophy; and the work of our generation is clear: it is to ascertain what is and what is not true, by patient and trustful investigation, and to have unbounded faith in truth. To later generations it is reserved to bridge the chasm that may now seem to separate truths from truths; and to find a higher and profounder unity than we can yet imagine.

> "This fine old world of ours is but a child
> Yet in the go-cart. Patience! Give it time
> To learn its limbs. There is a Hand that guides."

VII.

THE TEACHING OF ENGLISH.

BY J. W. HALES, M.A.

"Antiquam exquirite matrem."

"Hail, native language, that by sinews weak
Didst move my first endeavouring tongue to speak,
And madest imperfect words with childish trips,
Half-unpronounced, slide through my infant lips,
Driving dumb silence from the portal-door
Where he had mutely sat two years before :
Here I salute thee, and thy pardon ask
That now I use thee in my latter task."

It may seem strange that there should exist any necessity for advocating the claims of the English language to a place among the subjects of English education. But this is not more strange than true. None of our better schools, with certain notable exceptions, dream of giving any attention to it. There is a gross want of adequate treatises dealing with it. No encouragement is given to the studying such treatises as these are; consequently, the Englishman grows up in mere ignorance of his native tongue. He can speak it, because he has heard it spoken around him from his earliest years. If he has been born and bred in what is called well-educated society, he speaks it "with propriety." He shudders duly when he hears it spoken with impropriety. But his accuracy is of a purely empirical kind. If society were suddenly to countenance and adopt some outrageous solecism, there would be nothing for him but to submit. The language might be changed just as manners are. Propriety in the one case is pretty much what it is in the other. In a word, the ordinary knowledge of English is altogether one of facts, not of principles; is thoroughly superficial, not fundamental. English is an unknown tongue in England. Something is known of French, of German, of Latin, of Greek—of most languages, with this remarkable exception.

But I propose now confining myself to a consideration of its absence, not from the country at large, but from our schools.

To begin with, how comes it to be conspicuous by its absence from our schools? While in French schools, French is taught; in German schools, German; why is English excluded from English schools? The principal answers to such a question are: 1. That a deep-rooted prejudice in favour of Latin, as the basis of what linguistic education there is, has been handed down from generation to generation, ever since the Dark Ages. 2. That another triumphant judgment has pronounced that the English language is too irregular to be capable of being systematically taught. Such has been, and is, the power of these two prejudices, that the English language never has had, and has not that attention paid it which, as the medium of communication between so many myriads of people, as the obvious and natural basis of their education, to say nothing of the great literature belonging to it, it might naturally expect and demand.

With regard to the predominant influence of Latin, I

shall here say the less, because that subject is discussed at length in another essay contained in this volume. But I must point out how detrimental to the study of our mother-tongue that monopoly has proved. It has thrown it completely into the shade, has dwarfed and stunted it. It has driven English away from the doors of our better schools, "to seek a shelter in some humbler shed." The heir has met with no favour; a stranger has occupied his place. No doubt much of this fatal estrangement has been due to the narrow spirit in which the so-called classical studies have been pursued, which cannot live on in the light of a broader scholarship. In that linguistic dispensation which seems dawning, no language is called common or unclean. Latin can no longer stand aloof from the languages of modern literatures as if they were some inferior things, of suspicious contact. That old exclusive *régime* is gone by for ever; a truer, more catholic philology recognises the interest and importance of subjects that have for many centuries been regarded with the most languid indifference, or the supremest contempt. Thus, whatever conclusion may be arrived at respecting the time and attention that may be still given to the old monopolies, there can be no doubt that the manner of the study of these should be thoroughly revised; that that Pharisaic element which still lingers tenaciously, should be most carefully expelled from it; that modern languages, instead of being industriously ignored, should be perpetually recognised, both to illustrate, and to be illustrated. But till this current century, the influence of Latin has not only not been helpful; it has been deleterious. The classical languages have been the only wear; and so satisfied and delighted with them have men been, that not a native thread, not a home-dyed colour, not a domestic pattern could be tolerated. When in course of time the growth of a class that could never affect to be learned, but yet needed some instruction, made imperative the paying some slight attention to the language of the people, then most severely did the influence of Latin damage the rising study. The vulgar grammar-maker, dazzled by the glory of the ruling language, knew no better than to transfer to English the schemes which belonged to Latin.

"Jungebat mortua vivis."

He never dreamt that the language, for which he was practising his rude grammatical midwifery, might have a character of its own, might require a scheme of its own. He knew, or thought he knew, what the grammar of any language ought to be, and he went about his work accordingly. What chance had our poor mother-tongue in the clutch of this Procrustes? The Theseus of linguistic science, the deliverer, was not born yet. So the poor language got miserably tortured, and dislocated, and mangled. Who can wonder if it failed to thrive under such treatment? if it grew haggard and deformed? All the passers by were on the side of Procrustes; and, when the victim shrieked at some particularly cruel stretch of its limbs, they called it disorderly, reprobate, vicious. In these two ways then, the dominance of Latin proved baneful to the study of English; it for many a day made that study seem despicable and unworthy—in effect, suppressed it; and, when at last it could no longer be suppressed, then still it overshadowed and withered it.

Hence, then, arose that second prejudice mentioned above as obstructing the study. The language, coerced into subjection to laws foreign to its spirit and found rebellious, got a bad name, and the usual consequences followed. It became a proverb of refractoriness. It was anathematized as utterly lawless and hopeless. Its guardians did not understand its character; they judged it by their own narrow standard; they could not conceive that there were more things in heaven and earth than were dreamt of in their philosophy; they consigned this hapless nonconformist to profound neglect. It was mad, and there was no method in its madness, they said. They took no pains to investigate its hallucinations; these did not deserve so much consideration.

No wonder, then, the study of English did not prosper. Men were content with Latin; they were discontented with English. This discontent tended to perpetuate itself, as it restrained those investigations which, if pursued, would have put an end to it for ever. The language was in fact condemned without a hearing. And there was no appeal from the sentence of that ill-informed court which condemned it. The mere fact that the classics were in possession of the field, told with fearful power against the timid claimant for a place in it. Possession gives a vast advantage in all matters. In matters of education it gives an almost insuperable advantage. Parents are, for the most part, well content that their children should be educated much as they were. They are not likely to quarrel with the *propria quæ maribus* of their youth. Distance lends its enchantment to that and such like horrors. Moreover, as to what changes may be necessary, they put their trust in the schoolmaster to whom they confide their offspring. Schoolmasters as a race—whatever glorious exceptions there may be—cannot be expected to embrace readily alteration and change: they have learnt their part once and for all, and will not usually be anxious to unlearn or relearn it. They have mastered more or less adequately one particular system of training, and do not care to modify or abandon it. Then if we consider how extensive the machinery of any established system— how endless its hand-books, how enormous the literature belonging to it—we shall see yet more fully what a supreme advantage possession is, and what powerful incentives there always are to conservatism in educational subjects. The educational literature of English is yet in its very infancy.

These three considerations—the general unreadiness in schools to change their routine, the particular unreadiness to change it in the present case, the distinct reluctance to change it in favour of English, if any change at all were made—do, I think, sufficiently account for the forlorn condition in which the study of English now is, and distinctly show that no inference can fairly be drawn from that condition to the disparagement of its capabilities as an educational subject. They demonstrate emphatically that that condition is the misfortune of English, not its fault. The language has been weighed in the balances certainly, and found wanting; but this result has been due to the incompetence of the weighers. On this point I wish especially to insist, that English has never yet received a fair trial. Till very late years indeed it has been left in the hands of empirics and sciolists. Better men have occasionally wondered whether it was not worthy of more honourable treatment, whether it was in truth so bad as it was painted. "Ex nostratibus aliqui," writes Wallis in the seventeenth century, "quod tamen mirandum est nescio quam perplexam somniant et intricationem linguæ nostræ rationem, ut ægre possit grammaticæ leges subire." But our countrymen went on dreaming so. In a word, our language has been, ever since the Norman Conquest, the victim of prejudices. For more than a century it was thrown altogether in the background; not till the close of the fourteenth century did boys in schools translate their Latin lessons into it; not till the latter half of the nineteenth have boys begun to study it.

Now is it desirable that English boys should be taught English? And is the language teachable? or does that prejudice against it rest on some solid foundation?

As to the desirability that Englishmen should know something of their own language there can be little controversy. The most ardent disbelievers in the advisability or possibility of making English a school-subject do not doubt this. If we are to understand at all what we read, and not rest content with feeble glimmerings of its sense, then some knowledge of our language must be acquired. The question then is how this knowledge is to be acquired. The favourite answer is by learning Latin. What a singular method! When it is remembered what the prime origin of English is, and of what kind the connexion of English with Latin has been, one can only marvel at this answer, and shrewdly suspect that it is but meant to allay the distress of an uneasy conscience—a conscience murmuring at the utter neglect of the vernacular language, at the total devotion to an alien one. It may be urged that an acquaintance with Latin literature is invaluable for an understanding of English literature. This may be true. But it is surely most obvious that an acquaintance with English is simply indispensable for an understanding of English literature. But, whatever *à priori* verdict one might give on this method, how does it work? Does the smattering of Latin which the vast majority of schoolboys get, or the superior knowledge of it which is gained by the few exceptions, really perform this alleged service? I think it rather obstructs it. It lights up many English words no doubt; but on the whole, it leaves the language in its previous darkness, or even in a deeper gloom by throwing films of misconstruction between it and the eyes of the student. Practically, what knowledge of English the ordinary Englishman has, is "picked up." It is of a desultory, irregular, incoherent kind.

But is English teachable? One might imagine the language showing the same indignation at such a question as the Jew showed when seemingly suspected of incapability of revenge. "Hath not a Jew eyes? hath not a Jew hands, organs, dimensions, senses, affections, passions, &c.?" I have already explained how it comes to be possible that such a question can be asked. The inflectional virtues of Latin and Greek have blinded the world to all other virtues. English, mostly lacking them, has been stigmatised as wholly grammarless.[1]

---

[1] Gascoyne in his "Steele Glass" (1576) bids his readers pray—

"That Grammar grudge not at our English tong
Because it stands by monosyllaba
And cannot be declined as others are."

But inflections are not the soul of grammar. A language does not become ungrammatical when it passes out of that stage. The main function of grammar is concerned with more perpetual and imperishable matters. That function ceases only when a language loses its articulateness — ceases to serve for the expression of thought—ceases to be a language. However deficient the English language may be in case-endings and such grammatical landmarks,—in power of expression, in delicacy, in elasticity, in versatility, it is not deficient. So that it presents endless varieties of that grammatical culminating subject of inquiry and interest—the sentence. What an inestimable, inexhaustible mine of study is here! Then the very compositeness of the language adapts it singularly well for the teacher's use. It furnishes him at once with abundant material. He must be dull indeed who can be at a loss for subjects for lessons in English. No doubt, should English once take its place as a vulgar school-subject, innumerable text-books would quickly spring into existence. Consider of what a long growth our existing Latin and Greek school-book literature is; and consider how unsatisfactory it still is!

What I should wish to propose is, that the linguistic studies of all our schools should begin with English, should then proceed with the dead languages in the case of boys who are likely to have leisure to study them to any profit, and in other cases should proceed with English and living languages.

The study of language in English schools should begin with English—should begin at home. The way of learning is, and must be, rough and thorny; and I do

not expect what I now propose will make it smooth and
all roses. But if the road can be improved at all, if
but a few flowers can be got to grow along it, and the
torn feet can find a moment's respite, this is well worth
the doing. Obviously, what is most earnestly to be
wished for and aimed at in the formal commencement of
a child's education, is to excite his interest in his studies
—to give them some meaning to him, let him have some
inkling of their use. Their full meaning will not be
revealed to him for many a year; that will grow more
and more clear to him all his life long, if he develops
into a thoughtful man. But some meaning, some
practical significance his studies must have for him
from the beginning, if he is to pursue them with
pleasure—that is, with the highest degree of profit.
He cannot stretch a hand through time to catch the
far off interest of years. If, then, he is to learn intelligibly, he must see that there is some sense in his
studies, that these are not mere arbitrary burdens laid on
his youthful shoulders. Otherwise, things will go but
drearily with him. He will repeat with the mouth, not
with the understanding. His memory will be well
stocked ; but, what is vastly more important, his mind
will remain listless. Now, if we introduce a boy to the
study of language by putting into his hands a Latin
grammar and bidding him master the declensions, how
will the case stand with him? How does the case stand
with him? What wretched drudgery those early school-
days are! Is it one of the "penalties of Adam" that
they should be so? Is it altogether boys' fault that
their elementary tutors find them so recalcitrant? Is it
wholly through the dulness of their nature that they do

not love the Conjugations at first sight, or conceive a passionate attachment for the Irregular Verbs? What a queer thing their nature would be if it did kindle in them either flame! At all events, it does not. And the ordinary boy's early life is spent in a war of independence against his Primer. What is the genitive case of the Third Declension to him, or he to it? Then, for the teacher, is the work more inspiring for him? Can his enthusiasm relieve and dissipate the direful tedium? Can he brighten these lack-lustre exercises?

> "Pater ipse colendi
> Haud facilem esse viam voluit."

"Through me you pass into the city of woe," might well be inscribed over the doorway of the lower departments of our classical schools. "All hope abandon, ye who enter here."

I venture to believe that if the commencement of the classics were postponed for a while, and the time so saved devoted to some attention to English, great advantage would accrue. Consider how expedient and profitable it is to turn to account the boy's powers of observation, to enlist them in the service of his education. Why not, then, if you wish to provoke him to the study of language, bring them to bear on the language he hears spoken around him? Here is a world full of interest all round him. Why not encourage him to gaze well at it and air his nascent faculties there, instead of rudely dragging him forth into a *terra incognita*, where to him prevails outer darkness? Can such a wild, precipitate relegation profit? You divorce peremptorily his studies and his daily life, so that he cannot discern any sign of any association between them. You dismiss him into a far country amongst voices that are strange and harsh to his young ears. Why not rather win him to listen to the voices that speak around him? Are the words they utter not profitable for doctrine? Do they contain no lessons that are worth the learning? Are they, too, not the constituents of a mighty language?

Let his study of language begin with his native language. Let his first lessons in that science be based on that language which is already to some extent familiar to him — illustrated, interpreted, made meaning by that. Surely, this is the rational course. Having gathered so from the specimen that lies ready to hand, some notion of what a language is, let him, if you please, proceed to another language, dead or living. Will not that terrible listlessness be now alleviated? Will not a light now fall on the pages of his Accidence? Will not what seemed so utterly perplexing, meaningless, irrelevant, now wear some significance in his eyes?

To use afresh the old metaphor I have used above, the road will not indeed be all levelled and smoothed; awkward stones, sharp thorns, sudden ruts may still trouble the wayfarer; but it will no longer be a road which leads nowhere. He who plods along it will rejoice in the knowledge that it will lead him to a worthy destination, and he will sometimes catch a glimpse, in the far distance, of its fair lofty towers.

But it is necessary to explain more fully of what kind this early initiation in the study of language is to be. Can English so take the place of Latin? In what way is it to be taught?

The pupil comes to the teacher with the power of expressing his ordinary wants and ideas already acquired. He is already a master of language, to a certain extent. This power, this masterhood, such as it is, he has acquired by imitation. Along with it he has gained what power of thinking he has; for what the body is to the soul, that are words to thought. The pupil, then, is already able to wield in some sort the great instrument of language. But he does not know his own power. Is it not time that his attention should be called to it? —that he should be made aware of the crown that has descended upon his head, of the sceptre that has been placed in his hand? Why treat this young prince, with his regal endowments, like some beggar with never a rood of land or a single subject? The supreme necessity now is, to awaken in him a sense of his power,—to tell him of his kingly gifts, of the nature and extent of his dominion, that he may without delay do his endeavour to order it aright and secure its future prosperity. It is no time just now to augment his empire; that is large enough in all conscience. It is time to attract his eyes to this great instrument of language that he wields, in the form in which he wields it. Other forms he may hereafter grasp and handle; all the more intelligently if he is taught now to manage this one. It is time now that he should look at and explore this one. All philological questions may be, for the present, deferred. Etymology, history, and the like investigations, shall come in their time. He should now study language purely and simply as the medium for expressing his thoughts. He should be taught to observe how faithful a mirror it may be of his ideas, if rightly adjusted,—how flexible it is, how sensitive, and, above all things, how law-directed and law-obeying. He should be made to feel that great truth that the Greeks realised so fully when they attached to the word meaning "Speech" the further signification of "Reason." In other words, he should be shown that language is logical,—that it is not capricious and arbitrary in its arrangements, but reflects the operations of the mind. In fact, he should be made thoroughly familiar with the *sentence*—with the sentence in all its varieties, simple and compound; should acquaint himself thoroughly with the relation to each other of the various parts of it, with the modifications of the general sense that each one produces, with the significance of the order in which they come, and the results that would ensue from any transposition or inversion of them,—in short, with the subtle, delicate, vigorous expressiveness of the sentence.

I hope this suggested course does not look visionary. Boys are capable of far higher intellectual effort than the present memory-exercising system evokes. They can use their thinking powers, if only they are permitted and encouraged, not compelled to be parrots and stifle their better intelligence. This study of the sentence seems calculated to gradually awaken, develop, order these powers,—to shorten that "period of darkness" (as the Arabs called the ages that preceded Mohammed) that spreads now over so many precious years—to call into order and beauty what is at present for so long a while without form, and void. Boys act like rational beings when they rebel against tasks that can scarcely be said to require or exercise any intelligence. No wonder so many of the ablest men were the most troublesome and insurrectionary when at school. Nor let anyone think that this suggestion aims too high. If a child can ask questions such as would puzzle the greatest philosopher, let us remember that the greatest philosopher can say things such as the simplest child could understand. In very truth the philosopher is sadly wanted in our schoolrooms. The better arrangement, the enlightenment of facts is wanted. To be sure, the pupil will not comprehend at once the full force and excellence of any principles given him; but the bare facts with which he is now fed, does he realise them at once? At all events, whatever prominence you may concede to principles, the instruction ought always to be based on principles which will, in process of time, unveil themselves to him. Like the loveless old hag, in the old story, who, when the knight in obedience to his promise has, amid the mingled scorn and pity of his fellows, married her, turns out of a sudden an exquisite beauty, so the lessons of one's boyhood, however dull and dreary at the time, ought at last to be found the containers of what is true and beautiful. They ought at last to be recognised as the harmonious limbs of a well-formed, soul-inspired body. Are they so recognised? Or are they found a sorry collection of odd members, many a one of them mis-shapen and distorted, that could never have been compacted harmoniously together, with a spirit to rule and glorify them? Such are facts when they are not connected with principles. Yet is what is called classical instruction at our schools anything better than a more or less copious superfusion of facts? The logical study of the sentence would, at least, in one respect, help to repair this distressing dullness. "A beam in darkness—let it

grow." That boys would be found equal to the study—
I believe they would conceive an interest in it—can be
shown from instances. The "compound sentence" in
Latin is studied at several of our higher schools with
much success. Thorough able teaching of a high intelligent sort is brought to bear upon it, and the fruit
is good. What was dark, is illumined. But in schools
of a much lower social order, the "analysis of sentences" has been proved to be a perfectly possible
lesson-subject for pupils of no considerable age. Before
the adoption of the Revised Code, it was very commonly taught in National and British Schools, and
found to be within the reach of pupils who enjoyed so
few out-of-school advantages as do the children who
attend them.

I venture to believe then, that by beginning our study
of language with English, and beginning it in the above-sketched way, great gain might be secured both in
respect of the study of language, and also in respect
of general intellectual awakening and activity. "We
free our language," says Ben Jonson, advocating the
claim of the national tongue to some formal attention
and treatment, "from the opinion of rudeness and
barbarism, wherewith it is mistaken to be diseased;
we show the copy of it and matchableness with other
tongues; *we ripen the wits of our own children and
youth the sooner by it, and advance their knowledge.*"
And yet Jonson knew no truer mode of dealing with
English than binding it to the framework of the Latin
grammars of his time, and constraining it into the same
shape. He saw clearly enough what facilities of education were being wasted, what pearls were being trodden

under foot. But he, and many another thinker [1] before and since, saw and deplored this wilful waste (what woeful want comes of it!) in vain.

In schools where, rightly or wrongly, Latin and Greek form the staple of the studies, I am convinced those languages would thrive the better, if the medium through which they are taught were better understood. At present we teach *ignotum per ignotius*. Our grandfathers avowedly followed the same method with regard to Greek. The grammars of that tongue over which they groaned and detested life, were written in Latin. The old lexicons rendered in Latin the meanings of the words which that bewildered young ancestry "looked out." That remarkable arrangement has been repealed. But has the young student of to-day a much superior knowledge of the now current, the obvious, medium of instruction? May not his posterity wonder how he could make satisfactory progress, when he understood so meagerly the language in which his learning was tendered to him? We teach our children to walk, before we send them to the dancing-master. How obscure, how incomprehensible, must be, and is, a great part of the school-books in vogue, because the users of them have not been taught something of their mother-tongue! How can a boy be expected to know what a case is— what is meant by the subject, by the predicate of a sentence, by a dialect, by illative, causal, and other innumerable like terms which abound in his grammar, if he is not taught? An intelligent boy, we are told,

---

[1] See quotations from Mulcaster's "Elementarie" (1582), and Brinsley's "Grammar School," in "Education in Early England," by F. J. Furnivall, Esq. (1867).

will "pick up" these important bits of knowledge.¹ But what of the boys that are not intelligent? And is their name unit or legion? And in the case of the intelligent boy, is this "picking up" method quite safe and satisfactory? Will his ideas be sufficiently clear and lucid, or will they not rather be somewhat obscure and turbid? Yet in these matters definiteness and accuracy are essential. A confused notion is worse than none; and the clever boy, as will happen under some systems of education, is worse off than the dullard.

In schools whose pupils are not destined to proceed from them to a University, or to a life of studious leisure and opportunity, English should, I think, be made the prominent linguistic and literary study. Their time is too limited for any pretence at mastering Latin and Greek, and should not be squandered *operose nihil agendo*. What hope could they have of ever enjoying Virgil in the original? That poet will but become to their imagination the sort of magician—the sayer of dark sentences—that he was to the Middle Ages. They will dig but little gold from that profound mine: they cannot give to this work the necessary *labor improbus*.

Διώκει παῖς ποτανὸν ὄρνιν,
πόλει πρόστριμμ' ἄφερτον ἐνθείς,

for is not the public detriment grievous, when the energies of young scholars are misdirected and wasted? But it may be said that though the youth cannot reach the goal, yet the running is good for him. This is quite true; but there are goals and goals, and each one with its own

¹ What tutor has not perpetually to notice and deplore his pupil's ignorance of English? I have again and again found errors in the compositions of pupils, at the University and elsewhere, that sprang solely from inability to understand the English original.

course, its own difficulties, its own advantages. Which one is the best for this youth? I may presume to suggest that that study has many recommendations, which seems most possible to pursue in what moments of leisure the student may have in after life. Would there be much hope of his returning to his Virgil, and pushing on his studies in that direction? (Of course I speak of the ordinary mortal, and not of any exceptional luminary.) I think not. His imperfect knowledge of the language, coupled with its excessive difficulty, his ignorance of the ideas which permeate and inspire it, his consequent incompetence to appreciate and sympathize with its sentiment and tone, seem to render any such hope preposterous. For him in all truth it is

> "not better done, as others use,
> To sport with Amaryllis in the shade,
> Or with the tangles of Neœra's hair."

He does not know how to conduct himself before such presences. He knows nothing of their classical ways and arts. To him they seem uninteresting and frigid. In fact, he is not at all at his ease in their society, he cannot converse naturally with them, justly estimate and admire their calm placid beauty, their noble, dignified grace. He must find society more accordant with his tastes and abilities. For such an one, surely his native language and literature should be made the foundations of his linguistic and literary education. On these he will be able to build subsequently, to continue the structure commenced at school:—and consider how broad these foundations are. It is not unfrequently said that these subjects do not present sufficient difficulties to the learner. This is an ancient traditional objection, which surely cannot survive much longer. It is the voice of times that knew nothing whatever about the English tongue, that did not perceive it had idioms and characteristics of its own; in whose mind familiarity had bred contempt. I suppose to a Greek, the use of those fine, subtle particles, whose precise influence is to us so difficult to determine, seemed perfectly obvious and natural. Was Virgil conscious how well-nigh insuperable the language he wrote was, what a world of trouble his ablatives were creating for his future readers, what a forest of *cruces*? Should English ever become a dead language (a wholly improbable supposition) would it be thought devoid of difficulties? Would the scholiasts and commentators find no place for their acumen? Indeed, are they now without work, the editors of our English classics, the authors of treatises on our English language? Is Shakespeare's diction always so transparent? Can the reader never help understanding what Milton means? To go back to earlier English writings, any one who opens Mr. Morris's *Specimens of Early English*, for instance, may soon encounter difficulties in abundance, difficulties not only of a verbal kind. But I have already, above, glanced at this accusation that English is ill-adapted for the teacher's purposes. I do not think it has much weight.

Much more might be said on this subject. But I shall not now attempt to say it. I shall be now content if in any way I have excited or fostered a doubt in any reader's mind as to the wisdom of the educational course at present followed in this country,—as to whether we avail ourselves satisfactorily of the means at our service, or rather, strangely ignore and neglect them.

VIII.

ON THE EDUCATION OF THE REASONING FACULTIES.

BY W. JOHNSON, M.A.

ACCORDING to the custom of certain public schools, a classical teacher enters upon his duties as soon as he has taken his degree as a Bachelor of Arts, without undergoing any professional training, without attending any course of lectures on education, without having read any book on the subject. He is supposed to conform to the traditions of the establishment to which he attaches himself, and in case of doubt or obstruction to apply for advice or support to senior teachers and to the head-master. His outfit for this enterprise may consist, and certainly did, twenty years ago, often consist of a few score classical volumes read and pencilled more or less carefully, a few drawers full of manuscripts of his own composition, or copied from the stock of a private tutor, and a few commonplace books containing the notes taken at college or university lectures. It is the same stock with which he would have entered on the business of a private tutor at the university. He is fortunate if he has been kept waiting for a vacancy long enough to have spent a few months at Dresden, Rome, or Tours; for it is in the first few months after the degree that the academical mind passes through its fermentation, nor is there any time of life in which knowledge is acquired more rapidly or assimilated more thoroughly. If one could afford to remain unemployed, and the school could dispense with one's services, it would be in the highest degree desirable to assure oneself a considerable interval between the undergraduate's excitement and the schoolmaster's servitude. It is not that one is put into the grooves of professional duty blindly or even hastily, since it generally happens that one has been able, as a lad of eighteen at school, to observe the processes of the master; and to the college student not many topics of conversation are more familiar than the defects and absurdities of his school, few convictions stronger than that of his being himself intended by Providence to supply and amend them. The incepting Bachelor is likely to be at once fervent in admiration of an idealized institution, and of one or two living persons belonging to it, and bitter in contempt for the actual practice of most of the men who are making a livelihood out of the business. Having earned his appointment by success in the dead languages, he is instigated on the one hand by the wish to communicate what he has himself learnt from honoured academical instructors, and on the other hand by a generous impatience yearning for a very different kind of knowledge. The very skill in classical composition which he has gained in ten or twelve years of training seems to him, on his first professional attempts, incommunicable; for the young boys who are thrown upon him are surprisingly remote from him, and he cannot remember what he was at their age.

The more he tries to bring his pupils up to the standard of erudition fixed for him at college, the more does he marvel and shudder at their feebleness. He has lived for four years with robust intellects; he has now to live amongst incomprehensibly small and shallow minds. Enthusiasm forbids him to believe that boyhood is stupid and frivolous; surely it must be the parents, the governesses, the preparatory schools, the selfish and narrow-minded people who rule the public school itself, that are answerable for the failure. Could one but bring to bear on these obscurantists the spirit of the university, surely the face of things would soon alter. What is it that is needed, one asks. Conscientious accuracy, syntax treated deductively, rigid Atticism, unbending orthodoxy in Latin idiom, constant reference to the latest German authorities, unflinching surrender of old-fashioned formularies, a sort of Protestantism in scholarship,—this is what the young schoolmaster, so far as human frailty allows, professes and practises. This he does strictly in the spirit of duty, denying himself all the while; for in his heart he has always liked something else, let us call it history, or philosophy, far more than Porsonine. In fact, he thinks philology, or the critical study of Greek and Latin literature, rather dry and rather shallow: he teaches what he knows of it, which is indeed far less than he at the time imagines, because he has been told by his *Alma Mater* to count it a jewel, and experience convinces him that it is convertible into very substantial British gold. If he had his own way, he would be preaching the superiority of Bossuet to Luther, the importance of Celtic affinities, the craniology of the South Seas; or, if drawn back by the old Muses, he would at least rather descant on Bopp than on Jelf. But to a certain extent, with certain modifications, he must serve the world; and, inasmuch as scholarships and fellowships are manifestly won by prosody and the oblique oration, he must give his fifty or sixty hours a week without an audible murmur to parsing, and scanning, and saying by heart: only he does all this, he flatters himself, with more integrity than his elders. To this ascetic missionary spirit come the first holidays as an emancipation of the mind. From the images in the mirror one turns to the live things moving on the bank beyond the river. At a leap one plunges into that which one believes to be the philosophy of the present, or at least of the esoteric present which is to leaven the coming age. Then, if human affairs were but conducted at all methodically, then would be the time for initiation into society, for the give and take of London life, for contact with cheerful and enlightened men. But circumstances push the young schoolmaster into moping, varied only by desultory reading. He has lost the precious sympathy and the wholesome mirth of undergraduate friends. His intellectual appetites must be fed without social cookery. He is to fill up, as best he may, by uncritical and uncriticised reading, the lamentable gaps which a so-called liberal education has left in his mind. A strong will, no doubt, would take him to the persevering study of law or physics, or of a modern or of an Oriental language. But men of strong will do not so very often become schoolmasters: the work of schools must be done by men who have for the most part not enough energy for sustained inquiry: the classical teacher is generally a possible clergyman in his strength and in his weakness, not a lawyer, nor a man of science, nor an archæologist. Let it be supposed then, that into the hands of such a young man as we have imagined, a successful versifier with a leaning towards modern culture, but with no genius, no fixed resolution, no encyclopædic training, in fact, a very imperfectly educated man, falls a book of force and breadth, opening up like "a great instauration" noble vistas of knowledge, convincing him of his miserable ignorance, and making him believe in some occult force of reason that works below and across the currents of public habit and of rhetorical influences. Is it necessary to tell any reader of this volume, that there are such books? Does any one read to the end of these pages, who has not, some time or other, felt the trumpet-sound of passionless reason, putting to shame his hereditary scruples? No need to name an author; no one can safely do so: utter a name, and you are henceforth to walk with a label round your neck. It is enough to say that, if Cleombrotus by reading one book was lifted into the belief of his immortality, a young Englishman also may have been by one book of a fellow-countryman impelled, in spite of tangled and conflicting sentiments, to fall into the interminable procession of those who find no rest till the secrets of the universe are disclosed. There is a great gulf between those who are satisfied with examining and renovating the mental products of past times, whether they be ecclesiastical antiquaries, or editors of old books, or imitators of old word-melodies, and those others who study the past chiefly out of gratitude, partly for warnings against error, but are all the while straining beyond the duration of single lives towards the enlargement of fruitful knowledge and the progress of beloved mankind. Once having tasted of this great river, how could one turn back to the cisterns of dead literature!

A teacher once for all inoculated with a taste for inductive reasoning, however incapacited himself by nature and by habit for really partaking in discovery, can hardly fail to have his mind, such as it is, set upon undertakings different from the collation of parallel passages in the ancient authors. Might he not even then, when leisure and freedom from worldly cares were lost, gather together some scientific information, and fertilize therewith the ingenuous youth subjected to his influence?

There can be no study of science without constant reference to number, weight, and linear measurement. He, therefore, who has been cruelly left for twenty years of adolescence to drift about without these anchors and compasses, must renounce the notion of being a man of science. Granted: yet he may create an inquisitiveness; he may open for others the doors of chambers which he may not himself explore. In such a case it may seem possible, and, if this be an illusion, it is at least an honourable illusion, to attend lectures and give out some of the teaching in a form available for younger minds, to collect books, to pick the brains of better educated friends, to skim the history of science and put the biography of inductive philosophers in as fair a light as the lives of orators and poets, to encourage any gleam of a talent for observation, to encourage in particular the instinct of the collector, and as far as possible to turn collection into classification, to propound little puzzles in pneumatics or the like, to get together and display a little apparatus of scientific instruments and toys. If such attempts have been made, and have produced but little effect, set down the failure to weakness of purpose; but conclude not that they were in themselves erroneous attempts. Fifty years ago it would have been thought rather paradoxical to deny that parents and grown up people generally ought to open the eyes of the young at table, and in walks, to the curiosities of nature. The very Romans, whom the philological educators profess to honour, learnt and taught all that they could of the properties of matter. When the philologists stooped so low in accommodation to the spirit of the age as to ingraft on linguistic teaching a year's course of comparative geography, and preluded this geography with a chapter on the solar system and a diagram to explain the seasons, they were unconsciously conceding a principle, they were introducing science. If horror-stricken at their own act, let them take comfort; they were doing what Virgil wished to do, and Cicero thought he had done.

It is not pretended that one who gives his spare hours and his spare cash to a smattering of scientific information, which is to be beaten out into a mere film on the memories of boys, has any right to be reckoned even as a camp follower in the army of searching adventurers. Nothing short of an incorporation into the school-work in which boys are systematically examined, with all the dark background of penal necessity, can be held to do justice to the claims of science. Without a perfect obligation a study has no root in a school.

And yet it may seem strange and sad that a man actually living with boys, and having no other object than their good, should not be able effectually to do what an intelligent man can do for his children; elicit their curiosity by directing their attention to natural phenomena, and, without consideration of reward or punishment, open their minds to contemplate the forms of life, and explore the sequences and uniformities of the inorganic world. It is painful to enumerate all that we leave unnoticed; the "natural questions" which a Seneca would have asked, which we, the distant heirs of Seneca, either slight or dread. We force our pupils to say in Latin verse, that sounds to me almost as the voice of the Fairy Queen summoning the rhymer, "Happy is he who hath been able to learn the causes of things, why the earth trembles, and the deep seas gape;" and yet we are not to tell them. Virgil humbly grieved, but we grieve not, that we cannot reach these realms of wonder. A full-grown educated Englishman climbs a few steps to a telescope standing by Napoleon's trophy, gazes for a minute, comes down awed with a new sense of the earth's motion: so quickly has the splendid sphere we call Jupiter passed from the field of vision. It is then a new thing to him to feel and know that the earth is moving. The bright nymph, who brings messages from the gods, is well called the daughter of Wonder, Iris Thaumantias. The English Theætetus is condemned, for fear of being desultory and superficial, to keep aloof from those who can make him wonder and inquire. On the first of July, every year (says a naturalist), whether it has been a cold or a warm June, the spiky purple loosestrife rises into her place on the banks of the Thames. It is no hindrance to the growth of a literary taste to be taught something of the earth's relations to the sun; of the insignificance of atmospheric changes compared with that solar power which lies beyond the shallow rain-clouds. It is of the very essence of poetry to look at the flower and think that, by reason of the sun's stellar course carrying the planet with it, the flower does not blow twice in the same point of heavenly space. What would Lucretius have thought of men who knew, or might know such things, and were afraid to tell the young of them for fear of spoiling their perception of his peculiarities? How would Ovid flout at us if he heard that we could unfold the boundless mysteries contained in his germinal saying, "All things change, nothing perishes," and passed them by to potter over his little ingenuities. If our minds were well stored and active, we might incidentally throw out many hints about plants and animals, and stars, we might rid boys of many illusions about sound, light, and heat, without making any deduction from the hours given to the study of language and literature. As it is, our laborious games absorb much of the time which, in the days of Miss Edgeworth and Mr. Joyce, would have been spent in training the eye to observe things passing in field and hedge-row. Games are so absorbing that they prevent boys, even when not playing but sauntering, from thinking or talking of any other topic; and in the holidays there is hardly a father who tries to divert his son's mind from dogs and horses; nor can I bring to mind more than one or two that have sent their children, when obliged to stay in London, to the museums and lectures, which might, to a great extent, supply the deficiencies of school. With all the worship of the horse, no boy knows, by way of home-taught knowledge, what is the true name for a horse's knee. With all their love of boats, they think that a heavy boat, other things being equal, goes faster than a light one down stream. Several boys have a decided taste for machinery, and in particular for locomotive steam-engines; but even these boys cannot state the principle of the engine.

Ignorance and indifference such as this cannot, I am sorrowfully convinced, be cured by the occasional propounding of scientific puzzles, by the display of scientific toys, by reproducing in talk what has been carried away from lectures.

I have tried all this, not indeed with perseverance, but with genuine eagerness. The attempts were made mainly in conformity with the teaching of that very remarkable man, who ought not to be forgotten, the late Dean of Hereford, Dawes, of King's Somborne, whose village school was, about 1849, the hope and delight of all who wished to make peasants think. His pamphlet, suggesting many charming household experiments, was obeyed faithfully in my pupil-room; the only easy day of the seven was made a day of labour, week after week, in preparing experiments. What a man of no genius and of no sort of scientific or mathematical training could do by hunting amongst friends for information, was done strenuously. Physical geography, in those days a rather popular subject, was engrafted, as far as possible, on the school exercises in comparative or historical geography. Visitors were pressed into the service to give lectures on the mechanical powers, on astronomy, on geology. Tables of specific gravities and heat-conductivities hung on the walls, with zoological charts, and hydrographical and geological maps. Once a week a paper containing four or five questions, got up by reading scores of volumes of scientific voyages and travels, was hung up for volunteers, questions such as these:—(1) "A navigator keeps dipping his thermometer into the sea to take the temperature of the surface water: he finds a sudden change, and infers that he has come to a shoal. Why?" (2) "A bridge built partly of cast, partly of wrought iron, is insecure. Why?" (3) "In surveying at sea they take a base line by sound, by observing how many seconds intervene between the flash and the report of a gun fired in a boat some way off. They multiply the number of seconds by 1090, and so get the number of feet between ship and boat. But they have to add a foot for every two degrees of thermometer above freezing-point. Why?"—In setting these questions, which were always intermingled with zoology, much use was made of the Admiralty Manual of Scientific Inquiry. The questions were in a great measure the fruit of undisguised "cramming," so much so that he who set them cannot himself at this distance of time answer some of those which remain amongst his papers: but to read for this purpose such books as Ermann's Siberia, Wrangel's Siberia, Darwin's Voyage round the World, Forbes on Glaciers, Carpenter's Zoology, Reid on Storms, Herschel's Discourse on the Study of Natural Philosophy, and the like, seems, on calm reflection, a more satisfactory employment than the reading of Copleston's Prælectiones, or Muller's Dorians. Of what are called results obtained, no boast shall be made. It was at least better to have tried and failed than never to have tried at all.

On reviewing these early attempts at the enlargement of boyish minds, it now seems that, over and above the insurmountable obstacles presented to an untrained teacher struggling alone against his own misconceptions as well as the littleness of others, there must have been one fatal defect the mention of which would supersede the need of reference to any other hindrance. There was hardly any subject-matter for criticism. The boys did no exercises: nothing but a few papers of answers to a few questions, and perhaps a map or two differing from common maps in the notice taken of economic geology. It is a superficial and disappointing work to communicate knowledge to young boys without frequent reiteration and close examination. In evidence given before the Public Schools Commission certain eminent philosophers declared their belief that the elements of science could be with ease made known to young boys; and on the high authority of Mr. Faraday[1] the Commissioners seem to have at once formed an opinion to the same effect. But Mr. Faraday has probably never examined those children whom he used so charmingly and brilliantly to keep listening and watching for an hour, and whom at the end of the hour he would invite so winningly to his magic semicircle. No one who witnessed that truly beautiful spectacle of a sage surrounded by happy sparkling faces of children could think any teaching of school-

---

[1] This was written before Mr. Faraday's death.

masters worth mentioning. There never can be in any school such a teacher. The remembrance of him as he appeared in those hours is delightful and unique. Yet there is no sacrilege in doubting whether he would have found on the morrow of one of his lectures anything like an accurate reproduction of a tenth of the lesson given *on paper* by a tenth of the learners. No child would ever forget that he had seen a diamond burnt; but few would have been able at the end of a week to prove the hollowness of flame, or the heaviness of carbonic acid gas. Up to a certain age boys are generally eager and attentive listeners, and when their attention is kept up not only by a sweet and noble manner, but by marvellous demonstrations, their eyes and souls seem to vie with the carbon burning in oxygen. But we cannot, as Mr. Faraday told the children, burn a diamond every day. The man of genius cannot do the school's drudgery.

Without demonstrations, a lesson in natural history or in natural philosophy would not be very different in method from a lesson in grammar. With demonstrations, it would closely resemble a lesson in geography. The terminology of a science can no doubt be learnt by boys; but it would be learnt through a long course of forgettings and remindings; and it is the regular schoolmaster, not the lecturer, much less the man of originality and research, who will stand the wear and tear of this Sisyphean labour. Nor indeed would the reasoning faculties, beyond the rudimentary powers of attention and memory, be expanded by this study of terminology. A show of mental activity is easily made by recourse to a vulgar art and a cheap force. The emulation of young boys will keep up a phosphorescence without the combustion of a solid. You may think boys are improving their minds when they are merely playing a game. Classwork with the *young boys* is very much like a game in which the master is the principal player. In the earlier years of public school life the liveliest boys are making scores in school as in the playground. One in a hundred has a real desire of knowledge for its own sake—knowledge apart from imaginative excitement. The tutor may teach the individual pupil just as the father can teach his son, and half an hour of this is worth some hours of competition in class. But we are to find some method which will at once nourish the love of truth and subject whole classes to discipline, some task which the schoolmaster can accomplish a thousand times without special preparation, and yet with a certainty of bringing his mind to bear authoritatively on subject minds. There are two processes in what may be called the classical method of instruction; construing with parsing, which may be called the oral analysis of sentences, and composition with the altering of exercises. In certain schools a long and unbroken tradition, sustained by much genuine faith and honest energy, has established these habits of literary work on a footing which seems to be secure from scepticism or egotism. It seems, after long practice and much consideration, that there is a solid and sufficiently broad theory for these empirically established habits. Giving up the old distinction between demonstrative and catechetical teaching, one would say that oral analysis and the correction of exercises are two forms of criticism; and the theory is, that effectual instruction is critical instruction. Using the terms

rhetoric and logic in the mediæval sense, I will venture
to say that I was taught by men who applied criticism
to rhetoric, and I have taught myself to apply criticism
to logic as well as to rhetoric. With many oscillations,
and much infirmity of purpose, I have for twenty-two
years, with classes of sixty, of forty, of thirty, with sets
of pupils varying from twenty to three, and also with
single pupils, cultivated what is called taste, or the art
of expression, in conformity with an excellent tradition,
and in obedience to academical authorities of the highest
order. Nor is it in this paper asserted or implied that
propriety of language is not a more attainable result of
classical training than correctness of thought. But it
has of late years become manifest, that what was taken
for classical taste by those who did battle against useful
knowledge was, to a great extent, irrational imitation
and phrase-mongery. Taste after all is not a mere
cultivated instinct or perception, like an ear for music.
It is discrimination, a kind of reasoning. A logician
need not be ashamed to study those curious artifices by
which Virgil heightens the effect of his statements; in
"hypallage" and "hendiadys" there is scope for rational
choice. It is one thing to put together dissimilar words,
as Tacitus does, for poetical effect; another thing to use
two similar words where one will do, as Cicero does,
for mere copiousness of sound. The monstrous fatuities
which disfigure Æschylus are condemned by the clear
head of an Aristophanes, and can be proved to be
bad. Amongst the worthies whose names are used
as bludgeons to beat us with, there was at least one
whose taste was inextricably combined with his reasoning powers, Mr. Fox. He would not have abetted the

defenders of the classical faith in teaching boys to wrap their truisms in the drapery of Cicero; but he would have encouraged them to state a case or tell a story like Herodotus, Euripides, and Ovid. Think and write like Mr. Fox, and you will use Latin unaffectedly and straightforwardly to do justice to your subject: you will not choose a subject which will enable you to bring in your stored phrases. The desire of doing at schools what is done at our universities has led to very absurd results with ordinary schoolmasters, who have made it their object to get Greek verses written, like the Porson prize exercises, by tesselating bits of Attic idiom, and have broken their hearts in hopeless attempts to get Latin prose written as it is written by Oxford professors. It is only after an incalculable amount of trouble bestowed upon these desperately hard falsettoes that it has become a fixed resolve to insist upon boys' exercises being intelligible by themselves, and their phraseology strictly subordinate to the subject-matter, and also to make corrections or additions which explain themselves, and fit exactly to the text that has to be amended. Require of a boy an exercise which will make sense, however humble, without a commentary from its author. Strike out every couplet that is not needed, every clause that returns upon a preceding clause, every preamble which is not sufficiently backed up, every inferential expression that is not warranted. This is a more salutary operation than the attack upon idle adjectives with which some critics of the last generation were inclined to be contented; it is the ploughing of the subsoil. And then to alter an exercise, so as to do justice to the young author's intention, treating him with just so much respect as he deserves, filling his slender wandering rivulets with a sufficient flow of words, but carefully following the main direction of the stream, unless he be wholly in error, breaking up a long period for clearness, if needs be, varying the cadences to please the ear, making effective contrast by mere arrangement of words without particles, not to speak of all the pretty little artifices that are taken from Ovid and Livy—surely this is almost a fine art, the gardening of the mind, and a rational method withal.

The objection will be raised that poetic diction is just as much as rhetorical vapouring a kind of falsetto, and that the study of poetic diction is as unfavourable to the pursuit of truth as any other system of artifices. Now there are certain arrangements made in versification which need no defence: for instance, to say "they run, the enemy pursuing," instead of "they run pursued by the enemy," is an artifice suggested by the exigencies of metre, though adopted by prose writers merely for the sake of variety. The exigencies of metre in Latin verse, whatever mischief they may do in the way of exaggeration or suppression, do not, like the demands of rhyme in English verse, induce one to enter upon a thought or an image that nothing else would have engendered; and it will appear on comparison that the Latin verse of young people, even their lyric verse with its semblance of emotion, is more honest, more sincere, than their English rhymed verse. The artifices of which a specimen has just been given are as innocent as algebraical substitutions, to which they are analogous. But beyond these metrical contrivances lie the figures of Virgilian rhetoric, which are the weapons of more advanced versifiers : to use them rightly is a proof of keen discrimination, and in using them no one can deceive himself or his reader, since they are felt to be departures from literal truth : they are not more deceptive than the red chalk or the sepia of a drawing.

There are, it is readily admitted, only a few who can arrive at the rational use of poetic diction, nor is it my wish to recommend the expenditure of so much labour as it requires. Granted that we have not time to spare for this, I maintain that we shall not do well to substitute Ciceronian prose. Whatever may be said of our attempts at writing like Virgil, it is not good to imitate the copiousness and subarticulation of Cicero's periods, because they never have been imitated successfully even by the best scholars, and because the habit of writing that kind of Latin is likely to hinder the formation of a direct, lucid, and solidly impressive method of making statements. The Oxford Professor of Latin gave a bit of evidence to the Public Schools Commissioners which hits the nail on the head : it was to the effect that, whereas a verse is within the grasp of a boy's understanding, a Latin sentence is to him an impenetrable mystery. Another Oxford man, in a light and pleasant defence of classical instruction, has amused himself by playing with an English sentence and exhibiting many ways of turning it into Latin prose, advancing from the boldest and clumsiest to the most elegant and idiomatic rendering. When such a man of genius as Mr. John Henry Newman deigns to lecture on the art of writing Latin he is something more than an authority ; but an experienced schoolmaster knows and feels sorely that this mastery of Latin idiom, attained by Oxford men after some years of College tuition, is quite out of reach at school, and that the labour bestowed upon trying to make boys write elegant Latin prose is even more fruitless than the study of Latin versification. Few things can be more difficult than to get a boy to appreciate the best Ciceronian prose; and as it is after all one of the curiosities of literature it seems strange that it should be so very highly valued at Oxford.

What then is the province of Latin prose in a school? There are two ways of dealing with it for the cultivation of the reasoning powers, both subjected to much more limitation than might be wished. It is expedient to practise translation into Latin prose from those English writers before Addison, whose grooves of thought are parallel to the simplest Latin style; and here we should avoid the mistake of those who set passages out of histories of Greece and Rome on the illogical assumption that English written about the ancients goes easily into ancient languages; the truth being that it is much easier to translate Johnes' Froissart into Latin than Gibbon, or Arnold, or Merivale. This kind of translation is so easy as to be no substitute for verse-making as a test of mental vigour, and it does not do much for the reason; but it prepares you for a higher kind of work. Having attained some sort of skill in rendering simple statements from one language to another, one should go on to select passages from the rational authors of the eighteenth century who write on solid subjects, such as Robertson, Adam Smith, and Paley, and from translations (if need be) of such French writers as Montesquieu, and Dumont, the friend of Bentham. Here one would be studying something valuable for its own sake; translating is perhaps the most effectual way of securing attention to the meaning of a philosophical passage. But better still is an abstract or reduction, like the engraving of a picture on a smaller scale. Whichever is attempted, one must not be shocked at a certain amount of barbarism in the Latin; for the old language will not bear the full modern thought. It would be better to write Latin like Bacon or the translator of Bacon, and at the same time bring out the whole meaning of a modern philosopher, than to skirt the fences, to evade the difficulty, for the sake of a certain elegance. In any case, the Latin language must be a hindrance to the full culture of the reason. With all its merits it is not a proper vehicle for philosophy. If we are debarred from the use of any other, we must make the best of it; nor is it too great a tax on patience to search up and down for something that will go into Latin without being frivolous. It has been ascertained experimentally that such a subject as the influence of a solar eclipse on vegetables and animals (recorded in the journals of 1851), or Sir Humphry Davy's theory of the decay of buildings contained in his Consolations of Travel, can be treated by boys in Latin hexameters, and that the theory of Springs, of the Barometer, of Coral Islands, of Money, of Usury, of Parliamentary Representation, of Government Interference with Trade, can be handled tolerably well in plain but sound Latin prose. To enlarge the list of subjects both in verse and prose has been an undertaking carried on in spite of much discouragement and failure for seventeen years; and one of the conclusions is this, that literature, rightly understood, includes the cream of all philosophy, so that the literary teacher in

a classical school, having at his command the perfect
obligation of the weekly rent paid by the boy for the
enjoyment of his public school life in the form of "composition," is able, not indeed to teach any branch of
science, but to make boys understand where the sciences
lie, how they were put together, how they bear upon one
another, what is the vice of the spurious forms of science,
from what errors mankind has been delivered, and how
much remains under the seal. It is conceded that
"history" is in the province of the classical master. Let
this word, used by many in a feeble way to mean all
that is not philology or divinity, be interpreted broadly,
as Mr. Hallam, for instance, understood it. Let us be
allowed the three volumes of the Middle Ages, a book
which has now some right to be called a classic. Look
at its table of contents, and you will find the historian
taking stock of human knowledge for the end of the
Middle Ages. It appears that by history he does not
mean merely a record of alliances, expeditions, battles,
sieges, treaties, conspiracies, assassinations, and caprices.
He embraces, besides all this, law, church, school, and all
that belongs to them. If we follow him into his greater
work, the Introduction to the Literature of Europe, we
shall find a record of critical changes, not in the fortunes of monarchies, but in the psychology of mankind.
It is not pretended that all which Mr. Hallam sets
forth is to be taught at school: but it is most decidedly
asserted that nearly all this history of human progress
and panorama of things cognizable, expanded to include
the eighteenth and nineteenth centuries, ought to be so
far known to the literary teacher as to be thrown open
by him to his classes, in the hope that some few at least

will explore some chambers of the treasure house. It is a shameful thing to set exercises from week to week for a score or two of years, and never bid boys lift their eyes above some few periods of carnage and crime, such as the first few years of the second Punic War, the campaigns of Sertorius, and "the three battles" of Alexander; to let people grow up in the belief that luxury ruined Rome in the days of Augustus, and that the Goths came directly after Juvenal, to leave English Churchmen in ignorance of Augustine, and Benedict, and Anselm, to let English tourists walk the galleries with no recognition of what they are told by their guides and catalogues, to send men into Parliament as having taken first classes in history and law who could not answer ten questions in the Indian Civil Service papers on those very subjects. If there is a clear proof to be found of the frivolity of our classical education it is the habitual misconception of the term history, its miserable limitation to a tissue of homicide and perfidy stitched together with dates.

The champions of the philological routine are known to speak with great force on "cramming." Every thing that is not syntax or idiom is with them "cram." And yet they had themselves encouraged a considerable amount of hasty reading of commentaries and manuals, and even dictionaries. Any one, they say, can get up an English book just for an examination; it is no test of power or of taste. There is much truth in this, and it must be admitted, that, if the examiner frames his questions by doggedly following the headings of chapters, he is likely to bring upon himself a heavy and undigested mass of statement, which will almost overwhelm him when he has to read and give marks for the answers.

Nor can any occupation be at once more wearisome to the man, and more uninstructive to the boy, than such an examination. But let the questions be in some measure of the nature of "problems" as opposed to "book-work," let them vary from minute particulars to broad generalities, let there be a physical limit set to the answers by serving out papers which allow so much space for each question, let the manuscripts be to some extent treated critically, and returned with marks of praise or blame to their authors, and let the examiner take notes of the more remarkable answers, whether good or bad, so as to lecture upon the paper after it is all over; and then an examination in a book will be an intellectual process.[1] Granted, however, that there must be much crudity and looseness in the temporary knowledge taken into a history examination, and that it is at the best a less severe and stringent method than the correction of exercises, we are thus brought back to the consideration, that "history" is to be taught through composition, or, in other words, taught critically. But we are not to narrow it and emasculate it merely because pure Latinity requires the sacrifice. We are not to linger within the beaten track of Hannibal and luxury for fear of losing sight of our models. The Romans, whom we profess to imitate in their method of educating, wrote and declaimed on all available subjects. Our

---

[1] It is to be regretted that the University local examinations allow no opportunity to the examiners of explaining to the candidates what answer ought to have been given. Scattered as they are over the country, nothing can be done except by circulating a printed paper giving the right answers, and commenting on some of the prevalent and dangerous mistakes. This would cost but little money or trouble, and it would greatly enhance the usefulness of the examinations.

idol, Cicero, has a good deal more in him than his reiterated praises of eloquence and political virtue. He must have traversed the whole of Lucullus' library; he must have been "desultory;" he must have written on many matters with only a smattering of knowledge. The variety of his books rebukes his professed imitators; his example is followed more by those who try to enlarge the scope of composition than by those who seem to hold that, for boys, nothing can be too trivial. As a matter of fact, it has been found possible to treat, even in Latin, and with a considerable regard for correctness and purity, a very considerable number of subjects more complicated and requiring more reasoning than the maxims of Horace and the allusions of Juvenal. The schoolboy's theme is now-a-days a far less contemptible affair than it was. The improvement of style is, not perhaps, in the Latin, but in the greater attention to form. It has been found possible to get themes regularly laid out in little chapters or paragraphs, whether of the writer's, or of the teacher's, design. The exercise may be set with a plan clearly sketched out, and displayed on paper, or with only a few heads, or with a mere statement of the subject. It is tedious to do exactly the same always, and to allow no departure from a fixed type. The old scholastic plan of theme-writing, which many men now alive must have practised, ending like a sermon with a practical application, is not by any means to be despised; however meagre and stiff it may have seemed, it was far better than shapelessness. But it is applicable, perhaps, only to simple ethical subjects, such as envy, or forgiveness, or the fear of death, subjects by no means neglected by those who try to improve ratiocination, but not thought sufficient for the mental dictary. Even with ethical subjects it is desirable to analyse like Bentham, to examine, for instance, the difference between envy and jealousy, to consider forgiveness with reference to Butler's "resentment," to take remedies against the fear of death from the rich storehouse of Jeremy Taylor, and that not without weighing in the balance his multifarious arguments, so as to distinguish between what is, and what is not, fanciful or rhetorical. It should not be forgotten, that boys of promise are apt to prefer fantastic and paradoxical to judicious and truthful writers. If we wish them to be eventually cool-headed, we shall do well to introduce them to Sir Thomas Browne, and Sterne, and Charles Lamb, alternately, with Blackstone, and Mackintosh, and Mrs. Marcet, giving them their heads if they like to write out, in a new form, the whimsies and conceits, provided only they interpret some other time the sobrieties and simplicities. Suppose we have to teach boys who have, as a majority, perhaps, of hopeful boys have, a strong feeling about the divine right of kings, particularly Stuarts, with which feelings are associated many well-known longings and indignations; it is expedient to treat this mental affection homœopathically. In verses, if not in themes, ample verge can be given for the utterance of these transitory sentiments. The corrective can be applied, not directly, but by diverting the young mind to widely different objects, such as the character of Turgot or of Roger Williams, and at another time, by abstracting for translation the calm and plain arguments of a just writer like Professor Smyth. A teacher may be a Whig, and zealous for the faith handed down through the followers of Locke, and yet bear with those transcendentalists whom the best boys undeniably prefer to genuine philosophers. He may forego the right of critically condemning what he knows to be erroneous. But he can insist on a show of argument, on a reason given for the tenets. Make the young enthusiast show cause for his judgments; if not at the time, yet hereafter, he will discover the weakness of the pleading. Give him plenty of truth, or what you honestly believe to be truth, and he will know that other things are false by mere juxtaposition; and he will not cling to misconceptions which have been treated indulgently. Nor is there anything more to be avoided than undue pressure in attacking opinions held, or pretended to be held, by the young. It is needless to say how unfair it would be from the vantage ground held by the teacher; besides this, which is obvious, there is the mischief done by boring. In a very short time, anything like a parade of ratiocination becomes to people of our race nothing more or less than a bore. A very little pedantry, a slight infusion of Aldrich, a little jangling of the bells of the Positive Church, is enough to set against you the taste and sentiment of the pupil, if you are controverting anything which he is pleased to think he believes Hereafter there will be logical terms of some sort used as a matter of business in common teaching, and endured as a matter of course, just as the terms of grammar are endured. The authority which is already making "prolative verbs" familiar in the households of many country gentlemen, will no doubt, some day or other, bring into general use some of the compendious expressions with which a.

Whately would demolish a fabric of illusion; and then it will be a plain matter of business to speak to a boy of elenchus and middle term, just as we now speak of oblique oration. There is no more pedantry in the one than in the other. But at present we are not familiar with many logical phrases. Whately's "Easy Lessons in Reasoning" may perhaps be used in a school as a text-book, or some other manual might be written, more elementary than Mr. Fowler's, on purpose for schools, and if not wholly intelligible to boys, it would be to a considerable extent assimilated by the minds of the abler teachers, and through them would pass into customary scholastic language. It is even conceivable that an advanced class might have bound up in its grammar sequels to the syntax, resembling an appendix which treats of figures of speech, and containing explanations and examples of reasonings, as well as the elements of rhetoric. Meanwhile, it is here suggested, that a classical teacher should, if trained at Oxford, try to keep up his recollection of logic, and look out for occasions in teaching, and particularly in criticising themes for applying some of the rules of logic. If the art is new to him, as it is probably to most Cambridge men, he should make an effort to master it up to a certain point, examining himself by help of Oxford question papers.

No attempt, however, is made in this paper to put on a semblance of attainments, which the writer has no right to claim as his own. Such success as has been obtained, and it is but enough to encourage further endeavours, is due to no systematic grounding in logic any more than in physical science, nor have the suggestions just given been actually carried out thoroughly by the adviser. The reasoning and criticism found applicable to a boy's school in the enlargement of the old classical course are in some measure founded on books very imperfectly remembered, and on a few chance-sayings of well-educated men, but are for the most part hammered out in practice like rules for making verses and other pedagogue odds and ends. Such as they are, they have interested one or two Oxford men who have been thoroughly trained in logic, and they are thought to have leavened the instruction of some elder boys with something that may protect them elsewhere from delusions.

Philological teaching must be admitted to include etymology. The most old-fashioned classical teacher makes it his business to extort the "derivation" of a word. He would ridicule such an expression as "a cachectic state of health," because he would know that cachectic is derived from a word meaning "bad" and a word meaning "habit" or "state;" so that it is an absurd substitute for "bad." In the same way he would point out that "Toxophilite" ought to be "Philotoxite," and "Telegram," "Telegrapheme;" he would tell you the original meaning of "Pagan," "Bishop," and "Villain;" perhaps he would note with sufficient truthfulness, though not from a right legal point of view, the difference between "Prerogative" or "Privilege" and the Latin words of the same substance. So far, then, we have his authority in our favour, and if we look at the origin and history of a word we are but doing what we were ourselves taught in class to do. But the etymology of thirty years ago was insufficient. It did not guard one against error of more than one kind. Sometimes we err in making deductions, for we all reason in some sort of way, from the etymology, without regarding the deflection of the word in actual use from its etymological meaning: as if we were to argue that an university ought to be open to *all* persons or to teach all sciences, because it is derived from a word meaning *all*. Or we may be tempted to work from one "synonym" to another, forgetting that a word in connexion with other words alters its character as if it were compounded. In writing against trade, an amiable person once argued thus: "Profit" is interpreted in the dictionary "advantage:" to take profit, then, is to take advantage—it is wrong to take advantage of one's neighbour: therefore, it is wrong to take profit. Or again, we infer that a man is a schemer because he has broached a scheme, or a projector (to use a well-known example) because he has started a project.

These sources of error may be usefully pointed out to young persons. It is easy and expedient to teach them also that words are for the most part used relatively, and often have more than one correlative. "Realism" is opposed to "Nominalism;" but it is also used in art as opposed to "Idealism," and in books of education as the opposite of the study of language. "Faith" is sometimes opposed to "Sight," sometimes to "Reason," sometimes to "Works."

It is more important to distinguish between words used in their proper sense and otherwise. "Law" is properly a general command accompanied by a sanction; it is used by men of science to denote uniform recurrence without their intending to imply a sovereign will issuing a general command; and it is well known to students how this change of meaning is disguised in Hooker's first book. There need be no scruple about using words, as we say, *improprie*; only we ought to know that we are doing so, and it is not very difficult to point out this to the readers of ancient books, for the ancients do it openly, and Plato makes us vigilant. "Capital" used to mean in books of political economy the hoard produced by previous labour, applicable to the payment of wages in anticipation of profits, so that it was a positive term; we now find railway directors paying for repairs, not out of their receipts, but by a new loan, which is said to be added to the capital, so that an increase of capital merely means an increase of debt; in this there is no intentional juggling, and the transition is natural enough, but the word is changing its meaning, and it is the business of philologists to watch the change. Nor ought we to be less careful in noticing the use made in argument of common words. "Who rules o'er freemen should himself be free" is a good line and a sound maxim, surviving the attack made on it by the parodist; yet it will not pass muster as an argument. "Freemen" is used in the political sense, and political freedom is different from natural freedom or moral freedom. In plain prose, the ruler of freemen should be restrained by law, or else their freedom is at the mercy of his caprice; but, if restrained by law, he does not seem at first sight to be free. Yet the line is a good one in spirit; for the second "free" may be taken to mean free-hearted or free from passion—morally free, in fact. Such a play upon words is ornamental, and need not be illusory; but it ought not to pass unchallenged. Two clergymen of great influence have lately preached on Liberty, or Freedom, and have practised, in their use of the word, an elaborate shuffle. The man who holds a creed is above all men free, they say; he is free from doubt, free from fear, free from all sorts of vices. This is simply turning the word "free" into a negative sign; and any one who likes may be as eloquent on the word "not" as these preachers were on "liberty." Their text had originally a plain meaning: St. Paul said that where the men were full of the Holy Spirit, they enjoyed deliverance from the bondage of the Mosaic law. If the preachers choose this plain text for a motto, they may innocently engraft upon it any other doctrine besides that which St. Paul lays down in the context; but this is not exposition of Scripture, and they are as far as ever from having made good their paradox, that absolute submission to a dogmatic system ensures intellectual freedom. Sermons supply an inexhaustible stock of spurious arguments, and are a fine hunting-ground for logical critics. Newspapers also furnish them with serviceable materials. There was a good example given lately by a bishop of the legitimate fruits of Oxford philosophy. He was arguing about the admission of Dissenters to Universities; it had been urged on the ground that the Universities were national institutions: in what sense national? founded by the nation? founded for the nation? and so on with a truly Socratic investigation which furnished a good illustration of the maxim which the bishop quoted: "Beware of the trickery concealed in general terms," a maxim easily enforced by a classical teacher on hearers of a certain age. Without generalizing, how can we get on at all? it may be asked. Let us by all means generalize, and that roughly, or else we are imprisoned. But let it be constantly borne in mind that from the imperfection of our minds and of our language we can hardly, even by great caution, avoid overstating the generality. He who said that an university was national, was in a great measure right; yet the bishop did well to weigh and probe the term. If we wish for anything like truth, we should generalize provisionally, and offer our theorem to others for trimming and pruning. In no way do young people show their teachableness more than in bearing this retrenchment of sweeping assertions. The candid and patient lads of the Platonic dialogues are with us still; we are not to worry them like Socrates, but we are frequently to remind them of the inadequacy of the grounds on which in practical talk we are obliged for a time to rest. It may here be observed that the Socratic process of questioning, besides being excessively tedious, would seem to be too much like playing a game; and it has been pointed out already that a lesson which is of the nature of a game is good only for young boys, not for those who are on the verge of manhood. One may, no doubt with advantage, talk Socratically for a minute or two; for instance, "You do not believe in witches? Why not? Because none of your neighbours do? Then, if you had lived in the Middle Ages, you would have believed in witchcraft?" and so on, but only a little way. It is better to be content with the simple answer, "I do not believe that God gives such power to any one to hurt those who pray to Him." It is better to do like the good man who, having examined a village school, allowed himself to be questioned and broke down utterly when asked how many legs a caterpillar had, than to lead your Lysis up and down in quest of a solution, and reserve your own belief or your own doubt. Rough and hard exposure of error will do no harm if accompanied by open avowals of one's own knowledge and ignorance; ironical subtlety and evasive scepticism will make philosophy odious.

Without aping the Athenian dialectics, it is possible almost to form in a boy's mind the habit of weighing and scrutinising general statements and abstract terms. No knowledge of mathematics is needed to know what is meant by defining a term, and a real definition being kept in view as a standard, spurious definitions or inexhaustive descriptions may be tested. A boy knowing nothing of logic, and probably unable to understand Mr. Fowler's Manual, can, nevertheless, perceive what is and what is not a definition, what things can and what cannot be defined. It seems a very important thing that boys should be led thus to apply this primary geometrical habit to other branches of knowledge. There are a few definitions in political economy,—though it is, I venture to think, a sham science,—which are useful, if not in practical life, at least in education: since they are specimens of the scientific treatment of things in common life; and it is desirable always to keep the scientific method in view, even when we are dealing with matters which are not reducible to sciences. We must use many terms which we cannot define universally, but they are to be, for the particular occasion at least, held to single meanings, and he that is accustomed to defining is likely to keep closely to his chosen meaning. Besides political economy, every one is aware that in law-books and in legal arguments terms are used with precision and consistency. These terms can be learnt by young people and used correctly; if they do this, they will probably be careful in using political words; and if vigilant in political argument, they will in due time be tolerably self-denying in their use of ethical expressions. For instance, one who has a fairly accurate conception of money, so as not to confuse it with wealth, has gained a step in philosophy: an examination of several scores of boys and girls scattered over England, proved to the Cambridge local examiner that this was not at all an easy acquirement, and yet it has been reached by many students of the classics, whilst engaged in Latin theme-writing. That the right conception is acquired can be proved best by questions elsewhere called problems, such as this: "When a ship is wrecked and the cargo is insured, is it correct to say that there is no loss sustained?" If they answer that the underwriter sustains loss and no one else, they have not learnt to think correctly of money and wealth. Accustomed to such topics as these, a boy of superior mind might be asked to compare two apparently conflicting dogmas: "Virtue consists in conforming to nature," and "goodness is not of nature, but of grace." The difficulty of tracing the senses of the word "nature" is here counterbalanced by the special interest which our pupils take in theology; and a rational answer, on paper, may be expected from many students who have not been trained on any philosophy; but a more neat and precise solution will be given by one who has had some practice in the scrutiny of phrases, and the disentangling of ambiguities. Even if not answered at all, the question can hardly fail to stir the mind a little; and, after it has been set, there will be more listeners ready than there would have been for an explanation.

It has been held by a gentleman of high official authority, that a boy should write nothing that is not to be criticised in his presence; and this excellent principle, if turned into a rule and obeyed, would get rid of a great bulk of papers done in examinations. But it is easy to satisfy oneself that examinations are valuable as stimulants of exertion; and a young person well trained by literary censure will, in doing a paper for marks, act to a certain extent as his own censor. Let it, however, be kept in mind that we use the word examination somewhat incorrectly if we merely read what is written, and assign to it a sort of pecuniary value without censure or comment; and this process should be, as indeed it is, only a rare interruption to the course of training.

Some classical teachers are familiar with a way of studying the Greek Testament which is proved, by the results of many years, to be effectual, not merely in making a few boys do remarkably well, but in bringing a very considerable number up to a very creditable level in ecclesiastical lore. Twice a week, once in a small set of pupils, once in a class of thirty, a chapter, or perhaps less than a chapter, is construed just like a paragraph of Thucydides, but with more discursive lecturing on the substance, with a strict requirement of accuracy in words, and yet with a resolute endeavour to compass the whole meaning of the whole passage. These may fairly be called catechetical lectures, and they certainly differ from ordinary classical lessons, in so far as the teacher gives out more of his own mind and is more anxious to make his hearers think. In such a lesson it would be felt that the desire of reaching the truth was too strong to tolerate any appeal to the vulgar motive of emulation. Of these two weekly lessons, one is accompanied with a special exercise, consisting of short answers, though not always equally short, to some seven or eight questions; this exercise differs from most others in passing through only one inspection, but it is inspected and commented on in the presence of the writer and of others, the oral corrections being often repeated for a succession of boys, so that one is likely to have it really inculcated or thrust upon the consciousness. Now, though the greater part of what is written for these exercises is copied straight out of books, if not worse, and it is on the whole a more mechanical or less intellectual task than composition or translation, nevertheless a considerable number of boys have a certain impression made on them, and show, when examined at the end of a schooltime, that there is a certain deposit of knowledge not merely verbal in their minds. Moreover, there have been many cases within recent experience of habitual and unobtrusive industry bestowed upon these exercises, which are not in any public manner rewarded or praised, and do not obviously tend to distinction at school or college. Besides genuine industry of a remarkable kind, there has been a curious and interesting originality, sometimes happily inseparable from the disclosure of a peculiar thoughtfulness and a strong character. But setting aside as irrelevant the moral charm of these singularly modest exercises, I wish to ask gentlemen of my profession to consider whether they do right in neglecting this method of instruction, I mean the combination of a catechetical lecture with a written paper of questions followed by oral criticism of the answers. Firstly, is not this the right way of teaching Christian literature or divinity? Secondly, is there any reason why this process, which can be proved on the testimony of unprofessional examiners to be successful, should not be applied to other branches of knowledge? And in particular, let those who insist on the substitution of English essays for other forms of composition, ask themselves whether boys are really capable of writing essays of any length; whether they would not be better employed on short swallow-flights of thought; whether they can safely be trusted to go far by themselves without the check of the leading string; whether there is anything more suited to their age than questions varying in colour and size to be answered neatly and modestly on paper.

Candour requires the admission that to the second of the queries just propounded this reply may be given, that there is no subject but theology in which boys take a sufficient interest for this kind of exertion. Over and above the fact that in Scriptural and ecclesiastical lessons a teacher is greatly supported by the general, if not universal, concurrence of his fellow teachers, and is conscious that he cannot even be accused of indulging a taste of his own, it is evident, on experience, that the boys whose minds are most worthy of culture, are more interested in these than in any other studies, except those in which they are consciously making progress, such as mathematics. It is rare to find one who cares for political philosophy, and even a select class soon tires of a first-rate book of the Burke or Guizot type; it is not rare to meet with one who enters into controversial divinity, who reads week after week without weariness Dr. Wordsworth's "Patristic Commentaries on St. Paul's Epistles," who will listen with animation to fine passages of Hooker, or Edward Irving, who will take Church history and hagiology in any form and to any extent. This is in truth a literary teacher's widest and most fertile field; and for that every-day kind of reasoning, which consists of testing assertions, cutting down exaggerations, dissolving rhetorical compounds, appealing from text to context, and establishing the inestimable habit of considering two things at once, one needs no other materials than those supplied by Churchmen. It is indeed melancholy to observe how ignorant clergymen are of ecclesiastical biography, an ignorance which can be justly traced to colleges, and so back to schools; nor is there any branch of literature which he, who has in these pages undertaken to speak in favour of early philosophizing, would more zealously encourage. But it seems to be the duty of a master in a public school to serve his country by keeping up the stock of Englishmen who may sustain that beautiful fabric of English justice and beneficence, which is to our modern world the pillar and the cloud; and an Englishman is not merely a member of the English Church. Our justice and beneficence are plainly based upon jurisprudence, and ethics, and politics; and if their principles are to be held firmly, and secured from passion and caprice throughout a manhood immersed in worldliness, there is no time to lose even at school in studying the philosophy of government, the duties of citizens, the grounds of the ethical creed held by society. "These are not topics for boys." Nay, but you cannot help their being handled by boys. For they read newspapers habitually. And if, as it follows, they are familiar with questions of morality and polity, who will deny that they need critical, I do not say dogmatic, instruction in morality and polity?

It is perhaps necessary to remind some readers that the schoolboys of whom we are speaking are the select leaders of great schools, and are equal in capacity to the first-year men of second-rate, if not of first-rate colleges. They are, it should be remembered, of the same age as the freshmen or even the junior Sophisters of the last generation; and I believe they are not younger than the ordinary students of Scottish universities. A few years ago, a lad taken from an English public school before he had finished his course found himself at Edinburgh writing, instead of verses and themes, English essays, which were read and criticised by Sir William Hamilton. It appears that the essays were too numerous to be all treated respectfully; they were not read in the presence of the writers; but, some time after they were shown up, the professor addressed the whole class on what he had noticed in some of their papers. It would seem that these were but hasty and boyish writings; but the evidence goes to prove that one who would have been a sixth-form boy at a school, was, as an university student, brought loosely into contact with the mind of a philosopher. In Professor Browne's well-known Lectures on Moral Philosophy there is hardly anything that would not be intelligible, and there is much that would be interesting, to elder schoolboys. There is a great deal of Adam Smith's "Wealth of Nations" of which the same may be said; and the same experiment has been tried on Mr. J. S. Mill's "Political Economy," omitting about two-fifths of it. Many other books might be mentioned, and indeed some have been named already as supplying materials for Latin writing. But it is enough to refer to one book in particular, which, if I remember its contents rightly, shows what might be the sort of philosophical preparation made by a very young man for legal and parliamentary labours, "The Life of Francis Horner." The name of this really well educated member of parliament is, it may be feared, not familiar to men engaged in teaching, perhaps not to politicians. But it will be found historically true that he was, though short-lived, singularly useful to his country, and that the influence he had in the times of Canning was due entirely to his philosophical temperament and philosophical power. His memoirs show with considerable fullness who were the authors, domestic and foreign, whose researches and discoveries he studied. Some, perhaps, of these books are now almost obsolete; others are still worthy of respectful perusal: but it is in the habits, aims, and methods of Horner, not in the very books he read, that we are to find an instructive pattern. When the Cannings were attending merely to "belles lettres," and probably never employing their understanding on anything at all difficult, the pupil of Dugald Stewart was reading, as a law student reads, that is to say, digesting and mastering, the best treatises on jurisprudence, politics, and the cognate theories. And it is to the Edinburgh men, more than to any public school or Oxford or Cambridge men (unless Oxford and Westminster take credit for Bentham), that we owe the enlightened legislators and the righteous government of the last forty years. I do not say that we owe all this to the Edinburgh men only: there is a confluence of causes. But, if we can trace good statesmanship to good education, this is the line of descent; and if we ever had an educator, it was Dugald Stewart.

It must be readily admitted that what may be called, in compliance with the customs of the enlightened Scotsmen, "moral philosophy," belongs on the whole to a university rather than to a public school course of instruction; and it is in a great measure with a view to preliminary training for Oxford that a few hasty inroads have been made by schoolboys across the border into the land of fatness. There was a time, now far withdrawn into the archæological period, when at Cambridge also encouragement was given to ethical and metaphysical pursuits, and there are traces still to be found of the system. But it must be remembered that no mere demonstrative teaching, or popular lecturing, nor this combined with a few prize essays, nor these two combined with the addition of a book or two in the course of three years to the subjects of college examinations, can be expected to secure accuracy, precision, and all that we pique ourselves upon in the classical method. Either the classical method itself, or something analogous to it, should be applied to the study of "moral philosophy" with its adjuncts: nothing less critical or less stringent will be satisfactory.

To repeat what has been already indicated, the traditional method of teaching classical literature, which we call, for brevity, the "classical method," consists of "composition," or written exercises minutely inspected and altered, and of "construing," with "parsing," and with etymological analysis beyond what is known under the name of parsing. This is known to constitute a real discipline, and it is for this reason that men honestly adhere to the old grooves of Greek and Latin. It is from a wholesome horror of sciolism that they cling to what they know to be narrow and meagre. Furthermore, it is because they know that students are not generally likely to be diligent unless there is a coercive obligation behind the attractive teaching, that they shake their heads at the missionaries of modern philosophy. There is yet another most important consideration. It has been found in the forty years that have passed since "useful knowledge" was broached and mechanics' institutes founded, that amongst those who are compelled at an early age to enter into lucrative business, and have but little spare time for mental cultivation, those studies thrive most, if indeed they are not the only studies that thrive at all, in which one is able to feel that one is "getting on." In other words, those branches of instruction wither in which young people are but hearers and not practitioners. The students at mechanics' institutes prefer something that is of the nature of an art or craft, in which they can measure from time to time their own proficiency. So it is with the leisurely class which supplies the upper forms of a public school. They also have their business, though it is far from being lucrative; they are for the most part working at athletics, and school with them, hardly less than with young artisans, is restored to its old Greek meaning of the time that they can spare for mental improvement. And if you ask them to add to this time by taking something from the cares of the world,—that is to say, from what we are wont to call their amusements,—they will make the sacrifice more readily for the sake of a progressive study, especially for entering on a new department of mathematics, than for the purpose of merely reading a book or taking notes of a lecture.

This desire of perceptible progress in the acquirement of skill is satisfied to a certain extent in the practice of composition. Probably it accounts also for the zeal which for some generations the young Romans displayed in practising declamation,—an art which, if they were consistent, the admirers of antiquity would revive. But oral disputation is too much like playing a game, and we have long ago distinguished between the puerile play of the mind and the calmer pursuit of truth, which is becoming to early manhood.

The classical method, characterised by accuracy, by constraining and chastening discipline, and by some consciousness of progress in the acquirement of craftsman's skill, we would, if possible, apply to what we have called, for the sake of convenience, moral philosophy. And this we would attempt in the last years of school life, relegating to the universities the technically logical method, or at the utmost combining with the classical method only so much technical logic as can be either attached to syntax or thrown into a popular manual like Whately's "Easy Lessons." Now, can any one help us to a practical plan for adapting this discipline to English books? It is easy to say that we are to write English essays, but how are you to prevent the schoolboy's essay from being either a mere transcript from a book, if done in the absence of his teacher, or a rambling and shallow tirade, if done without books in a schoolroom? I must personally avow an impatient weariness when my friendly advisers plead for English essays. As an occasional effort, the essay is good enough; for instance, if a class has been reading the Annals of Tacitus, you may at the end of the school-time shut them up for an hour or so to write an essay on the character of Germanicus, or on the growth of imperial absolutism. That is to say, the essay serves fairly to try a boy's intellect in a rather longer flight than usual, and over historical ground it will fly tolerably straight. But, by the supposition, we are looking for something that cannot be treated merely as history. We need something that will bring out in shape and form something like a view of a philosophical topic. We need an exercise which cannot be written quickly, which is sure to give the censor plenty to do, which will bring two minds, the older and the younger, into stimulative contact, which forces us to distinguish between the thought to be expressed and the manner of expression. The use of the English language by itself has been, if I am not misinformed, tried and found wanting in Scotland and in New England; the fruit of essay writing has been shallow and tasteless fluency. Men of genius, with an academy to formalize for them, might have made the English language a classical language, and it might have been brought to pass that, as a Frenchman studies French and learns how to write French as an art, so an Englishman might have found a discipline in his mother tongue. But at the best this would, for scholastic practice, fall very far short of the use of a second language. That part of the paper work which we call translation, whether in the form of epitome or at full length, must be foregone by the English essayist; and we should be left to the cyclic monotonies and platitudes of that "original composition" which school reformers dislike. Paltry as original composition in Latin verse may be, it would be a relief after the amorphous garrulities of the young essayist. And, though no doubt we can do a great deal in the etymological analysis of English words, which has been already touched upon as an unfathomable mine of knowledge fit for schools, yet we should miss the parsing; for no ordinary schoolmaster can find a nourishing diet in English syntax; and it is obvious at first sight that, unless we read Mr. Carlyle's works, there could be no "construing."

I have challenged the friends of modern philosophy to devise for schoolmasters an adaptation of the classical method, plainly averring that we cannot be content with an offhand exhortation to English essay writing. In default of any hopeful proposal from gentlemen who are not themselves teachers, I would ask the reader's attention to a suggestion which was made several years ago before the Public Schools Commissioners, and which subsequent experience enables me to repeat with more confidence. It is briefly a proposal to substitute the French for the Latin language as a vehicle of youthful thought, and to resort to French instead of English books for the study of the rudiments of science and philosophy, with a preference of historical dissertations to formal treatises. It seems certain that the oral part of the classical method is easily transplanted in its integrity to the French language, which is, moreover, taught more solidly and effectually by simply doing just what we do with a

Latin book than in the more elocutional or phraseological way of those who now teach French in England. It seems probable, but my own experiments are not yet quite sufficient to warrant a positive assertion, that the paper work, setting aside verses, can be done as completely and precisely in French as in Latin, with the enormous advantage of overstepping the limits set by the poverty and forced purity of Latin. Dividing paper work into translation, epitomizing or abstracting, written answers to questions, and original composition or essay writing, I speak positively as to the first only, which has been tried for many years, though not as a matter of universal habit. I have sufficient reason for believing that epitomes or abstracts of French chapters or treatises can be made in English, and I should have no doubt that the converse could be done. Answering questions in French on paper is an experiment hitherto untried, except in matters of light literary history; but there seems no reason why it should not be done with science, history of all kinds, and philosophy. French essay writing has been occasionally tried with success, and if reduced to formal themes would be quite feasible, as soon as the classical teacher had acquired enough knowledge of the idiom to alter freely, an amount of attainment not beyond the horizon of younger men. For a few years there would be a lack of competent instructors, well grounded in mathematics, skilled in Latin and in French. But there is a natural progression up to a certain point which may be reckoned on. The pupils of those who with an imperfect knowledge teach and learn simultaneously will be, when grown up, in advance of their preceptors; a second generation will be nearly competent; a third or a fourth will be as familiar with French as with English idiom. It must have been so with the Latinists of the Renaissance. When Ciceronian elegance was substituted for barbarous Schoolmen's Latin, the first literary teachers were pioneers, themselves struggling with the thorns from which they would extricate their disciples; but a lifetime was long enough to see the complete deliverance of the taste of Europe. Once agree to put French on the footing of the classics, and you will soon get a fair supply of Englishmen able to handle it properly. A year or two spent in Paris, after taking the Bachelor's degree at home, would enable a first-class man to gain a diploma or certificate of fitness to teach French; and it would be far from disadvantageous to schools if this delay were secured, and this addition made to the young teacher's stock of wisdom. It might be required of some men that they should have become "Bachelors of Literature" in Paris, which cannot be done without passing a strict examination in French. Paris, instead of Rome and Dresden, would be the finishing school for the English graduate who means to be a teacher, and the time now bestowed on art would be almost enough for the rudiments of science. Art is strong enough now-a-days to take care of itself; and it may be doubted whether it has not, in the form of superficial connoisseurship, made some encroachments. At least, one is tempted to wish that more attention was paid by our young graduates to industrial processes and the applied sciences, and one would recommend the occasional preference of a manufactory to a mountain, of Jermyn Street to South Kensington, of handicraft to "bric-a-brac." We deceive ourselves if we think that we become enlightened and accomplished by looking at and talking about the contents of galleries and studios. We are not less mistaken if we imagine that we have acquired a modern language without having read much or composed at all. If sincere in our wish to be more thoroughly furnished with knowledge than were our classically trained predecessors, let us submit to being drilled and examined by foreigners, and by foreigners of authority and independence; we hardly get the truth from those whom we engage as language masters, for they flatter us.

The leading schools are in a position to demand these increased qualifications of those who wish to be on their establishments as teachers. It would not be unreasonable to go so far as to put off the final appointment of an assistant-master till he had reached the ordinary standing of a man called to the bar, and had gone through as laborious a preparation as the law student. Hitherto our authorities have affirmed, and not without some grounds, that a young man called from college to take a form, or even a house, in a school, will, after the commencement of his professional labours, take care to improve himself and supply all deficiencies. But, in fact, little is added beyond a smattering of modern languages and dilettante culture, which it would not become him to despise who confesses his own sciolism, but which he may, as a patriot, wish to see replaced by solid and well-proved acquirements. Others have lamented the slenderness of the outfit with which young English gentlemen leave school; a schoolmaster may in his turn lament that society, which is above and around him, is itself content to fetch so little from European capitals, and, in particular, that it is satisfied with so partial a survey of the magnificent literature of France.

In this paper there has been indicated a certain respect for the lucid and sober philosophy of the Locke-Bentham period, and a belief that the "middle axioms" of politics are wholesome food for students on the edge of manhood. The "advanced liberals" of the present day are, I believe, dieted upon intuitions which make them think Whig and Scotsman insipid; and fashion is against what is called the eighteenth century. But it is generally held that a certain economy must be practised in teaching the young, and that we may safely stop short of the latest modernism. It is argued in favour of the classics that they are sphered on high out of the range of party storms and prejudices; and if there is any force in this argument it applies to some of the writers who have a European reputation, and are not arrayed in our controversies. I find amongst the writers of France since the Restoration, including the Belgians and the Swiss who write in French, men who combine the sanity of Robertson with the moral loftiness of Burke, and who, because they are Frenchmen, have none of our badges fastened upon them. I would read these as I read Cicero and Tacitus, mainly because they teach political virtue, and teach it intelligibly as well as loftily. But this is not the reason on which my thesis allows me to dwell. I recommend modern French books because they are rational, and indirectly scientific: if not on science, they conform to the scientific mould. They present to the students models of statement, of limited generalization, of delicately shaded language free from ambiguity, of sentences perfectly articulated, and yet not too obviously logical to cause annoyance. It seems to be true that France, the hotbed of revolutions, has in mental government undergone no violent change; that it has preserved, not without abundant activity and contention, a considerable uniformity; that there is an unbroken succession from Malherbe to Victor Hugo, from Bossuet to Montalembert; that the French have escaped the dislocating agencies of anti-scholastic thinkers; that they are in literature the legitimate heirs of the Romans, and are still displaying the cognizance of Cicero and of Quintilian. Whatever may be their inferiority to the very best English writers, they are wiser than the ancients, and we are looking for wisdom; and the wisdom of the English cannot be by a classical or a critical method of instruction made to filter slowly into the understanding of a young student, whilst the wisdom of the ancients is not enough to guide a man through the complex duties of our life. As the world grows older there is an increase in the number, as well as an expansion in the range, of what a Latinist would call "doctrines" or "arts,"—that is to say, of bodies of cognate truths with their applications; and if we are to be enlightened men, we must take these, or most of them, synoptically: we cannot afford time in early youth to dwell long upon the curiosities of one particular body of truths, such as grammar, still less on a body of doubts and minute controversies such as what is called "critical scholarship." There is enough grammar in French for coercive discipline and for the shampooing of a dull mind; there is in it etymology, enough to be the foundation of that healthy nominalism which above all things charms us against delusions;

there is no textual criticism or conjectural emendation, no worship of aberrant phrases, no love of difficulty for its own sake; there is no film of imperfect sympathy to come between the writer and the reader and intercept the thought or throw it in several shapes on several understandings. Whether the subject be geology, or commerce, or the English Revolution, or the metaphysics of grace and freewill, the French writer teaches the English reader with no oracular haze between them, and what he states can be reflected without distortion by the interpreter. Seasoned with this rationality, one can go safely to another atmosphere. From the modern books we may go, provided with touchstones, to Plato and Livy, to Thucydides and Virgil; and, whilst revering the intellectual freedom of our heathen forefathers, we may honestly investigate their many errors; using them at once as patterns and as warnings; exposing the shallowness of their inductions, their employment of metaphor instead of argument, their subservience to abstract terms, the frequent breaking down of their rhetoric, their countless fallacies of observation, and the barrenness to which they were condemned by the estrangement of their literature from science.

IX.

ON THE PRESENT SOCIAL RESULTS OF CLASSICAL EDUCATION.

BY LORD HOUGHTON.

THAT the whole of the boyhood and the greater part of the youth of the higher classes of our countrymen should be occupied with the study of the language, literature, history, and customs of two nations which have long ago disappeared from the surface of our globe, and which, but for the common conditions of all humanity, have no more relation to us than the inhabitants of another planet, would assuredly, if presented to our observation for the first time, appear a strange abuse of the privilege which the wealthy enjoy in the long, sedulous, and uninterrupted education of their sons. And yet the problem has its solution, and the anomaly its excuse, in the story of the intellectual progress of mankind. The empire of the Roman language plays a scarce less important part in the records of mankind than the dominion of the Roman arms. When the central power had collapsed, when the legions had retired from province after province and left the outer world to what they deemed an irreclaimable barbarism, a new and unthought-of influence was yet to come from the same region, and to spread itself over portions of the world, not only inaccessible to the force of Rome, but whose very existence was then unknown. The old tongue became the instrument and auxiliary of the new spiritual authority that rose on the ruins of the material power; and though the Empire was for centuries Greek, Latin was becoming the expression of the thoughts and highest interests of the future civilization. And soon, while the modern languages of Europe by the side of it, and in all cases affected by it, were struggling upwards into individual life, it stood amid the inchoate and changing forms of speech in a distinct supremacy and perfection which gave it the character of the catholic and permanent utterance of the Roman race. So many of the vulgar tongues were but dialects or corruptions of the Latin, and others so interwoven with it in the process of their formation, that the conception of the Latin as the foundation of universal grammar was natural and just; and when, in course of time, it became the means of intercommunication among men from Sicily to the Hebrides, and made Augustine of Hippo intelligible to Pelagius of Wales, what other or better education was possible, than that Youth, wherever born, should be introduced into this great citizenship and community of mind and heart?

And therefore if in this latter time we have to set before us the question, whether it is wise and right that purely classical studies should retain the monopoly which they still possess in the instruction of the present and future generations of those classes of our countrymen who are free from the necessities and obligations of manual labour, and who can exercise and develop their intellectual and moral faculties to the utmost for their own pleasure and advantage and for the profit and guidance of their fellow-men, let it not be thought that there is any desire to derogate from the immense claims that the Latin language, even apart from its literature, legitimately maintains, as an agent in the advance and cultivation of the human race.

But this main utility, this intellectual convenience, greater than ever has been the dissemination of the French, or even than will be that of the English language, among the inhabitants of the earth, has literally ceased to exist. Latin is no longer a spoken tongue; even among scholars in the departments of theology and physical science,—where the advantage of addressing *ad clerum* arguments and facts, that the ignorant may easily misapprehend or misapply, might well be appreciated,—its use is rare and has an air of pedantry: and it is discontinued in our academic disputations and discussions, though retained in the proceedings of some foreign universities. The ecclesiastical allocutions, which are the most living forms of Latin speech, though addressed *urbi et orbi*, affect a small portion of our people, and even in Catholic countries require interpretation and comment. Occasional works of classical investigation and verbal criticism appear in the ancient scholarly costume, but they have a pretentious and exclusive bearing that repels even the capable reader. The complicated torture and linguistic anomaly of making Latin the vehicle for instruction in Greek is rapidly passing away from our schools, as well as the practice of illustrating the classic writers by annotations and dissertations of doubtful classicality: and in the study and processes of law, which had appropriated to it itself, in the lapse of time, a special and corrupt, but in its application throughout Europe a general and recognised, Latin diction, nothing remains, as far as British jurisprudence is concerned, beyond a few isolated and mispronounced expressions.

It has been reserved for an enthusiastic French Phil-Hellene (M. Gustave d'Eichthal) to propose that Greek should now become the Universal Language; but even this is not more hopeless than the rehabilitation of the Latin, and there is no more reason in the teaching of the one than of the other, as far as relates to any intercourse or communication with the actual world and living men.

It will answer no purpose of argument to depreciate the effect and worth of classical scholarship. Let us have as much of it as possible. There is no danger in this time and country of the existence of a class of *Gelehrten*, who should distract the energies of the nation from the broad highways of civic life and lead them into the by-paths of abstract study, so that, while thought and speculation might be busy and free, political action might be inert and shackled. The critic and the searcher, the man to whom the records and productions of these two wondrous peoples is an inexhaustible mine of intellectual treasure,—before whom these languages, in the unalterable passiveness of their structure, lie like the dead subject under the knife of the anatomist,—who combines the curiosity of the antiquary with the induction of the philosopher,—he can owe little, if anything, to the present formal routine of classical discipline. It is doubtful, indeed, whether, if he had first come to that study at the age of sixteen, with faculties already strengthened and regulated by any sound system of education, without any ungrateful associations of the daily recurrent task and the natural resistance of boyish distraction to lessons that have no connexion with its instincts or its observation, some four or five years of conscientious and willing labour, with all the stimulus of enjoyment in progress, would not effect at least all that is required within the modest range of an University curriculum, and leave him well armed and equipped for the campaigns and efforts of a further erudition. At any rate, it must be supremely indifferent to a man thus engaged, whether an infinite number of boys are learning one grammar or another, or construing one or other book, which it is clearly understood that they are to lay by and forget, as soon as they confront the businesses or even the pleasures of mature life.

For to the social phenomenon of all this elaborate study, which cannot be applied to any practical purpose, must be added this other peculiarity of the system, that, when once the ordinary British youth has bidden farewell to school or college, any attempt to prosecute, or even keep up, his classical attainments and interests would make him an object of curiosity, if not of censure and alarm, to all who might be solicitous for his future welfare. It is accepted that, whatever other advantages he may have derived from his public education—and they may be many—the knowledge of the ancient languages, which formed so large and indispensable a portion of it, may be at once abandoned without compunction or reproach. He has repeatedly learnt the Odes of Horace by heart, but at the age of thirty he will not be able to repeat one of them; he could once write a sort of Latin verse or prose, but that accomplishment soon utterly disappears, perhaps at no great loss to himself or others. There must be, however, some positive gain in even such a limited command of ancient literature as has been drilled into him, and if we were not case-hardened by custom, it would seem to us a scandal that it should be thus altogether thrown aside. The exceptions to this rule, of course, are numerous, and examples of men of too much mental vigour, and memories too well exercised, to abandon easily what they have acquired with much intelligent labour, will suggest themselves to all of us. Yet follow that young lawyer who has won high honours at his University, and whose talents and industry are undeniable: he throws himself with zeal into his new profession; he sets himself to master the knowledge that may, when properly used, gain him wealth and position; he would willingly pursue his former classical studies, but he finds no time for them, even in his hours of intellectual relaxation. For these he has his French or German—which perhaps he once learnt from his sister's governess, but lost at school—or the elements of physical science, of which he now feels himself shamefully ignorant—or it may be some art—music or drawing—for which he is conscious that he possesses a true natural gift, and to which he sometimes regretfully thinks that the supple fingers or eager eyes of his boyhood might have been profitably directed. So that he must content himself with the superior enjoyment which his classical remembrances and associations may give him, if he chances to visit the scenes of ancient history; or, if he becomes the father of a family, with the means of imparting to his children the rudiments of the same education which absorbed all his early life, but to which he has so rarely reverted in his later years.

With the clergy, whose occupations are for the most part sedentary and unambitious, the results might be expected to be different, but it is not so. Outside the Universities it is rare to find a clergyman, not engaged in tuition, whose intimacy with his previous studies goes much beyond his Greek Testament, and indeed it would hardly tend to his professional credit if it was known that he spent any considerable portion of his time in company with a literature not akin in thought and principle to his present duties. The old-fashioned conventional standard, which not only permitted, but encouraged, among ecclesiastics the familiar intercourse with heathen writers, and by which subjects indecorous or even sacrilegious when expressed in the vulgar tongue, became harmless and becoming when conveyed in Greek or Latin diction, is now obsolete; and the spiritual condition of the semi-pagan prelates of the court of Leo X. or that of the Catullus-editing divines of the seventeenth century is not very comprehensible to the modern religious mind.

If, then, the exclusive classical education, so prolonged, so elaborate, so costly, is acknowledged to be inoperative, as regards the retention of the languages and the interest in their literature, among all classes of society, except those, whose business it is to continue and propagate the study, and a few scholastic amateurs,—can it be maintained that the mental discipline which it enforces is of so peculiar and unique a character as, in itself, to justify this sacrifice of human intelligence and parental expenditure?

Admit all that can be adduced as to the superiority of these tongues in the regularity of their structure, the logical accuracy of their expression, the ease with which their etymology is traced and reduced to general laws, and the precision of their canons of taste and style,[1] can it be affirmed that these peculiar excellences are appreciable by the mass of schoolboys, and that these processes of thought cannot be evoked by any other instrumentality? Is the difference between these and other forms of speech such, that grammar cannot be taught efficiently in any living tongue, or that so refined a perception of style and taste in composition can be conveyed to the generality of young minds by these and by no other means? Now no decisive answer can be given to these questions till the test of experience has been fairly applied, and this can only be done when all the other separate and collateral circumstances that affect and distinguish the education of our public schools can be combined with other than exclusive classical teaching. When boys, in all other respects under the same intellectual and moral training, are submitted to different courses of instruction, when the grammar of living tongues is taught as accurately and scientifically as that of the dead, when the sense of beauty and fitness in diction is excited and directed by judicious exercise in the masterpieces of native and foreign literature, when diligence and aptitude in the one study or the other are equally considered and rewarded, then, and not till then, can it be positively predicated that the imagined attributes of a classical education are not referable to circumstances and treatment with which classics, as such,

[1] See Dr. Temple's evidence before the Royal Commission.

have nothing whatever to do, and whether the most enlightened advocates of the retention of the system are not unconsciously affected by a powerful literary superstition.

Powerful indeed,—so powerful, that its permanence and resistance to all attacks must rest on other grounds than even the intellectual approval of ages or the mental advantage of generations of mankind. It is no doubt in the social conditions and political habits of the inhabitants of modern Europe that such a belief must have been rooted, to maintain its literary supremacy through all mutations of thought and above all storms of public opinion. It is as the proper and recognised education of the governing classes, the honourable accomplishment of all aristocracy, that the classical teaching endures so firmly, even now that it has ceased to be the mysterious speech of the Church and when it is no longer the authoritative exposition of Law. For as soon as it became the qualification of a Gentleman to read and write at all, it was Latin that he read and wrote. From Charlemagne, learning his Latin accidence at the age of forty, to the royal pedant, King James I. of England, the best classical culture of the age was ever appropriate to the highest social station. For centuries the young fancy and fresh wits of the civilized laity were nurtured with the images and incidents of old classic life, and all gentle literature was mimetic of the ancient standards. All else, tongue and word, the vehicle and the substance of native speech, were common, of the people—vulgar.

And as the community of the modes of diction and writing extended itself from the learned to the powerful and wealthy portions of society, and distantly affected the formation of the manners, as well as the mind, of Europe, *Unus sonus est totius orationis et idem stylus*,[1] might be applied, without exaggeration, to all the societies that co-operated in the revival of letters, and a certain identity has come down among them even to this moment, in which we are discussing the question whether or not classical instruction must remain the staple of the gentleman's education. These effects extended to the transactions of daily life, the euphuism of speech, the formation of all that can be comprehended in the notion of Taste. There can, indeed, be no better illustration of these indirect influences than a certain condition of high society that existed in this country in the latter part of the last century. At that time the education of our public schools was no doubt very inferior in accuracy and extent to that now offered or enforced; yet among the patrician class there was a considerable body of men whose tastes and habits were coloured by classical associations and interests to an extent which at this day we can hardly comprehend. Few of them had any pretensions to large or precise scholarship, and their scope and purpose were well expressed by a word which some of them brought back from Italy, *dilettanti*, to which, however, no light or disparaging sense was at that time attached. "*Virtuoso* the Italians call a man," says Dryden, "who loves the noble arts, and is a critic in them;" and it was these men who introduced *Virtù* into the luxuries of British life. They touched the rough manners of their age with a jovial grace and a genial delicacy, and they applied their wealth to the acquisition of

---

[1] Cic. Brut. 26

those fine specimens of Greek and Roman sculpture which adorn our public and private galleries, and to the production of those sumptuous works of antique topography which enrich our libraries and have so few successors. To them we owe the foundation of the British Museum, the introduction of the Italian Opera, and the establishment of the Academy of British Artists. They covered the country with Palladian edifices, that only too often rose on the ruins of the pleasant, commodious, old English mansions; and they decorated the city with palaces of an architecture which Mr. Ruskin tells us has found its final form in Gower Street. The range of classical writers with which they professed an acquaintance was of the most limited, but, within it, allusions were frequent and well understood, so that Parliamentary quotations were not exhibitions of erudition, but familiar forms of rhetorical expression. The genteel multitude affected the habits of the more instructed; if the public taste was bigoted and confined, at any rate it knew what it wanted, and, if monotonous, it was never confused : the notion of a Gothic House of Parliament would have convulsed the clubs, but Mr. Swinburne's "Atalanta" would have taken the town by storm. Now it may be said that this was a poor result of what was contentedly regarded as the highest education, but it was, as far as it went, a positive gain; it was a Culture,—and, if the exclusive distinction of a special class, it was at the same time a bond of intellectual sympathy that went beyond it. To men of this temper, no scholarship seemed pedantic or superfluous : they valued all they retained of the old tuition, and they respected all that could make clear to them their own memories and intuitions. The acquisition of the French and Italian tongues was facilitated and encouraged, instead of being thrust out of education, by classical teaching, and something of the common speech of former times was at least desired and attempted by this modern society. There are, indeed, still to be found among our elders some few, mostly of those who have been actively engaged in public life, who cling with affection to this literature, often the only one to which they have felt inclined during their existence—a remaining savour of the old *dilettanti* fruit, which we must not look to see repeated in an after-generation. Among future statesmen we may have serious scholars like Mr. Gladstone or Sir Cornewall Lewis, but we shall not again have Sir Robert Peel discussing with Lord John Russell what was Mr. Fox's favourite among the Odes of Horace, or sprightly men-of-the-world exchanging their Virgil and translating Homer.

Yet, however imperceptible may be the effects of classical training in after-life, either in manners or in mind, as long as the fashion of the education endures, our higher classes will continue to subject their children to it, and the large portion of society which desires, at any cost, to give their progeny what seems to them the best start in life, will follow the example. Whilst a boy is placed, on his arrival at school, according to his classical attainments, the preliminary classical teaching becomes necessary, whatever be the sacrifice of other natural, opportune, or more available instruction, because no superiority of childly knowledge, either of words or things, would compensate for the disadvantage of an inferior position to others of his own age and ability in the new world of which he is to form a part. Our great historical schools derive such a distinct moral benefit from their association with the tone of feeling and habits of demeanour that prevail in our best British homes, that, apart from the less worthy consideration of the prestige or possible profit that their sons may derive from daily contact with the sons of the titled and the opulent, it will require some very strong impulse to decide what may be called the upper stratum of the middle class to accept for their families any education which almost appears a descent in the social scale. And yet it is precisely this class which is the most palpable sufferer under the present system. If indeed these chief laboratories of national instruction combined with their social prominence a large and systematic instruction in the requirements of active and industrial life, their tutelage would be the most effective apprenticeship to which a sensible father in that rank of life could entrust his son. Now, however, when the young manufacturer or banker begins what is to be the real business of his existence, he leaves irrevocably behind him every object to which his ten (or more) early years have been devoted, retaining little beyond some tastes in which only the idle or the independent can indulge with impunity, and a certain dim conceit of his own superiority over his fellows, who have only received a "commercial" training.

There are too many flagrant examples in the history of the human mind of the persistent adherence, not only of public opinion and private judgment, but of the religious conscience and the moral sense, to forms and ceremonies, after the beliefs on which they were founded have faded into shadows, to permit the hope that any amount of negative experience will bring about a reformation in the matter we are now considering. It is solely to a growing conviction of the necessity of larger and wiser instruction of our governing classes, if they are to remain our governors, that we must look as the source of any beneficial change. The first, and indeed the chief impediment to this result, is the extreme self-satisfaction with which not only our national pride, but the authority of our public institutions, regards the character of the present English gentleman. He is exhibited to us as an ideal of humanity which it is almost sinful to desire to improve or transcend; and it is, if not asserted, continually implied that if he in his youth were taught more or otherwise than he learns at present, some mysterious degradation would inevitably ensue. Now, without detracting from any single merit which is attributed to this high personality, never was there a greater confusion of *post hoc* with *propter hoc* than the theory that his actual excellent characteristics have anything whatever to do with the method of instruction which has been imparted to him. It is not pretended that he pursues, or ever resumes, the study that has occupied a fourth of his probable existence: it is not claimed that he has acquired a general taste in literature or arts, which will either serve as the basis of professional knowledge or dignify his hours of relaxation; it is admitted that he may become a landed proprietor without a notion of agriculture—a coal-owner without an inkling of geology—a sportsman without curiosity in natural history—a legislator without the elements of law: it is assumed that he may frequent foreign countries, without having acquired even a convenient intimacy with their language, and continually incur that ridicule which is especially disagreeable to his nature; and yet, in the face of all these admissions, every attempt to supply these deficiencies is regarded as little less than revolutionary. When a distinguished foreigner comes to London, it is almost impossible to collect a dinner-party in the highest circles who can speak with comfort and precision what he has a right to consider the present vernacular tongue of good society throughout Europe, and yet the study and exercise of the French language in our public schools are still little more than a caprice and superfluity, instead of being, as they ought, the substitute for that spoken Latin, which was the bond of intercommunication among civilised nations and the common dialect of gentility. But if an equality with the rest of the world in this respect is not required of the English gentleman, it might, at least, be expected that he should be furnished with all that constitutes the elementary education of the people, in the most perfect form that pedagogic skill and science can supply; that his reading should be that of a clear and intelligent utterance; that his writing should be neither "clerkly" nor illegible; and that his mechanical command of arithmetic should be secured by some comprehension of its mathematical principles; so that if, as far as he is concerned, the classical learning has been a fiction, he shall at any rate not be in a worse condition than if he had been born in an inferior station, and with only the ordinary opportunities of instruction. But unfortunately it is this humble standard which the gentlemanlike education overleaps, or rather does not condescend to obtain, and the children of the nobleman grow up, in all these respects, often inferior to those of the butler who stands behind his chair.

It has been a skilful calumny to attribute to the promoters of scientific knowledge in our schools the desire to fill the minds of boys with a quantity of unconnected facts, or to give the character of serious mental exertion to what is at best the exercise of puerile observation. That it is in itself an immense profit for a youth to learn how to observe, and that this habit may mould and direct all his future life, is undeniable; but it is precisely not the conglomeration of the facts, but the scientific method which is above measure valuable as a training of the adolescent mind. To lay early the foundations of certainty is to build up the man of principle and conviction, and has a moral purpose beyond any intellectual gain to be derived from the distinctions and functions of language. But there is no reason why the two should not go on together, and why grammar should not be considered in connexion with its sister-sciences.

"But there is not *time* for all these various subjects of instruction, and in trying to teach all you will teach none," say the opponents. Not time! Not time in thirteen or fourteen years of life—of that life when the faculties are most active, the memory most retentive, the will most ductile? Not time for the wealthy and the leisurely, for those who are destined to advise, direct, and lead the affairs of their country and the destinies of other men, to be taught aptly and completely the use of those instruments of intelligence which their less fortunate fellows have to acquire, as best they may, in some five or six years of boyhood, before they enter on the earnest strife of social existence?

And this is probably the form in which the decision of the question of the continuance of the classical education in this country will take place. If our public schools and universities can, as seems practicable, combine the ancient and honoured mode of instruction with the peremptory requirements of the present age, the presumption of classical superiority may not only be sustained but may become an admitted fact. Let a youth come forth from his academic career familiar with the phenomena of the world about him, apprehensive of scientific principles, comprehending the facts and deductions of the history of mankind, sufficiently at home in the great societies of Europe to enjoy their intercourse and profit by observation, and, in addition to these qualifications, a good classical scholar, he will not only himself be too conscious of the value of the accomplishment to permit it to be disused and forgotten, but his possession of it will elevate him in general esteem and assist him in many special objects of life.

For it is as the complement of European culture that these literatures can alone retain their hold over the minds of men. The East has now revealed the higher reservoirs of the stream of human speech, and the eye of the historian reaches to far more distant ranges of the civilization of mankind. But, though ceasing to be the only scholarly learning, they may well retain their parental relation to the ethical and political life, to the taste and intelligence of the modern world, if they are only raised from the degradation to which they are now submitted in the profitless drudgery of elemental instruction. They may become the exceptious and ennobling study of numerous persons who will find them interesting and useful realities, instead of being, as they now are, receptacles of dead names and phantasms, and impediments to practical knowledge and scientific truth.

There is a negative effect of the assumed universality of classical culture which it is worth while to consider, and, if possible, to remedy. No one is averse to showing his familiarity with Don Quixote, though he is ignorant of Spanish, nor does an absence of the knowledge of Italian or German prevent the enjoyment of Cary's "Dante" or Anstey's "Faust." Still less is an acquaintance with Oriental languages thought necessary for an interest in, and appreciation of, the history, literature, manners, and thought of Eastern peoples, from the "Arabian Nights" of our childhood, to Professor Wilson's Sanskrit Philosophy. Indeed, it is notorious that works of the value of Baron de Bunsen's "Bibelwerke," and Barthelemy St. Hilaire's researches on Boodha and Mohammed, have been produced without any assumption of Oriental scholarship. But there has come to seem something incongruous and offensive in any man's assuming to know or care about classic objects or classic letters, without having been taught to construe Greek and Latin. Thus a large field of converse and discussion is practically closed to numbers of educated persons perfectly capable of comprehending and criticising its meaning and spirit, and a serious intellectual barrier is raised, not only between man and man, but, almost universally, between man and woman, both in general society and in domestic intercourse.

Some relief to this defect would no doubt be afforded by the more frank recognition of the worth and use of translations into modern languages, which represent, as truly as may be, the graces of form and the essential merits of the original writers; versions, not merely accurate, but sympathetic with the matter and the style they are handling—of poetry by poets, of oratory by orators, of history and philosophy by affectionate students of the emotions and reflections of mankind. These should, by right, be the most effective material of school training, instead of being prohibited and regarded as substitutes for severe study and inducements to juvenile indolence. But the true encouragement to a more general and unpedantic cultivation of what is universal and enduing in classic literature and life, beyond the mechanism of language, would result from such an alteration of the habitual methods of instruction as would strive, first and foremost, to fill the mind of each pupil with the realities of the past, and to make the thoughts and deeds of those old existences as intelligible to him as the events of his own time or the workings of his own observation. Then, as he grew to manhood, they would be no longer a fairy or rather demon-world, which the activities or pleasures of the present and the aspirations or interests of the future equally authorise him to quit for ever, but an order of things in which he would feel a life-long concern, and which would mingle with all the conclusions of his increasing knowledge and the intellectual relations of his advancing years.

To conclude, it can be no abstract advantage, with the present political prospects of this country, and indeed of Europe, that any education should retain an exclusive or class character. The free and intimate association of men of different birth in professional occupations is accepted by our aristocracy with that good sense which enables them to maintain a social influence almost extinguished in European communities, and which is one of our best safeguards in the perplexities of the future. Any training which tends to keep up distinctions, whether real or fictitious, must injure that community of views and objects, which is so essential not only to personal comfort, but to advancement in any special avocation. We already hear the young ambitious Engineer or adventurous Colonist lamenting over his lost time and unemployed abilities, and speaking in no measured terms of reproach of what has been to him an inappropriate discipline, of which he so little appreciates the indirect and secondary advantages, that he regards the toils of his boyhood with unmitigated disgust. Is it impossible to make a satisfactory compromise between the just exigencies of our age and the honourable traditions of past generations—one more compromise in a country and among a people who wisely have made so many?

THE END.

www.ingramcontent.com/pod-product-compliance
Lightning Source LLC
Chambersburg PA
CBHW032025220426
43664CB00006B/372